The Fantastical Art of Jim Pitts

Volume Two

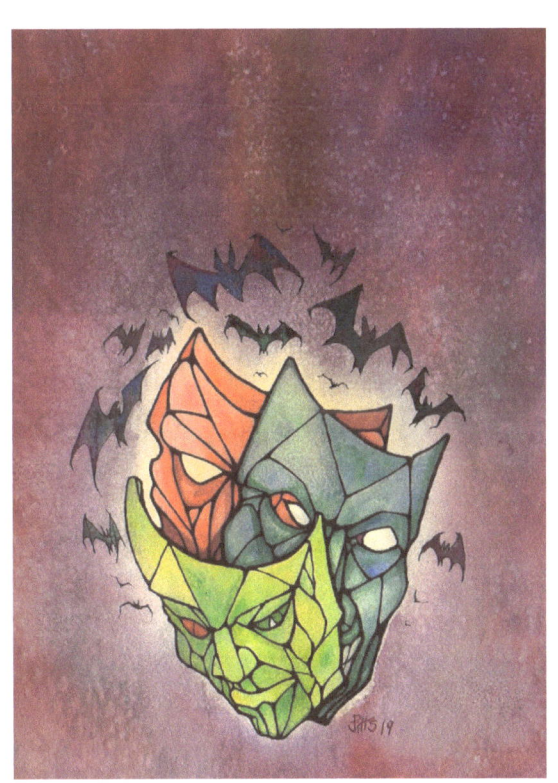

Rolling back the years...

PARALLEL UNIVERSE PUBLICATIONS

First Published in the UK in 2017
Volume Two of the soft cover version First Published 2019
Jim Pitts artwork copyright © 2017 Jim Pitts
All other artists and photographers retain rights to their own work
All written contributions are copyright the individual authors
ISBN: 978-1-9161109-1-5

THIS BOOK IS DEDICATED TO THE MEMORIES OF

**JOHN STEWART
DAVE MCFARREN
& KARL EDWARD WAGNER**

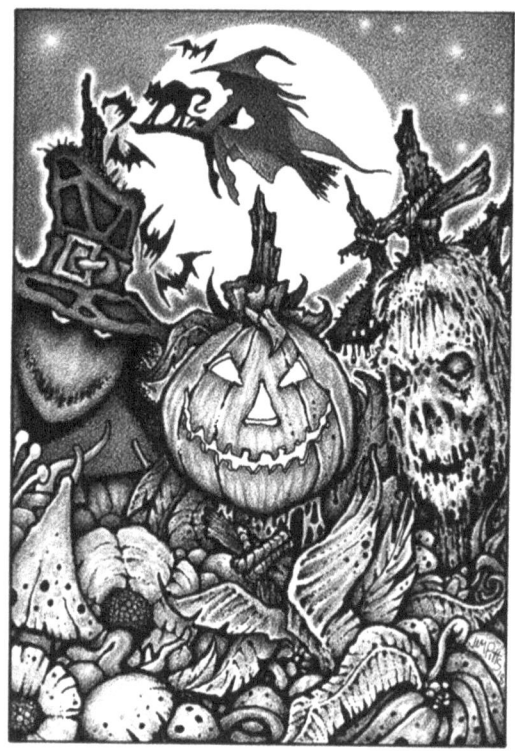

All rights reserved. No part of this publication may be reproduced, stored in a retrieval system, rebound or transmitted in any form or by any means, electronic, mechanical, photocopying, recording or otherwise, without the prior written permission of the author and publisher. This book is sold subject to the condition that it shall not by way of trade or otherwise be lent, resold, hired out or otherwise circulated without the publisher's prior consent in any form of binding or cover other than that in which it is published.

Parallel Universe Publications, 130 Union Road, Oswaldtwistle,
Lancashire, BB5 3DR, UK

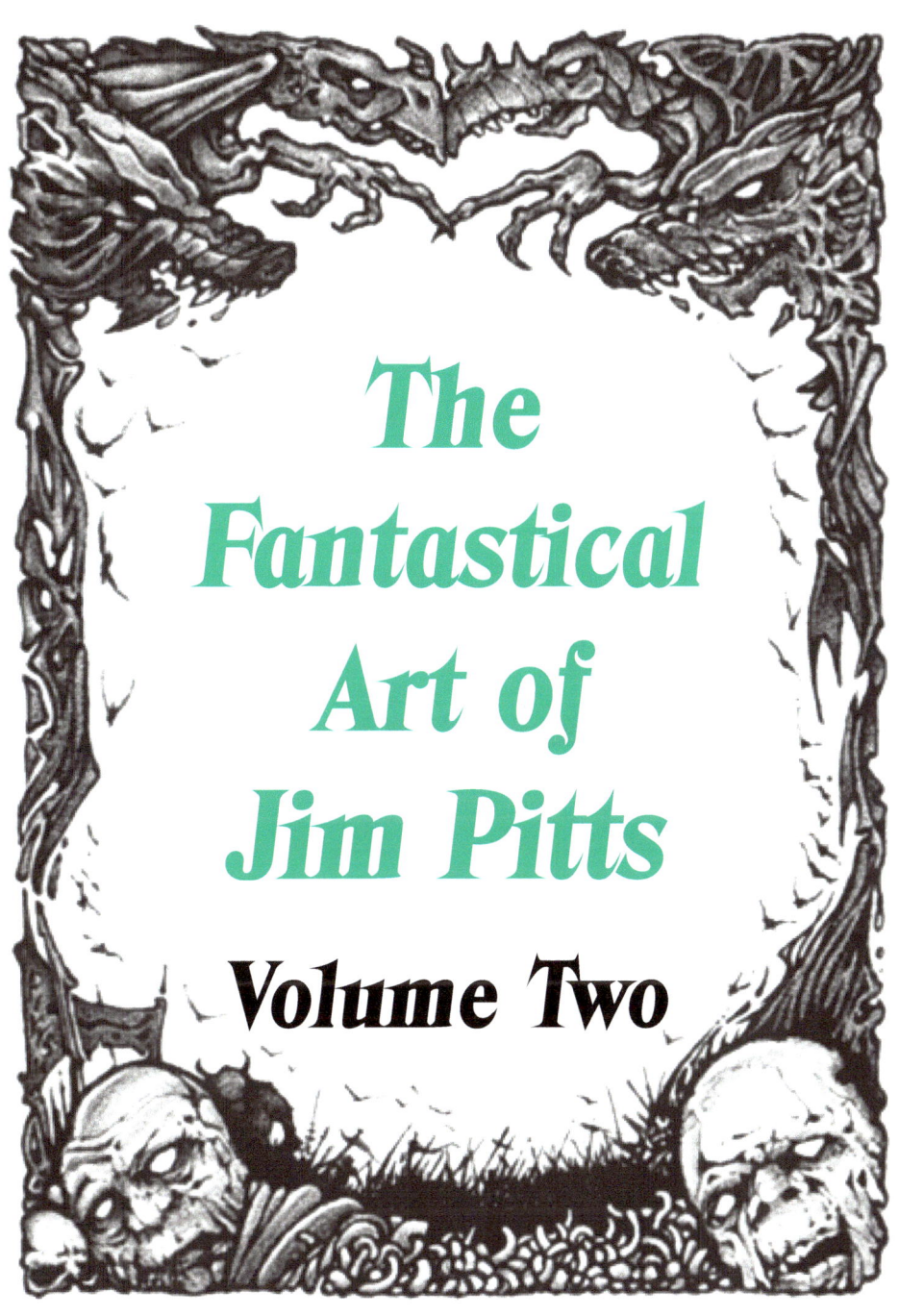

The Fantastical Art of Jim Pitts

Volume Two

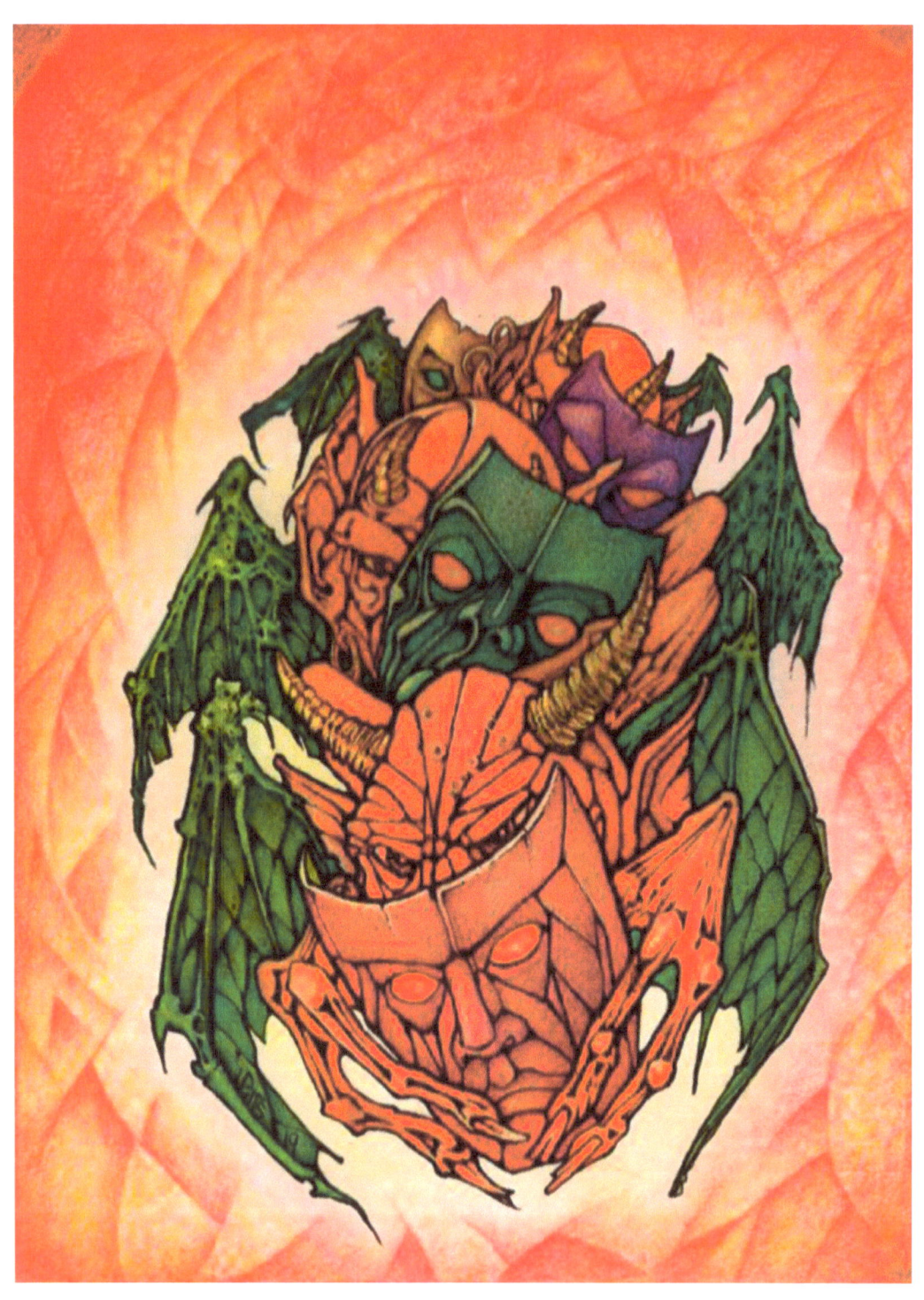

Cover artwork for *Phantasmagoria Magazine* #10, edited by Trevor Kennedy

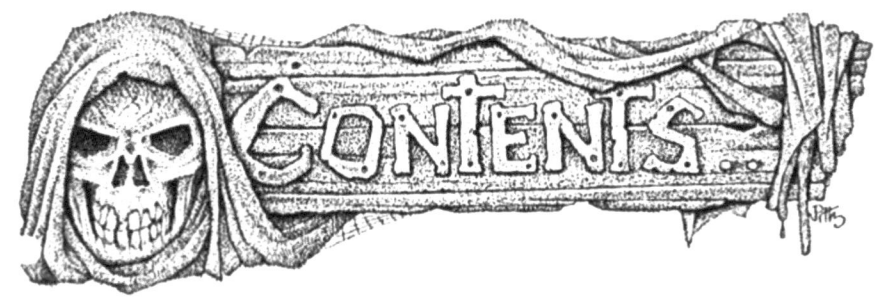

BFS Folio	6
Gaslight & Ghosts - World Horror Convention 1988	10
Jim Pitts: From the Dark Regions of the Voidal Universe to the Twisted Pulpworld of Nick Nightmare by Adrian Cole	14
In Pencil, Pen-and-ink, the Uncrowned Prince of the Primal Land! by Brian Lumley	26
Jim Pitts: Society Gent and Artist by Peter Coleborn	41
Skeleton Crew magazine	52
Northern Chills - Graham Hurry	67
Experiments in Colour	69
Fishhead - The Darker Tales of Irvin S. Cobb	79
Fear magazine - Artist in Residence: Jim Pitts	81
Marianne Dreams - Puffin Books	82
Shadows Over Innsmouth - The Great Collaboration	86
Some Sketches	94
The Hyborian Gazette	101
Looking for Something to Suck by R. Chetwynd-Hayes	103
Acknowledgements and Thanks	111

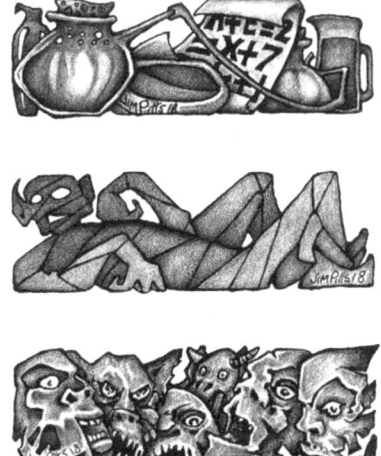

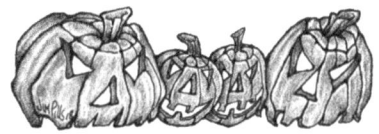

BFS *Folio* of Jim Pitts Artwork

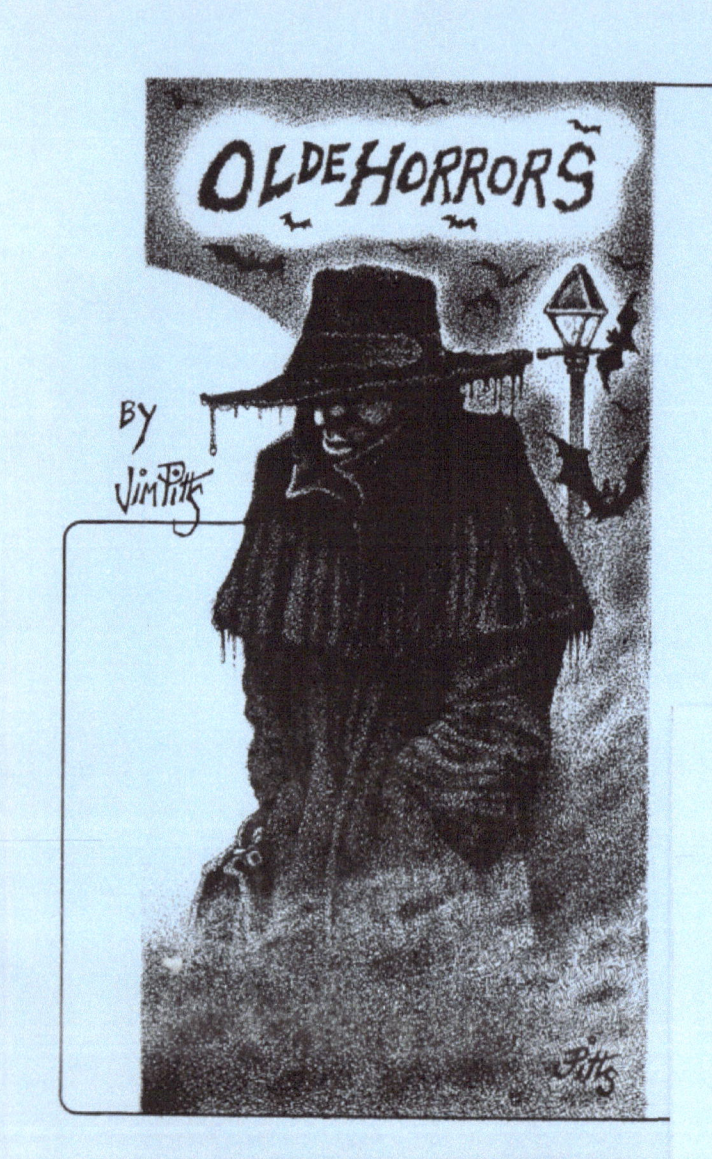

The cover depicts Jack the Ripper.

Back cover: the Living Dead

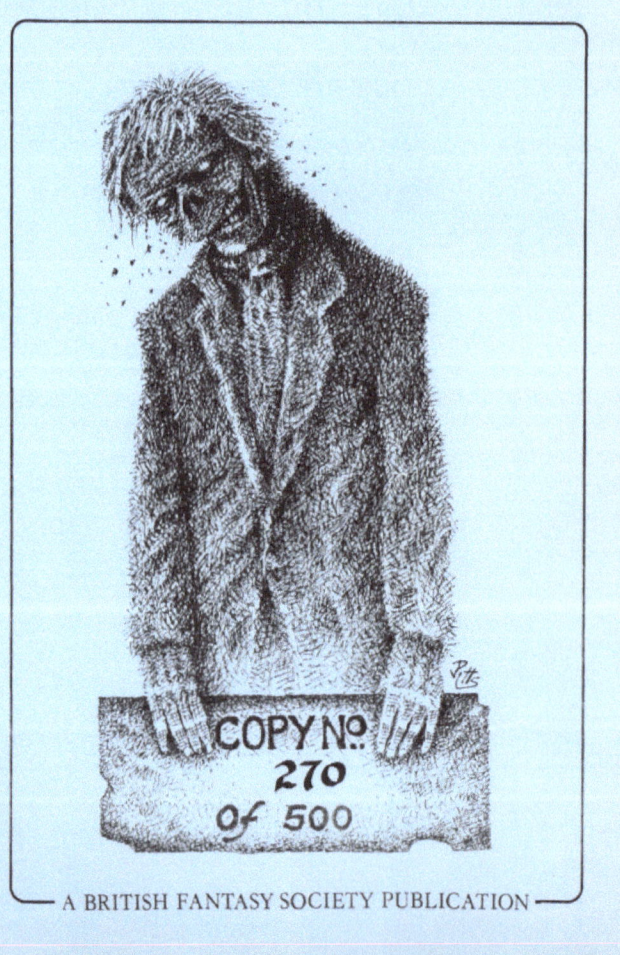

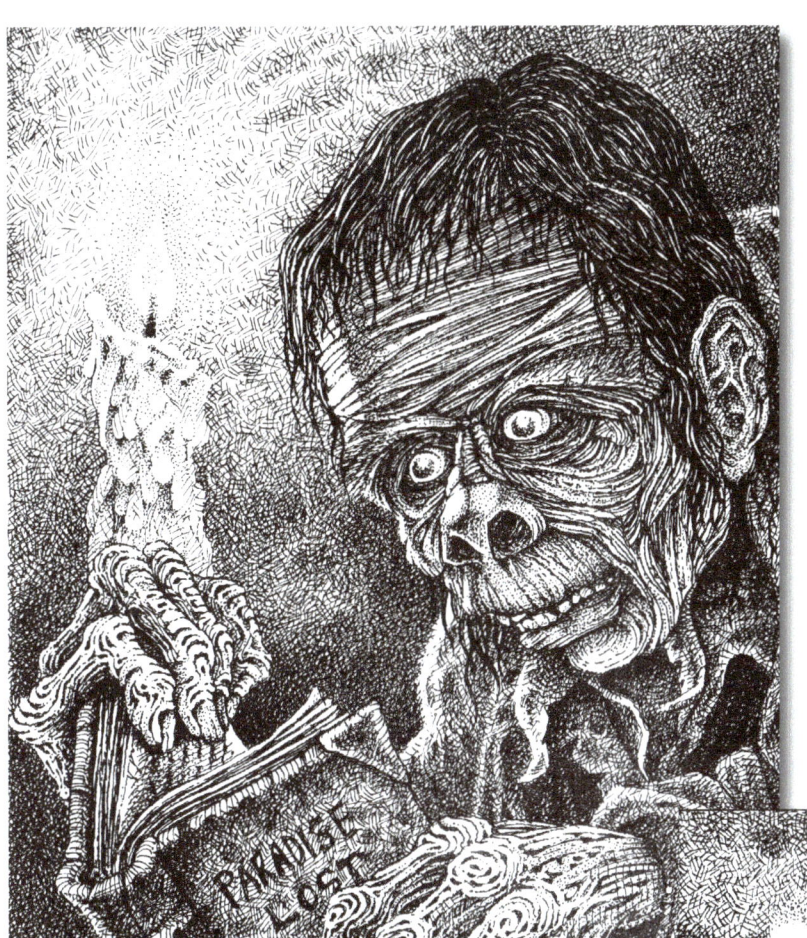

Mary Shelley's creature from *Frankenstein*

M. R. James - *Oh Whistle and I'll Come For You, My Lad*

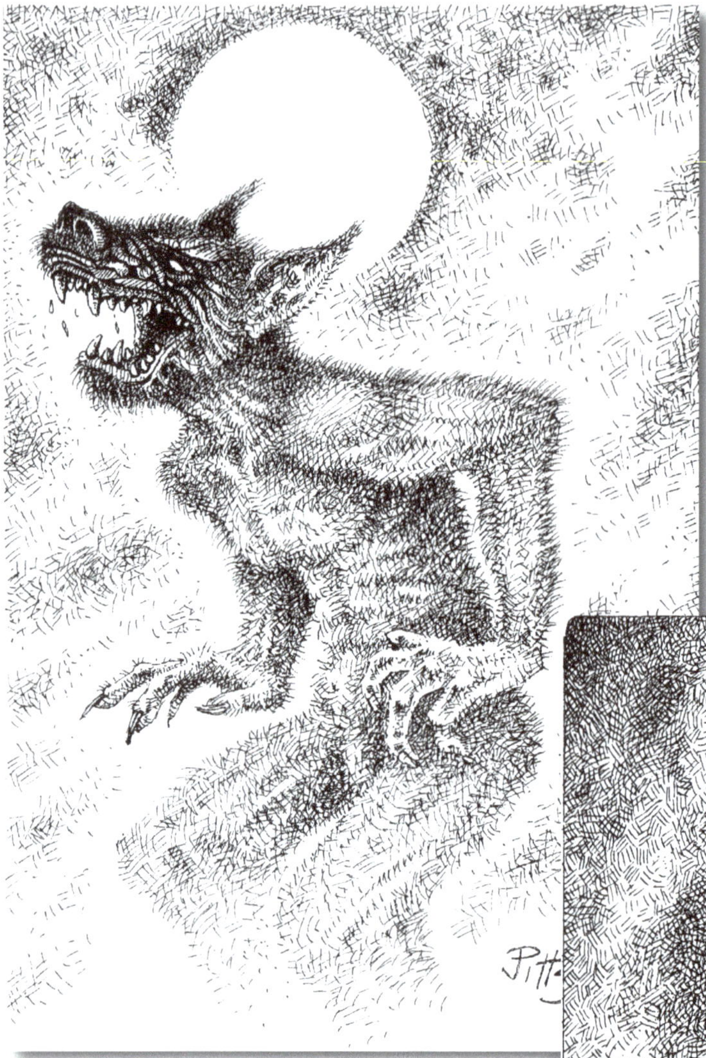

Guy Endore's *Werewolf of Paris*

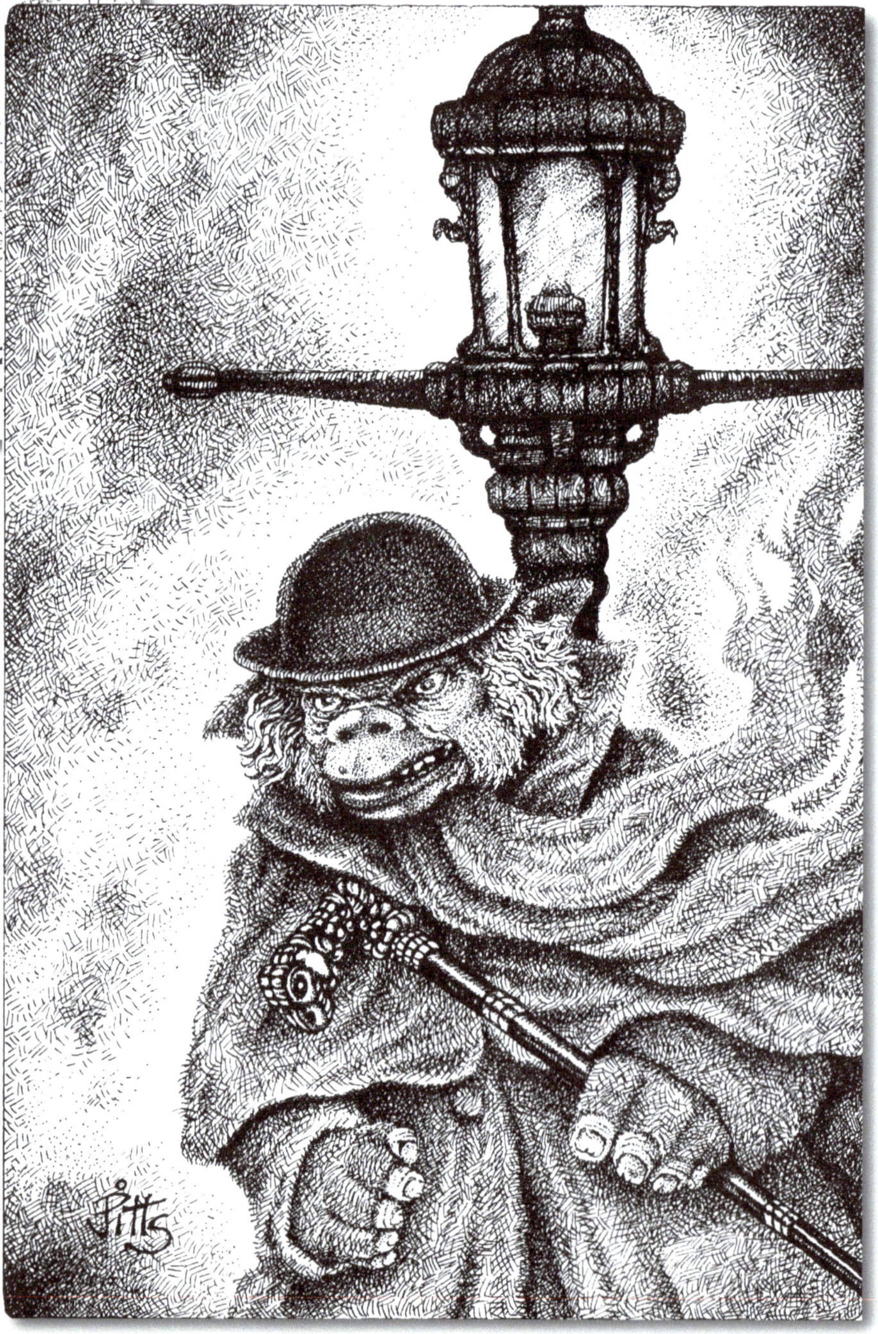

Mr Hyde from *Dr. Jekyll and Mr Hyde* by Robert Louis Stephenson

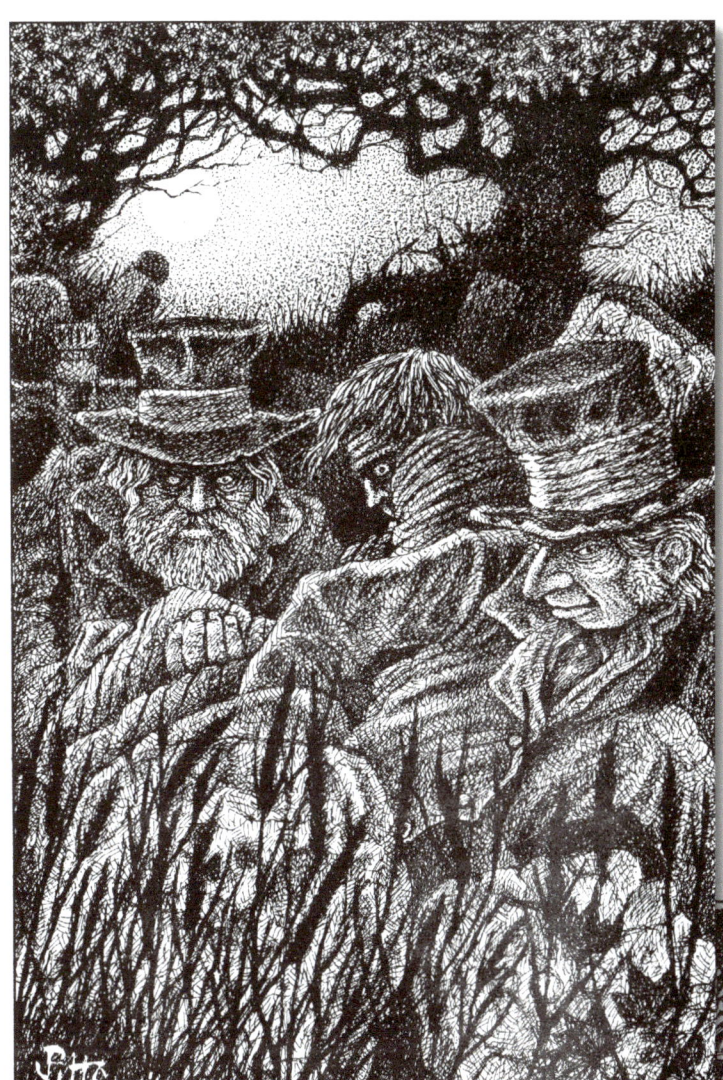

The Body Snatcher by Robert Louis Stephenson

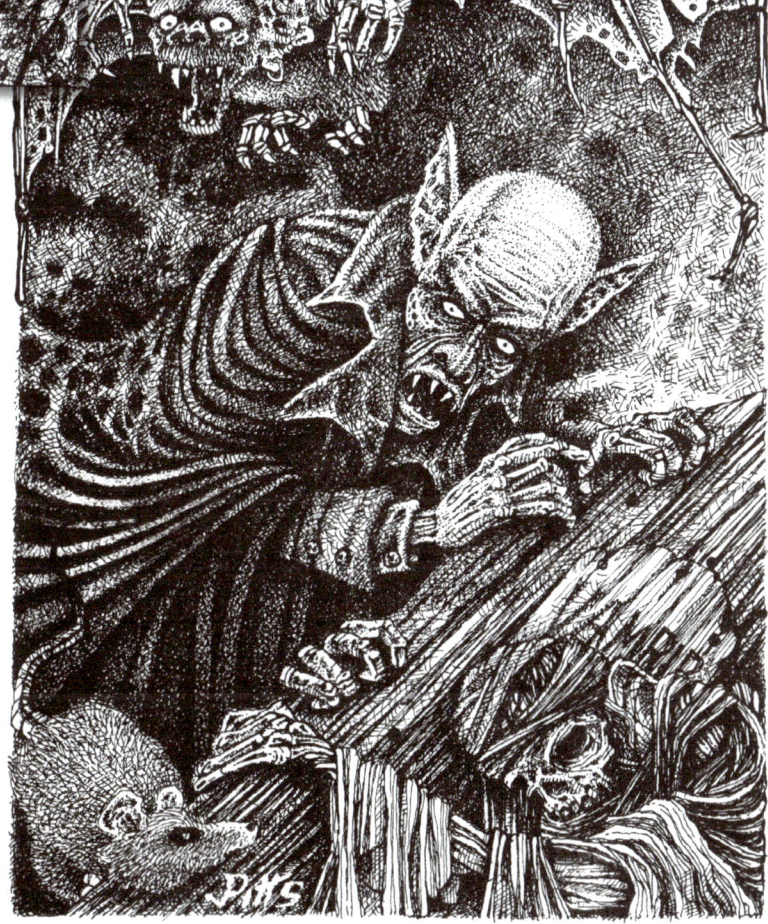

Vampyre

1988 WORLD FANTASY CONVENTION - LONDON
Gaslight & Ghosts
edited by Stephen Jones & Jo Fletcher

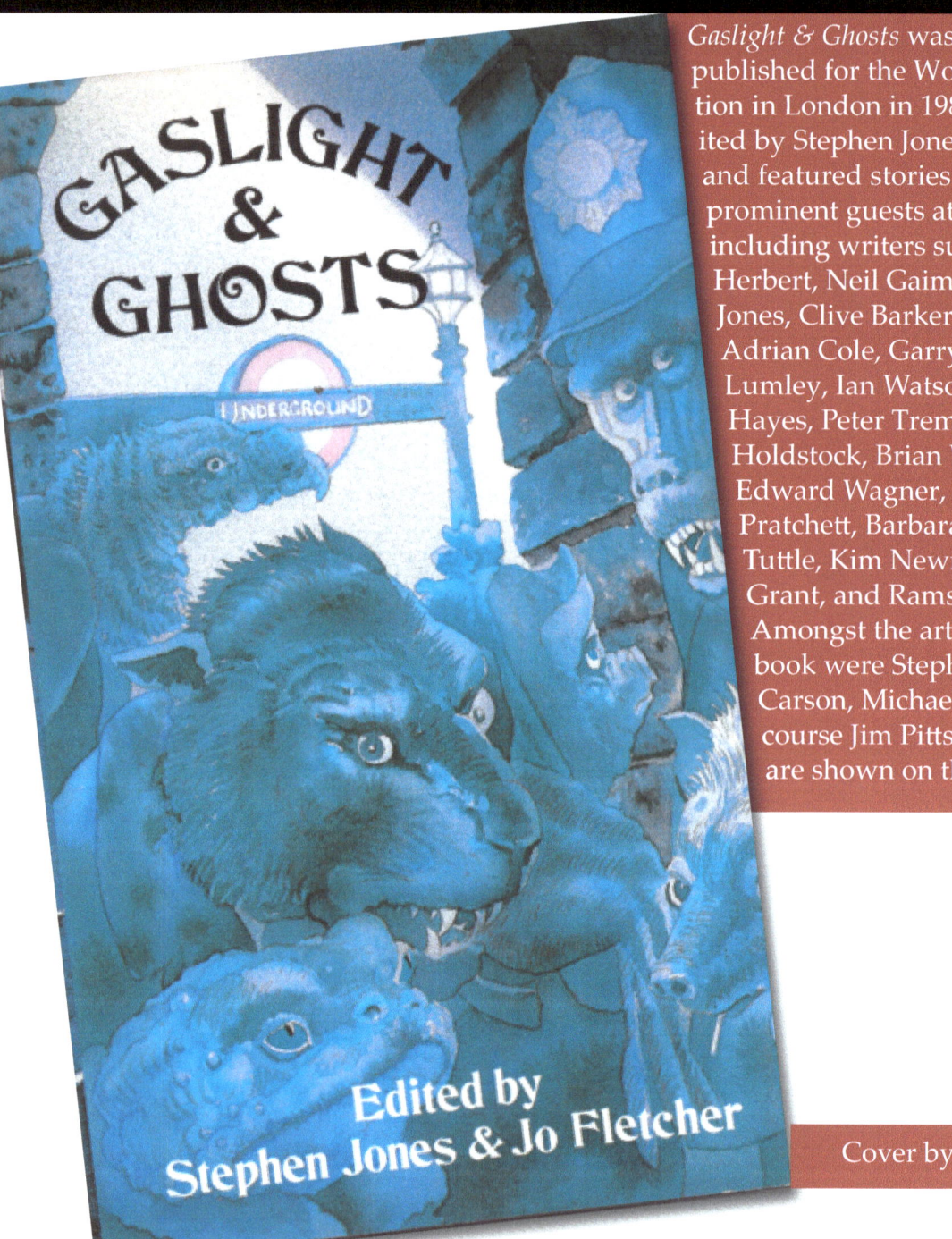

Gaslight & Ghosts was a hardcover book published for the World Fantasy Convention in London in 1988. It was jointly edited by Stephen Jones and Jo Fletcher, and featured stories and articles by prominent guests at the convention, including writers such as James Herbert, Neil Gaiman, Diana Wynne Jones, Clive Barker, Hugh Lamb, Adrian Cole, Garry Kilworth, Brian Lumley, Ian Watson, R. Chetwynd-Hayes, Peter Tremayne, Robert Holdstock, Brian W. Aldiss, Karl Edward Wagner, Mike Ashley, Terry Pratchett, Barbara Hambly, Lisa Tuttle, Kim Newman, Charles L. Grant, and Ramsey Campbell. Amongst the artists included in the book were Stephen Jones, Dave Carson, Michael Foreman, and of course Jim Pitts, whose illustrations are shown on the following page.

Cover by Michael Foreman

Jim's illustrations in *Gaslight & Ghosts*, edited by Stephen Jones and Jo Fletcher.

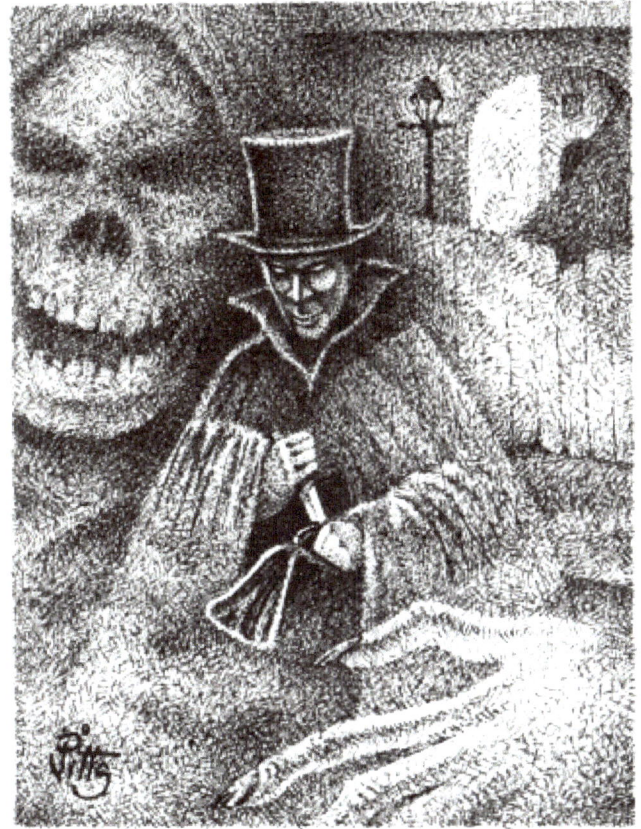

Illustration courtesy Jim Pitts

Top left: Jack the Ripper

Bottom: Demons

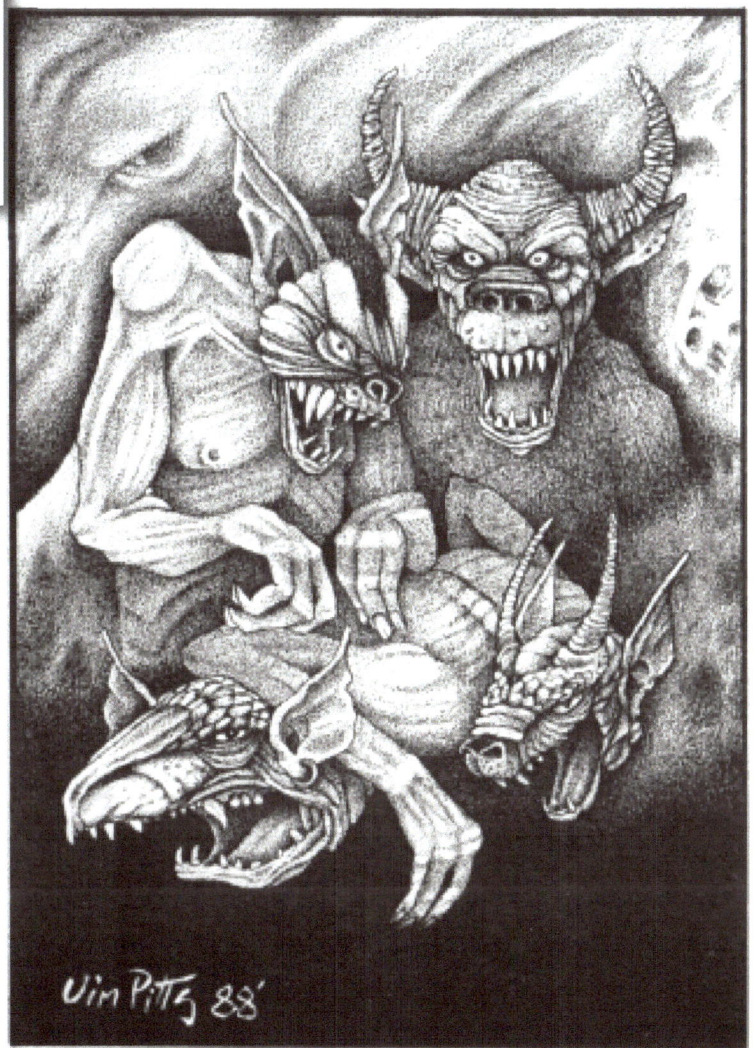

Illustration courtesy Jim Pitts

From the collection of Stephen Jones, Jim's depiction of a wizard - from the 1980s

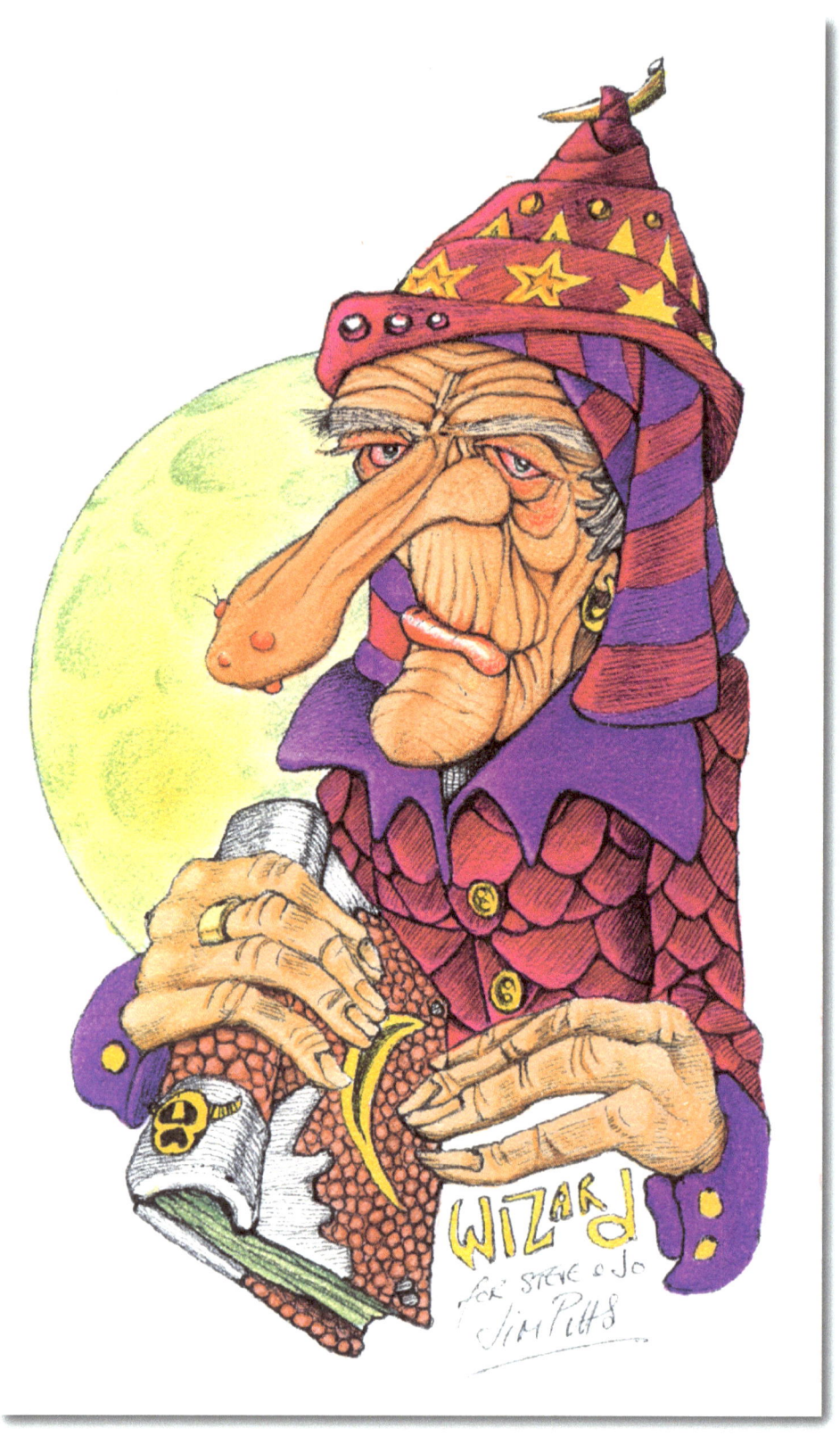

Original artwork for the front cover of *Oblivion Hand*, published by Wildside Press in 2000

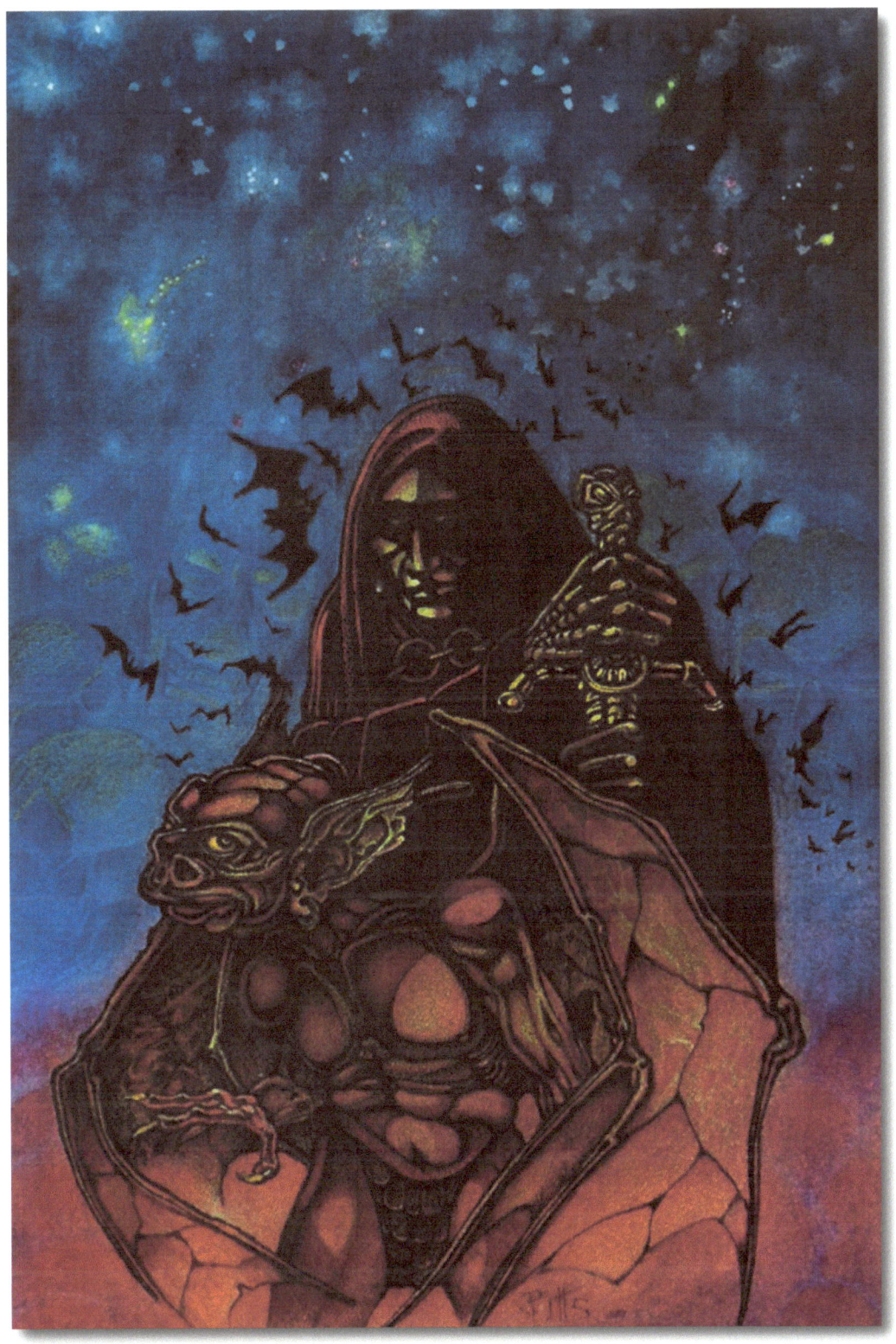

JIM PITTS: FROM THE DARK REGIONS OF THE VOIDAL'S OMNIVERSE TO THE TWISTED PULPWORLD OF NICK NIGHTMARE

A FEW REFLECTIONS by Adrian Cole

Back in the early 70s (I don't remember the exact dates) I began corresponding with Jim Pitts as part of a more general connection with the writers and artists who had become associated with the evolving British Fantasy Society. Jim's illustrations appeared in the BFS newsletters and magazine, *Dark Horizons*, and I chipped in articles and reviews, along with others: David Sutton, Stephen Jones, David Lloyd and Russ Nicholson, to name but a few. When I first met Jim, at one of the early Fantasycon conventions, it didn't take long for us to establish a friendship that has lasted to this day – we were, like most of us at the time, kindred spirits. Our mutual love of what was broadly called fantasy bonded us together.

We both enjoyed each other's work, so it was natural for Jim to be chosen to illustrate some of my pieces. My fiction at that time, still emerging from its earliest contortions, was a strange mixture of Edgar Rice Burroughs, H. P. Lovecraft and on to Robert E. Howard and other similar authors from the era of the pulps. Jim had a similar predilection for this type of fiction, and some of our conversations were very much a sharing of our tastes. As I recall, the first significant illustrations Jim did for my stories were for *Fantasy Tales*, the magazine launched by David Sutton and Stephen Jones. I'd written a King Kull pastiche for the first issue, and I'm sure Jim would have been asked to do the cover, illustrating it. However, copyright problems meant the story had to be pulled. Undeterred, I had a horror story, *Scars*, in the second issue, which Jim did do the cover for.

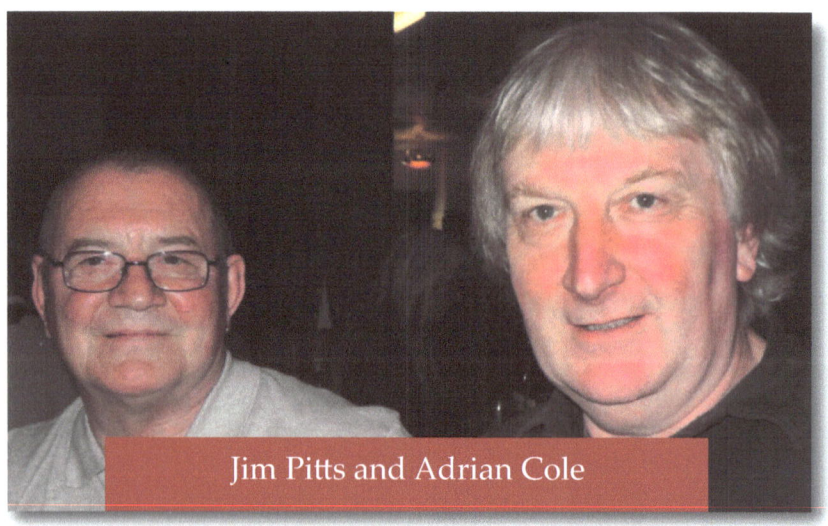

Jim Pitts and Adrian Cole

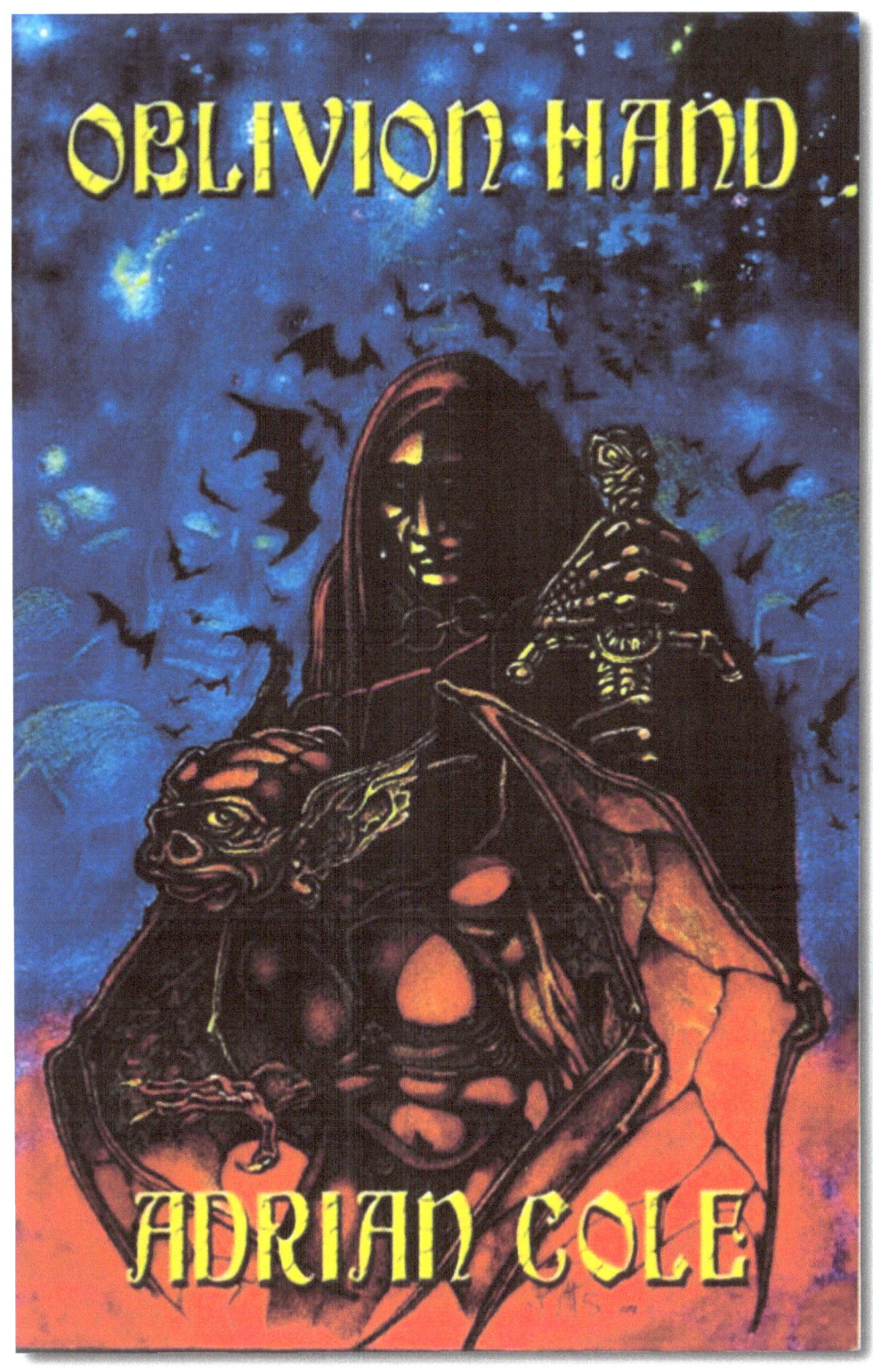

I had embarked on a fresh project (and I do know this was in late 1976) which was a series of bizarre adventures concerning a sword & sorcery character, the Voidal. This was no ordinary S and S clone, but a twisted mix of H. P. Lovecraft, Clark Ashton Smith and ideas inspired by the ultra-weird work of the French artist, Philippe Druillet. When Jon Harvey, publisher of the small press, Spectre Press, decided to publish the opening Voidal novella, *The Coming of the Voidal*, Jim was the obvious choice for its illustrator.

Jim entered the spirit of the story and produced some excellent full page illustrations for it, as well as some spot illustrations, and the chapbook appeared in 1977, launched, inevitably, at Fantasycon. Soon after that another Voidal story, *First Make Them Mad*, appeared in the 4th issue of *Fantasy Tales*, with a Jim Pitts cover as well as some very nice interior illustrations. Although I went on to write a number of Voidal stories, my character had a somewhat chequered career, some of the magazines he was due to appear in folding and various related projects collapsing – the Voidal did seem to have been cursed, certainly suppressed! Otherwise I'm sure there would have been far more Jim Pitts Voidal artwork unleashed.

I went on to concentrate on writing novels and was fortunate enough to be published both in the UK and the States and for a long time wrote very few short stories. I followed Jim's progress as an artist, however, and still met up with him and other friends from the early days. I vividly recall one Fantasycon where Jim won the British Fantasy Award for best artist, and as I was toastmaster, I had the honour and great pleasure to present him with the award, which seemed very fitting. (Actually, I presented him with the base of the award, as the pieces themselves weren't ready in time for the convention, which was, I believe, a somewhat unique occasion.)

I think it was in the late 90s when I was approached by an American publisher, Wildside Press, about doing some work for them and I suggested they do the entire Voidal canon. This would be all the original stories, revised and put into order, with a significant amount of new material, the whole saga culminating in the denouement. Wildside signed me up to do the books – a trilogy – and I suggested they approach Jim about doing covers for them, as he'd been involved in the early days and his depiction of the Voidal had nailed the character nicely.

I'd been out of touch with Jim for a while (indeed, with the fantasy scene as a whole) but was delighted when he agreed to do the work. The first Wildside volume, *Oblivion Hand*, was subsequently published in 2000, with a full colour cover by Jim – the Voidal and Elfloq, his familiar. Jim and I talked about what might appear on the cover of the second book. However, there were interior wrangles at Wildside, the details of which I know little about. However, these led to a long delay in the 2nd and 3rd volumes being published, and I'd given up hope of them coming out at all, at least from Wildside.

The original editor at Wildside had moved on, and in the meantime John Betancourt did want to publish the books, and when they came out, it was without Jim Pitts covers. The curse of the Voidal had struck, one way or another. (As an aside, I had done another book for Wildside, acting as editor on *Young Thongor*, and had arranged for another British artist, Bob Covington, to do the cover. Bob produced a beautiful piece, but it was lost when the original editor moved on and when the book came out, it had a cover by a different artist.)

For various reasons, both Jim and I were away from the scene for many years – I think in both our cases it was to do with work commitments. So, when I retired in 2011, and got back to writing and being published, I was excited to learn that Jim was also keen to start illustrating again. We began to communicate – our common link was Jon Harvey, who had also been away from things for years and who wanted to re-launch Spectre Press.

By then I had started writing and publishing the first of my Nick Nightmare stories, tales centred around my hard-boiled, wise-cracking occult private eye, whose exploits invariably pit him against the Mythos and other dark and demonic forces. Jon Harvey commissioned a novella from me and I duly wrote *Nightmare on Mad Gull Island*. Jon suggested Jim for the cover and interior art, and I wasn't going to argue with that! Jim then produced a beautiful wraparound cover for the booklet, and some suitably dark interiors. Peter Coleborn, of Alchemy Press, approached me about doing a Nick Nightmare collection, and to cut a long story short, *Nick Nightmare Investigates* was published in 2014, with suitably creepy endpapers from Jim, as well as his trademark spot illustrations inside.

We launched the book at Fantasycon (of course) in York, where Jim and I and Mike Chinn (who co-wrote one of the book's yarns with me) joined up with Peter and Stephen Jones (who co-produced the book) for a reunion that had more than a little nostalgia about it.

Having come back into illustrating, Jim has very clearly raised the bar with his work, in particular his colour work, which seems to me to have a new power and maturity about it. This is especially true of the cover he painted for my *Tough Guys* collection (Parallel Universe, 2016). One of the stories in the book is particularly bleak and I suggested that Jim use that one as the basis for his cover. I wasn't disappointed, and by people's reactions to it, it has clearly evoked a very positive response.

Where does our unofficial partnership go from here? Well, there'll be more. I have a novella due for publication in the highly praised *Skelos* magazine (issue 4) which is part of my on-going Elak of Atlantis series and Jim is working on the artwork for it, and we also have another new story due out in the summer from Jon Harvey's *Worlds of the Unknown* (issue 5), for which Jim is painting the cover. I'm sure things won't stop there.

Jim's work has always been very distinctive, with a style all of its own that's always recognisable. From the simplicity of his early artwork of the 70s and 80s, Jim has evolved in an exciting way and I'm sure this volume will attest to his development as an artist. It's been a privilege to work with Jim over the years and I'm looking forward to co-producing many more projects together.

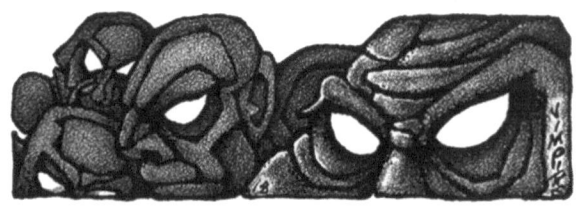

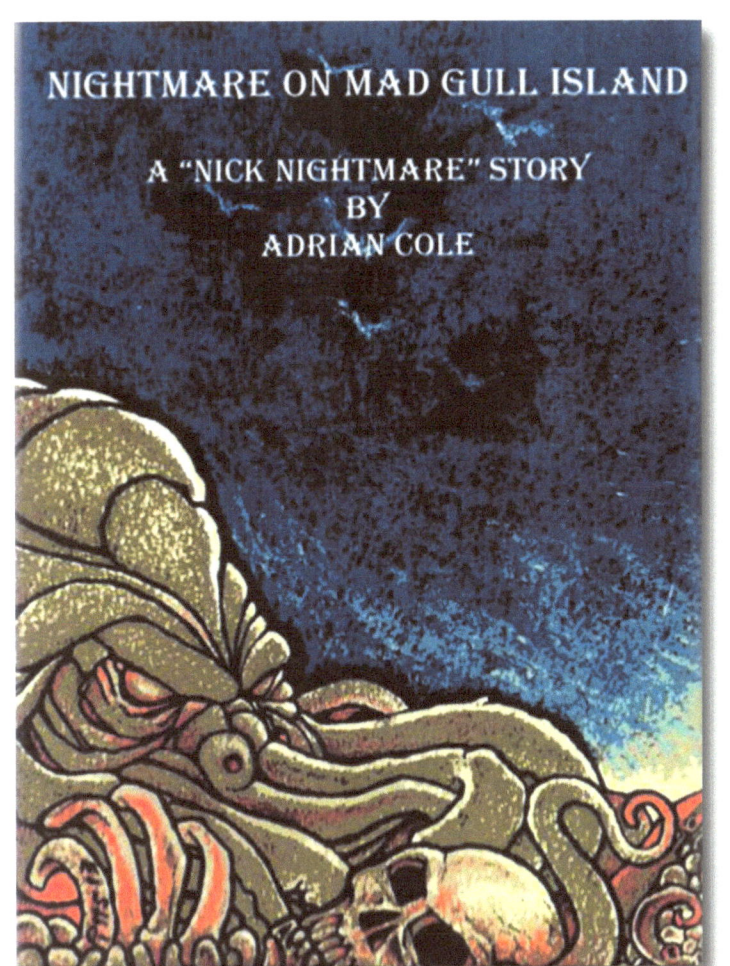
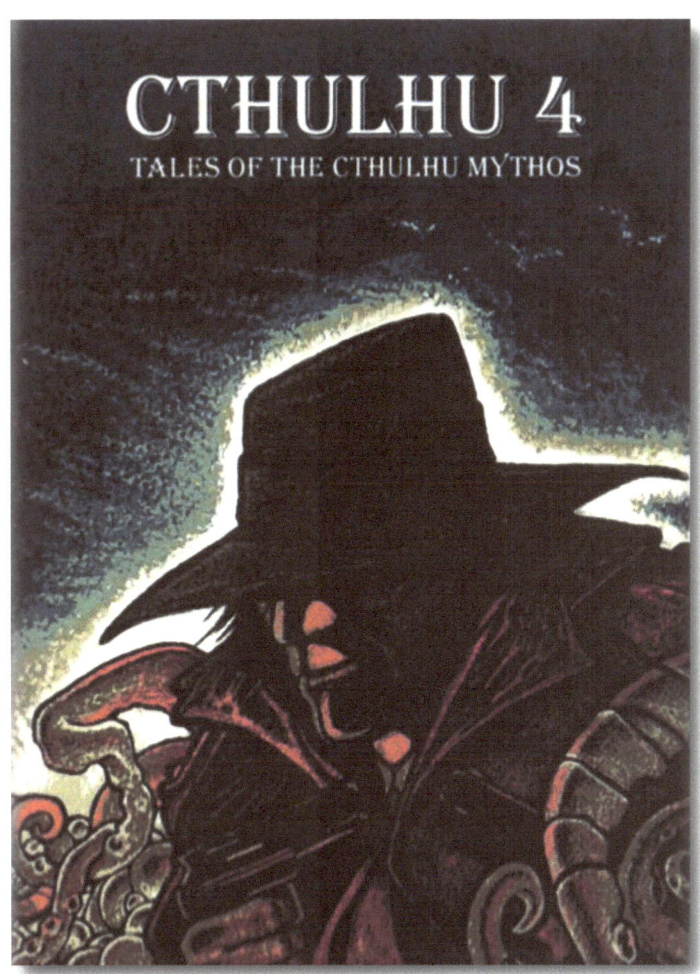

Back and front covers of *Cthulhu 4* - original artwork below

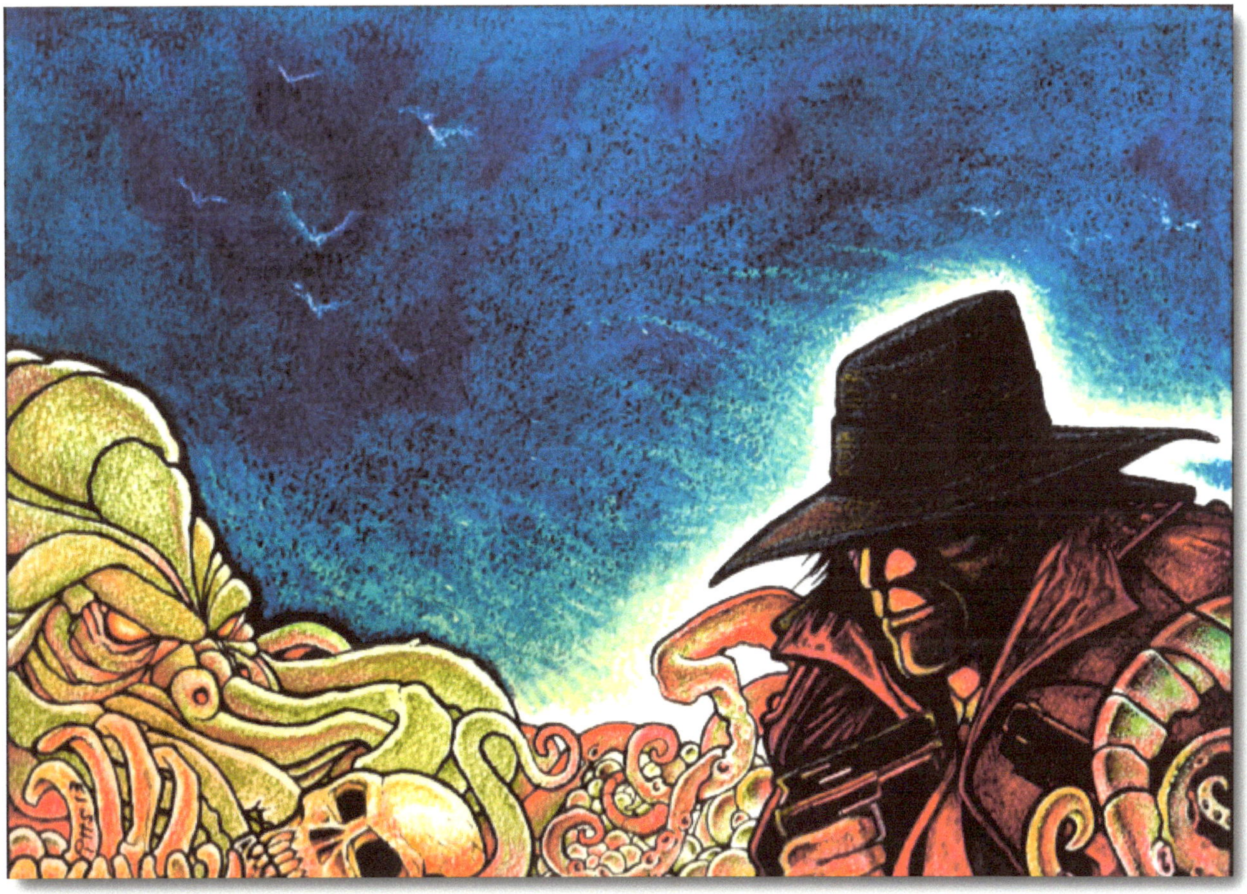

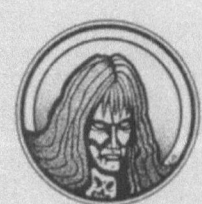

Adrian Cole's *The Coming of the Voidal*

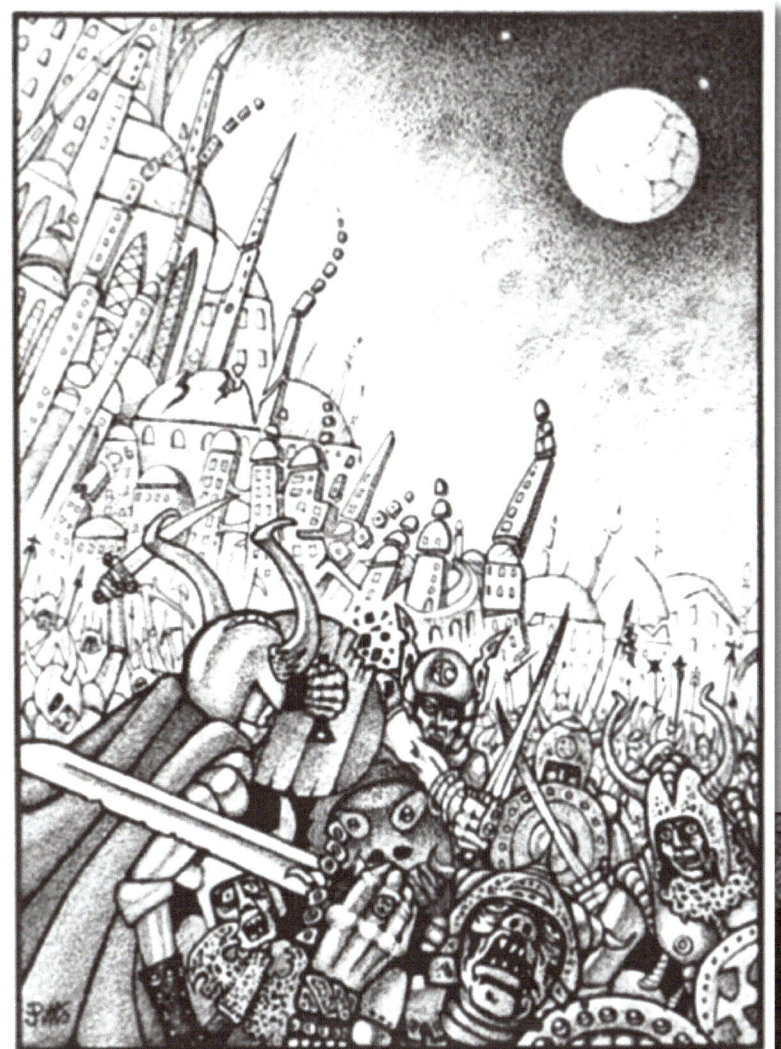
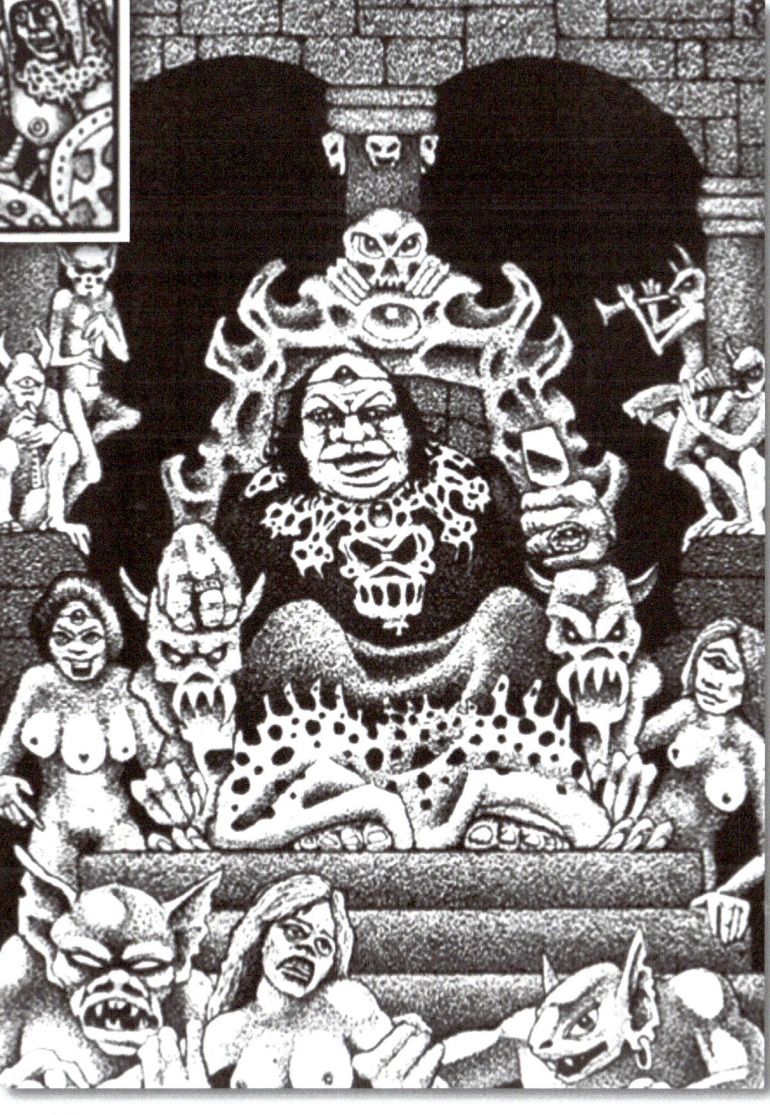

Adrian Cole's *The Coming of the Voidal*

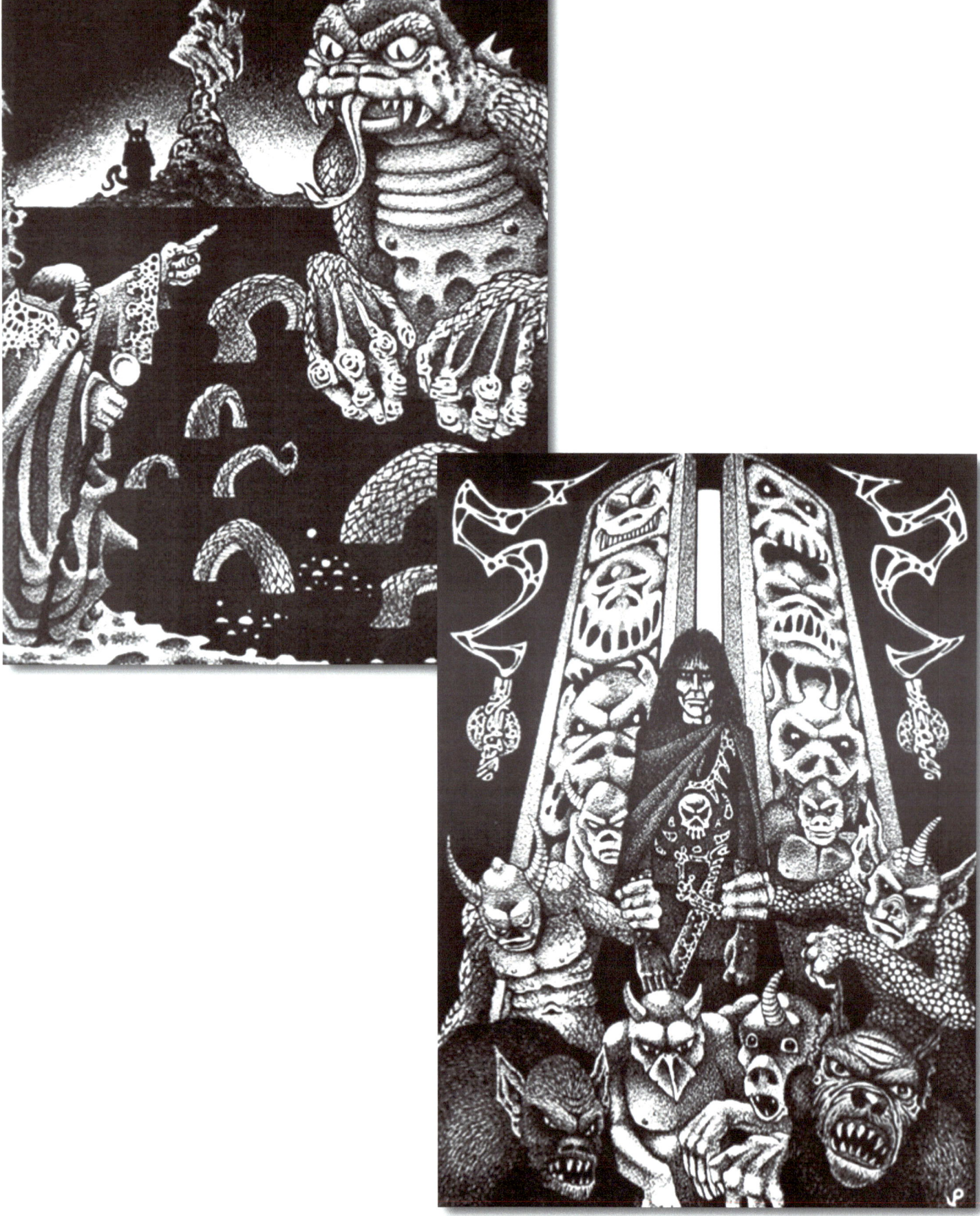

Adrian Cole's *The Coming of the Voidal*

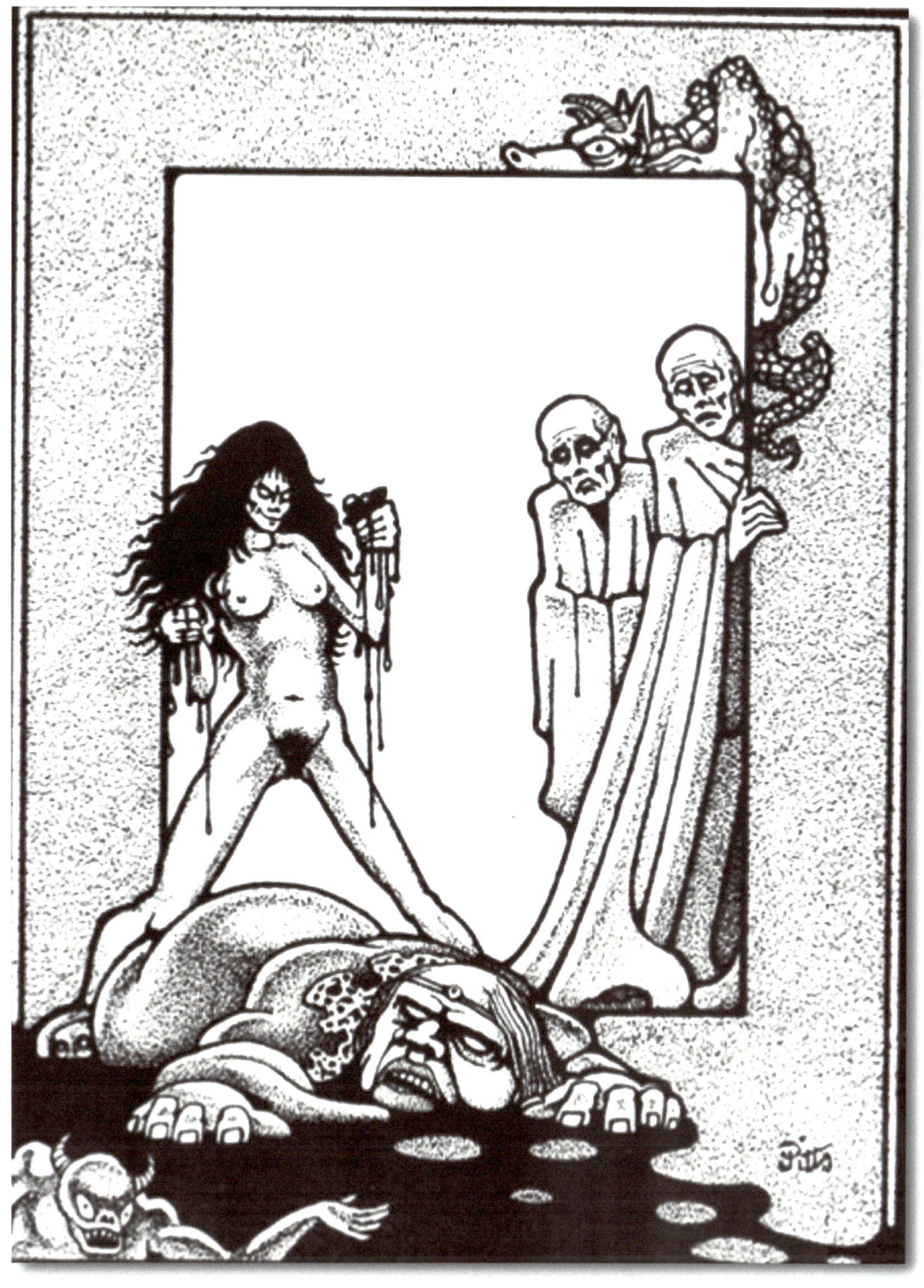

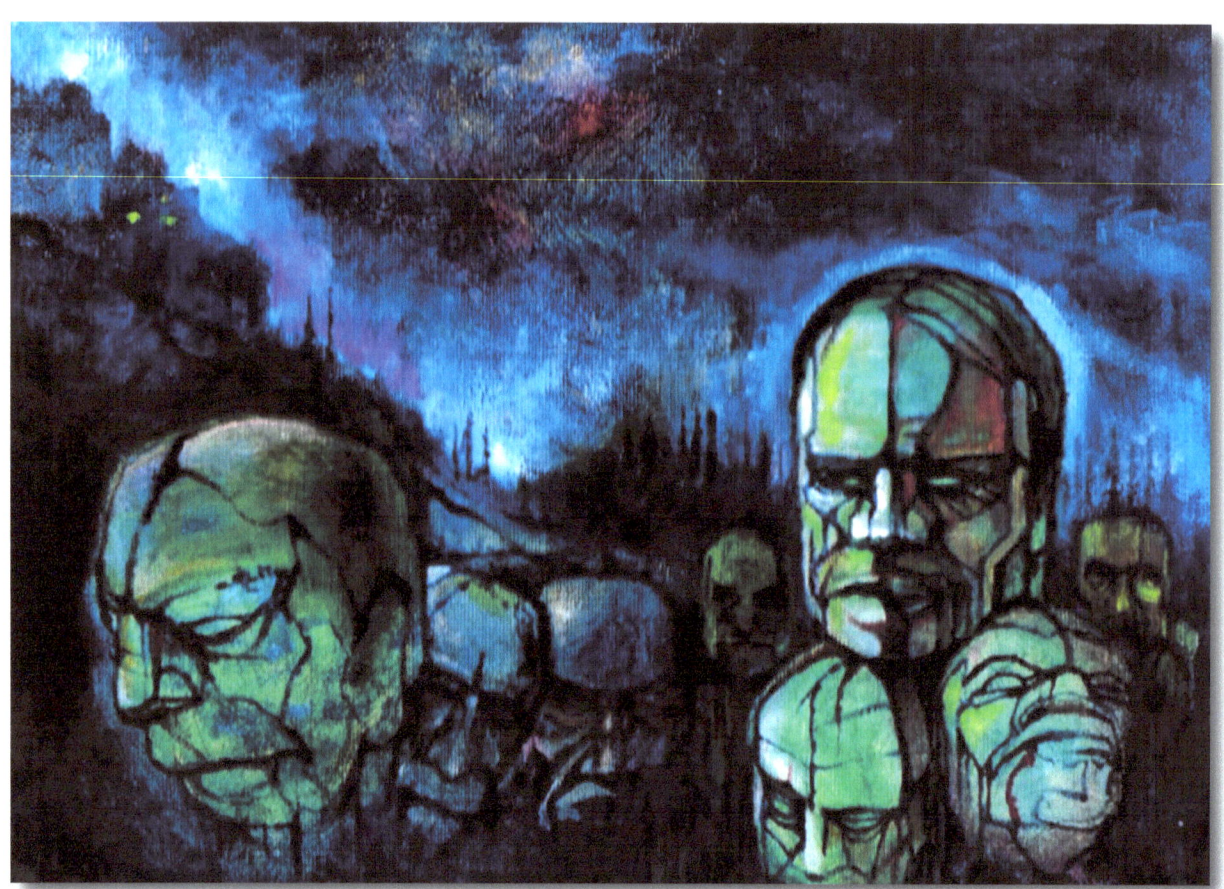

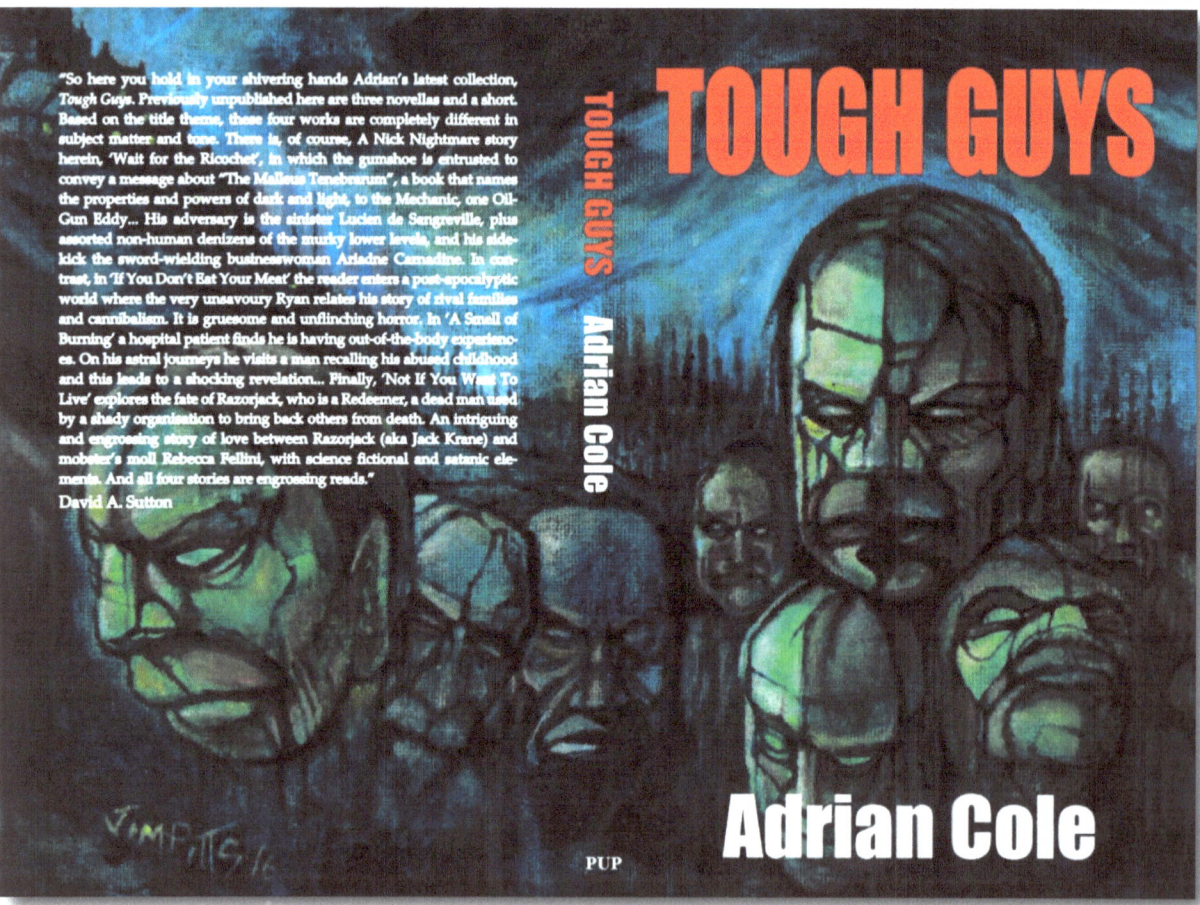

Tough Guys by Adrian Cole was published by Parallel Universe Publications in 2016, with a wraparound Jim Pitts cover.

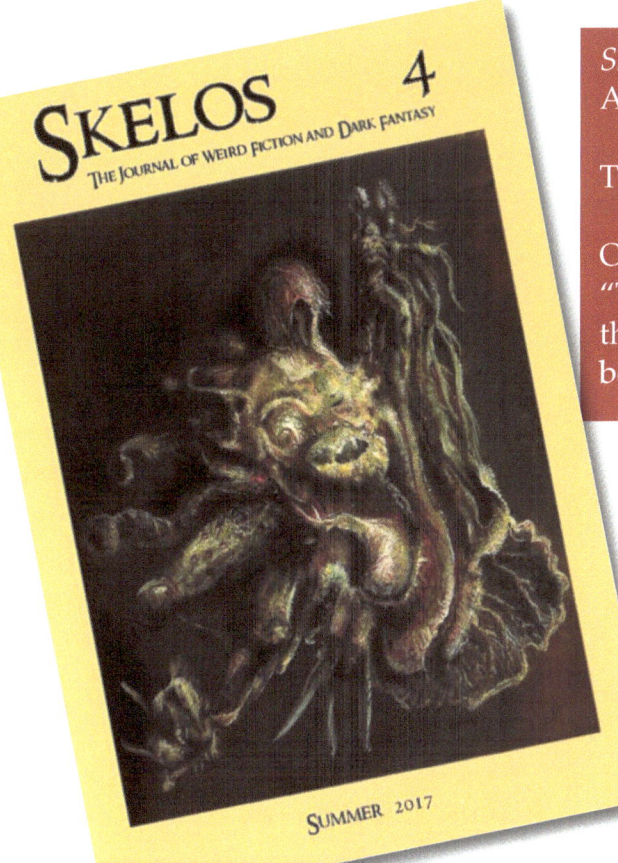

Skelos 4 - 2017 - featuring Adrian Cole's Elak of Atlantis tale *The Revenge of the Sorcerer*.

The illustrations below are the heading and tailpiece.

On the facing page is the main illustration.
"They felt the rancid breath of the huge sea beast as the thing came down with devastating force across the bow of the ship, smashing planks and timbers."

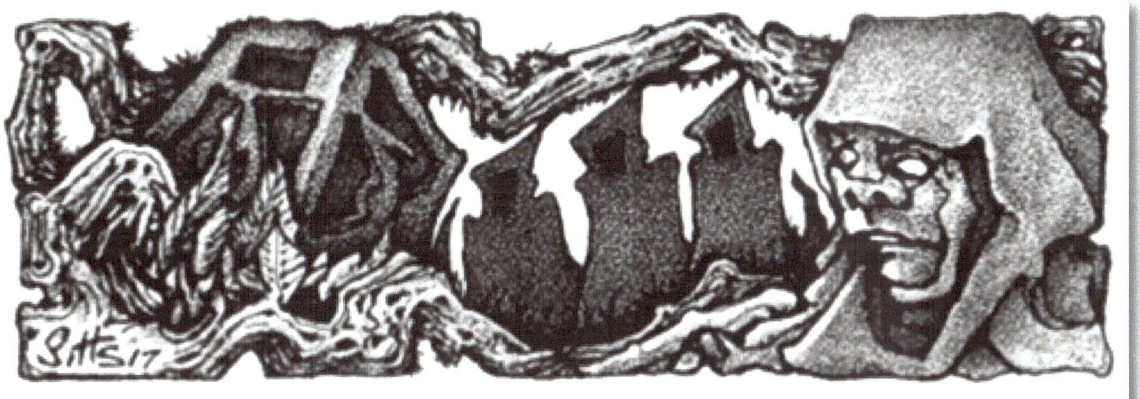

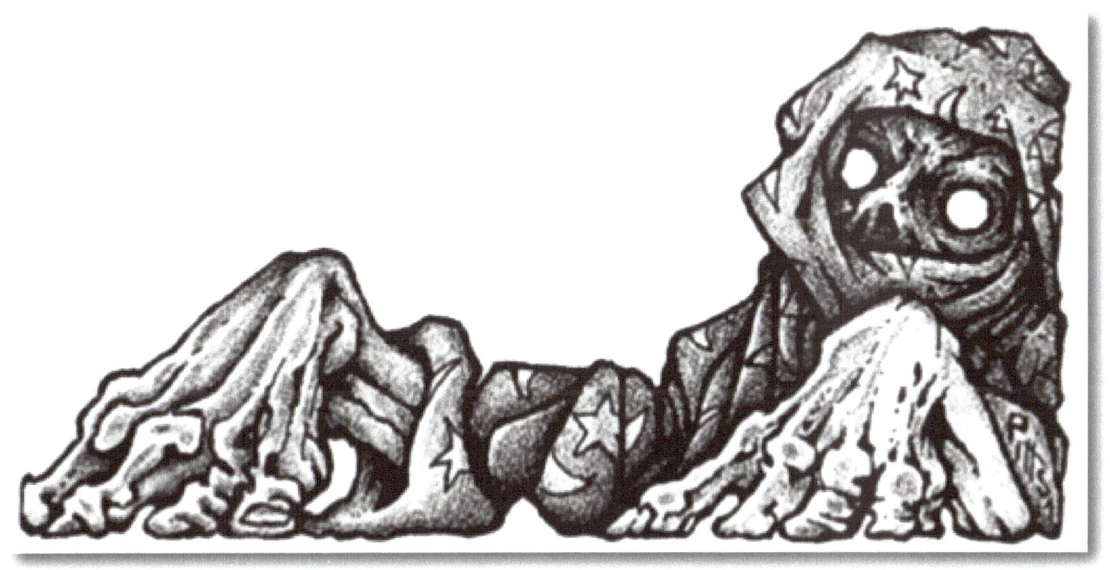

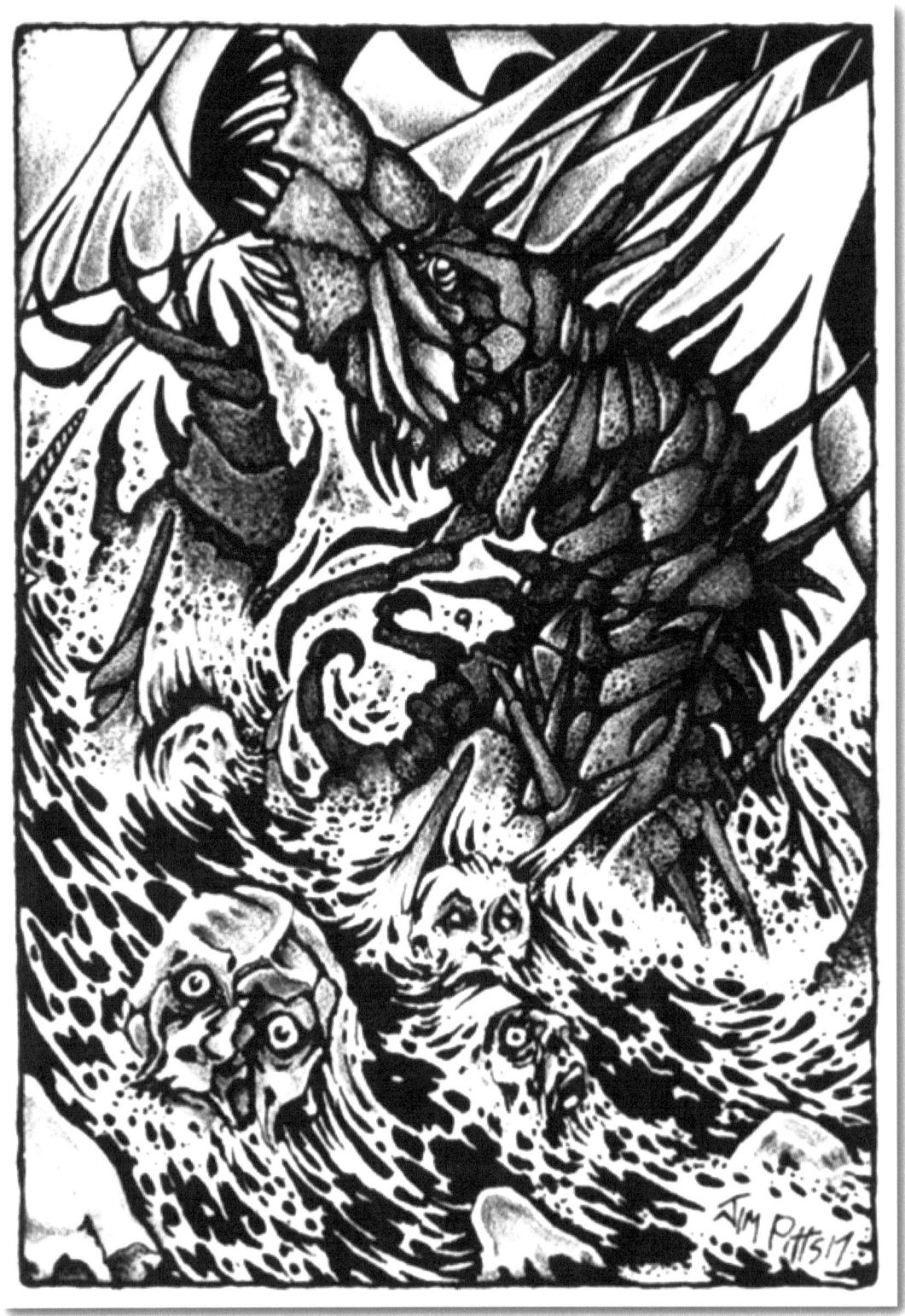

THE HOUSE OF CTHULHU
and other tales of the primal land

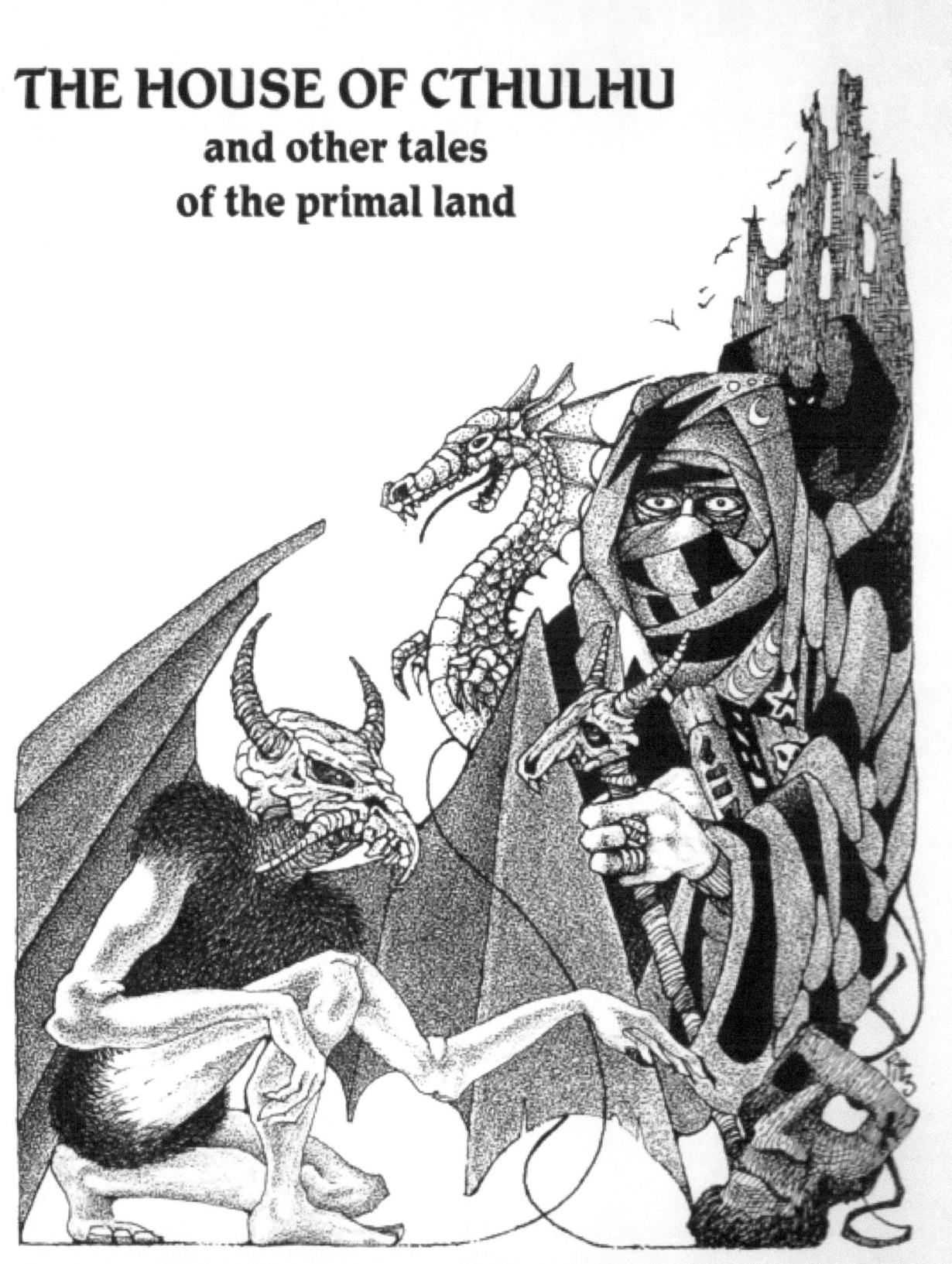

JIM PITTS: IN PENCIL, PEN-AND-INK, THE UNCROWNED PRINCE OF THE PRIMAL LAND!
by Brian Lumley

Jim Pitts? Yes, I know him, have known him for…well, it feels like ages! For I seem to remember we were well met in Theem'hdra, the Primal Land (in fact an island continent and the earliest of embryonic human civilizations, at the dawn of time), where I came across Jim sketching a struggling barbarian Hrossak caught up in the frantic but weakening clutches of a great wounded Roc-bird, and aeons later in several providential meetings of the annual British Fantasy Society in Birmingham in this our latest 21st Century, er, "civilized" world. For he and I, Jim and me, we've both been great travellers in space and time, if only in our minds, or in words and pictures.

But to know Jim in whichever space- or time-frame – in fantasy or in fact – is to know him for a true gentleman and something of a near-genius artist. And when it comes to fantasy art I think I know what I'm talking about; for I have enjoyed, even loved, the artwork of…oh, so many Science Fiction, Fantasy and Horror limners in my time. I'm talking about the likes of Virgil Finlay, Hannes Bok, Lee Brown Coye, Margaret Brundage, Richard Upton Pickman and many others of that ilk among those I term "the Old Masters" (far too many others to find space for here; for which, reader, forgive me and my dodgy memory if you happen to be one of the so-called "others") down to such comparative newcomers as the mighty Bob Eggleton (who even has an asteroid named after him, I believe as a result of his superb Science Fiction artwork), the fabulous Fabian (whose gorgeous colours are blindingly vivid but real as life), down to the immaculately inked works of the likes of Alan Koszowski, Randy Broecker and Allan Servoss; and that fantastic trio Dave Carson, Martin McKenna and, of course, Jim Pitts – the last-named three of which once combined their talents to illustrate in amazing intricacy editor Steve Jones' *Shadows over Innsmouth* from the Fedogan and Bremer publisher, as well as many individual illustrations for other magazines and books. And once again I'll apologize for the dozen or more artists I've missed.

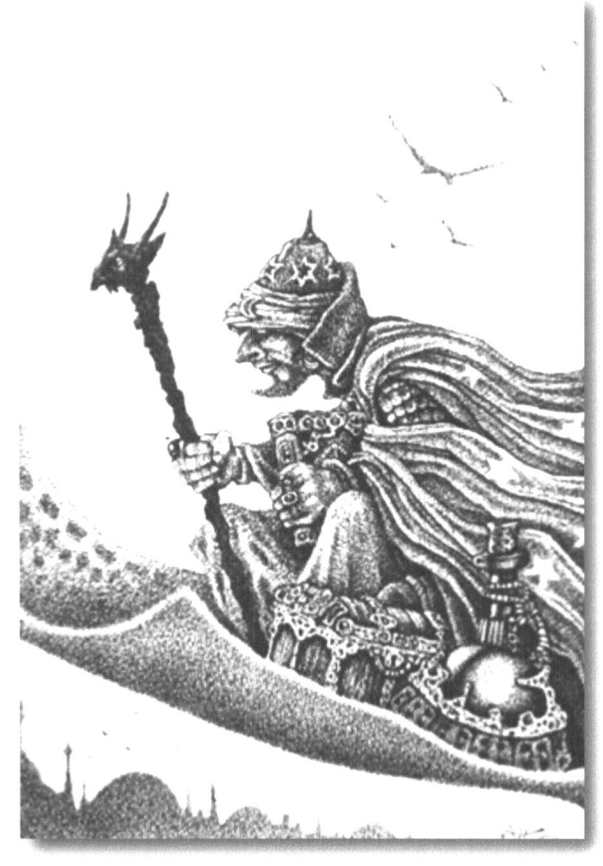

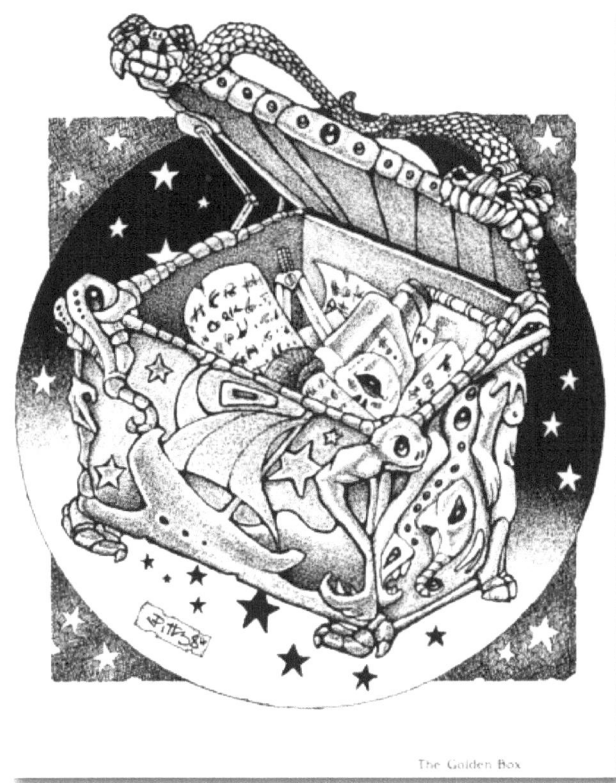

The Golden Box

Now, I'm not sure how much painted or coloured work Jim has done, but I've called him a prince in pencil, pen and ink, for a reason, and a very good one at that. Oh, indeed, for I've been fortunate enough to have Jim illustrate some of my stories and books…in fact several of them. From short stories and a jacket in editor Steve Jones' (once again) *Fantasy Tales*, to entire books from W. Paul Ganley's Weirdbook Press: such books as *The House of Cthulhu & Others* and *The Compleat Khash* in two volumes, of which trilogy I shall treat in that order.

In *House*…Jim's illustrations are fantastic! Especially the marvellous drawing on page 14 (borrowed from the very first issue of *Fantasy Tales*). Go out now and buy a copy, if you're fortunate enough to know where to find one! Some specialist bookstore, perhaps? And as for *The Compleat Khash*:

I'm happy to state that I've never got over my original delight at every one of this superb artist's illos in this Weirdbook collection…for they are simply, well, superb! And what author could possibly say less than that on seeing his stories given such visual life? This is where we first saw the barbarian Tarra Khash "in the flesh", as it were, battling that Roc-bird in primal Theem'hdra. And it doesn't stop there – in fact that's just for starters. Or rather, the inspirational jacket is just for starters, for the interiors – and once again I say all of them – are just as wonderful. I only wish I could show them here. But no, I can't, not all of them…though I can tell you about at least a few of them:

Such as the wizard Dramah aboard his flying carpet, his staff and runebook in hand, and the wizardly concentration of his mien as he speeds for home, passing high over that city of domes and spindly spires en route. But those birds in the sky, and the city below, and even the carpet itself – no matter how real to the viewer, these things – composed of nothing more than dots and scratches! Now how the heck did this artist friend of mine accomplish that? And then there's that small corner-of-a-page portrait of the treacherous Hadj Dzym on page 88, a character study if ever there was one. And more wonderful (or worse) still to come, in that full-body portrait of the hideous lamia Orbiquita, with a yet more monstrous lamia sister close by, scolding her. And this is only the first volume in the Tarra Khash saga…

But there – even though *Volume Two* of *The Compleat Khash*, *Sorcery in Shad*, contains almost as many gorgeous illustrations as *Volume One's Never a Backward Glance* – that's enough said on the Primal Land and the adventures of Tarra Khash…but it's not the end of our adventures together, Jim and I. For when Fedogan & Bremer release my next and what could well be my last book of Cthulhu Mythos tales and novellas, who do you suppose the publisher chose to do the illustration? Well, Bob Eggleton for the jacket, certainly – but as for the interiors:

Yes, you're right, and so are Fedogan & Bremer. As for me, I'm lucky because once again I've beaten my readers to it by persuading Jim Pitts to allow me an advance viewing of his astounding interiors. And you may rest assured that when *Eearth, Air, Fire & Water: Four Tales of Elemental Mythos Horror* is launched, you'll find that this master artist's headings and full-page delirious depictions will do for you what they've already done for me – for of course they're utterly monstrous! And I simply love them!

Jim, you see this glass in my hand right now…well, I'm tilting it to you, my friend, with my congratulations on what you've achieved, and what with your skills you will surely achieve in the future…

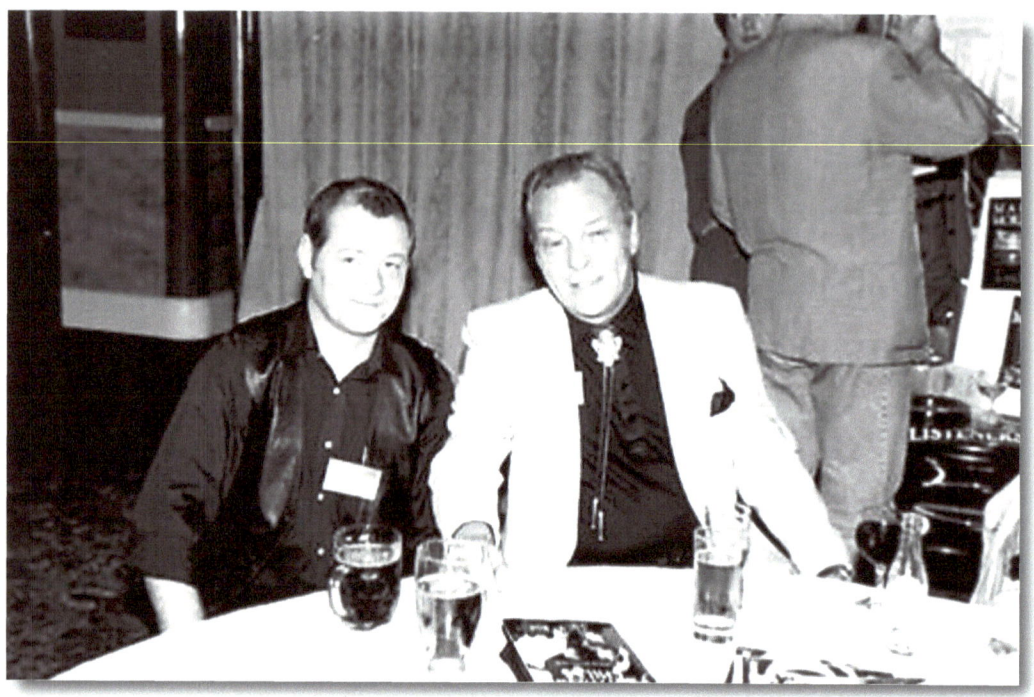

Jim Pitts and Brian Lumley enjoying a relaxing drink at FantasyCon.

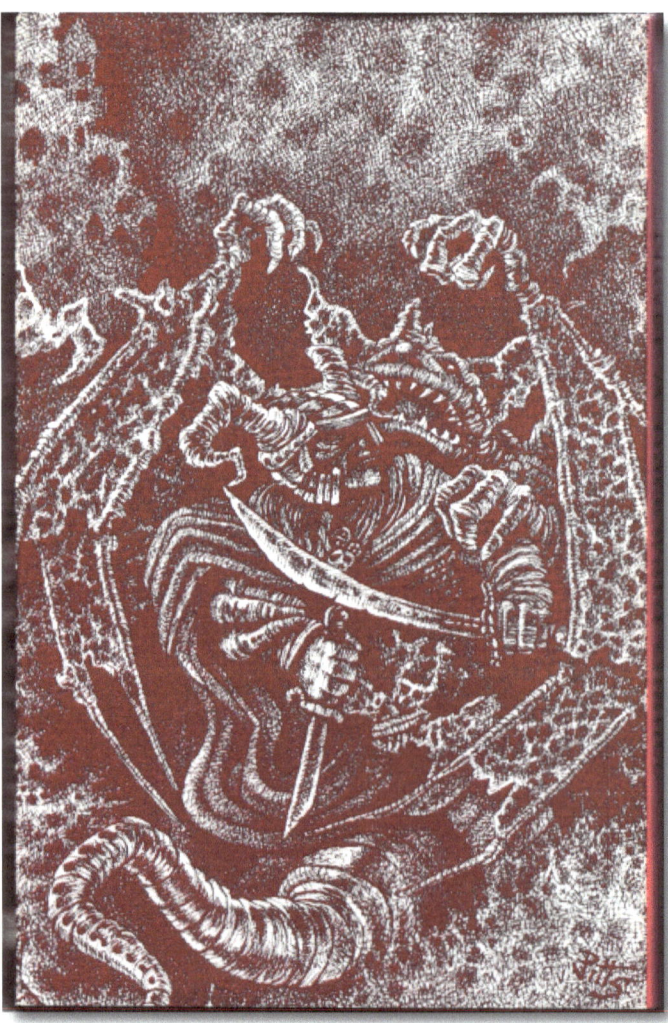

Front and back covers of *The Compleat Khash: Volume One*.

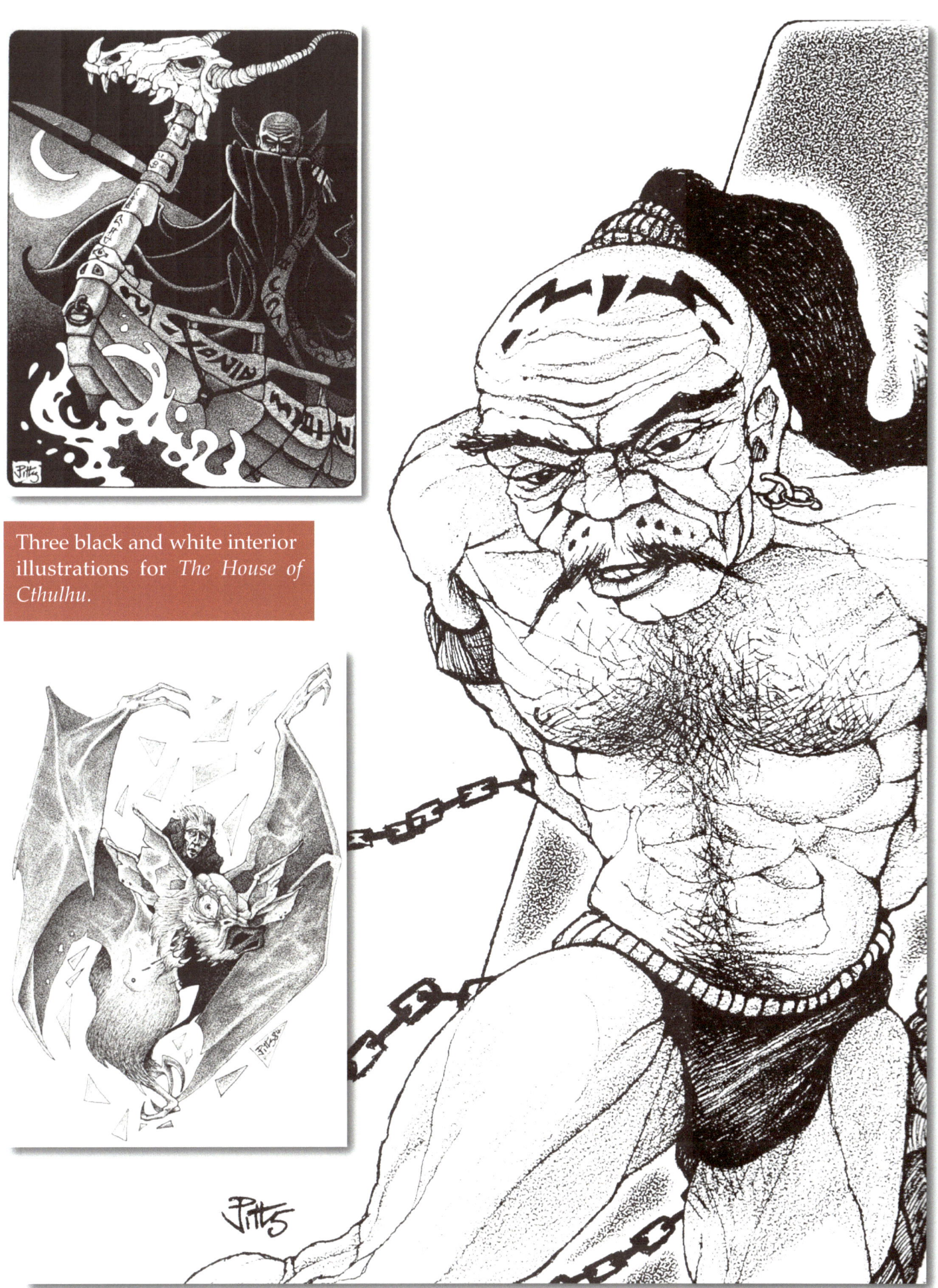

Three black and white interior illustrations for *The House of Cthulhu*.

29

The original artwork for the front cover of *The Compleat Khash*

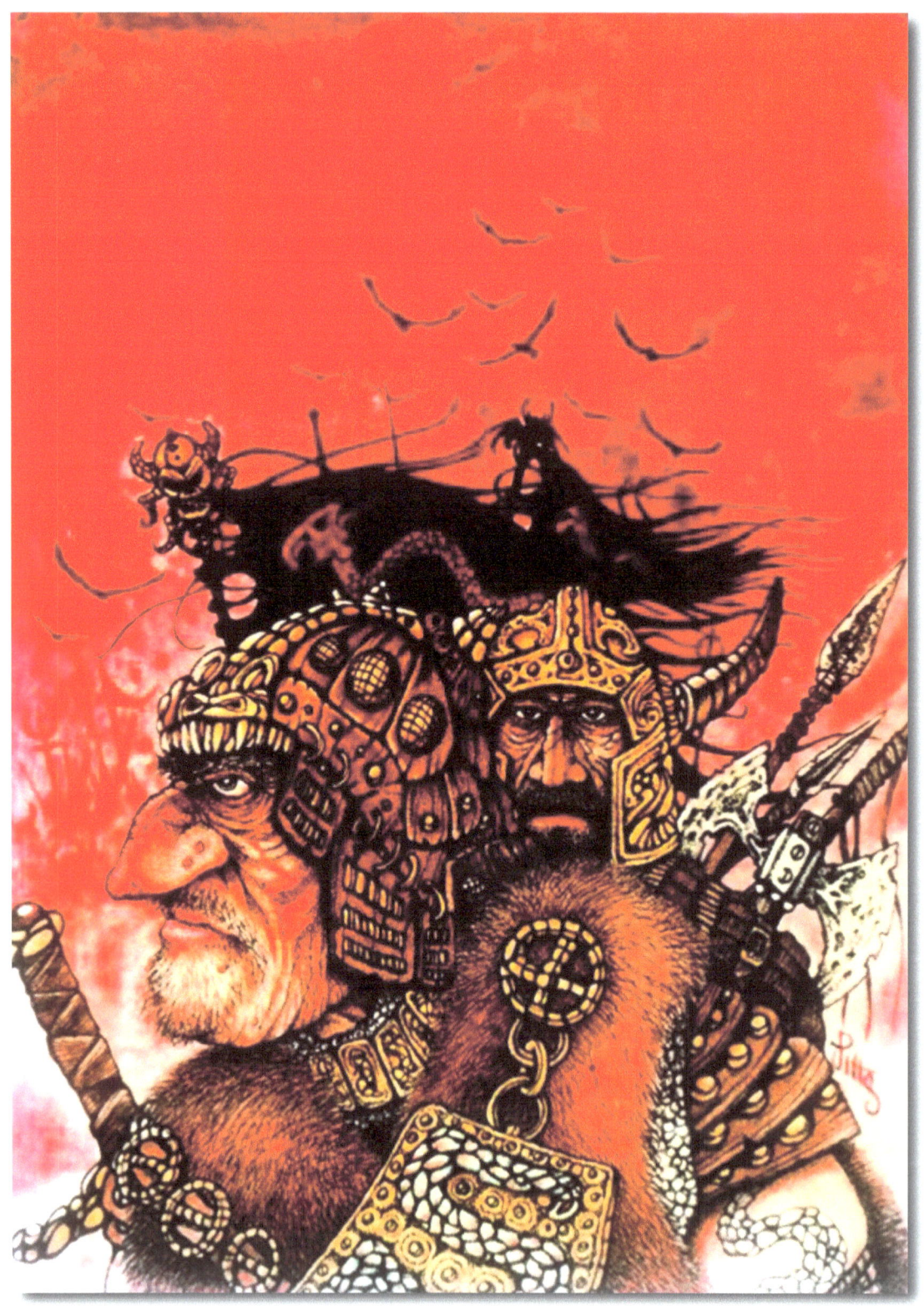

The front and back covers of *The Compleat Khash Volume Two: Sorcery in Shad* by Brian Lumley - published by W. Paul Ganley

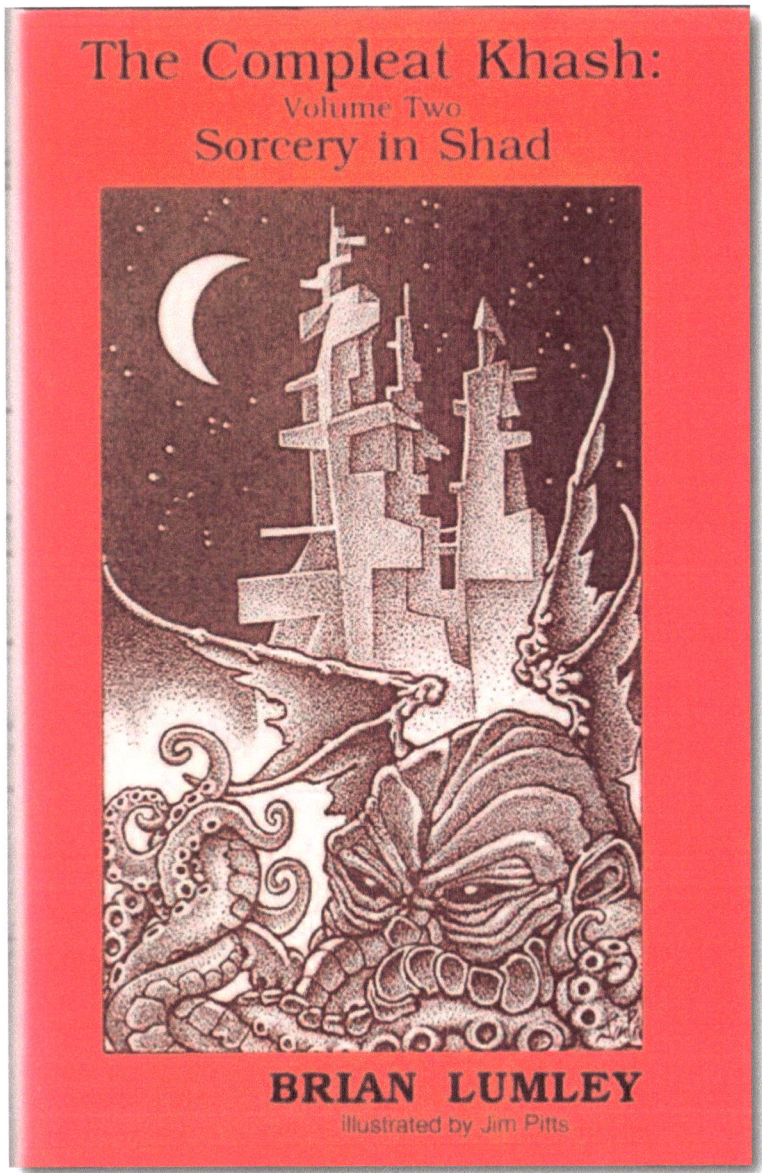

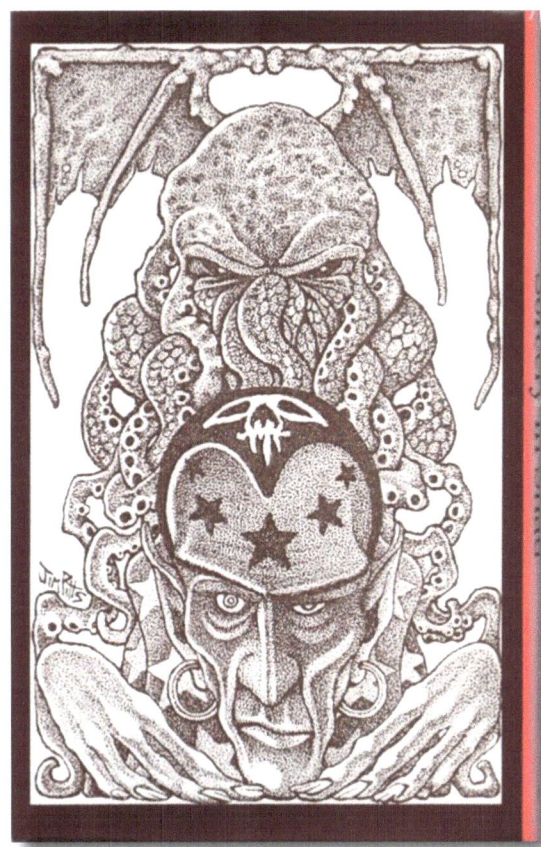

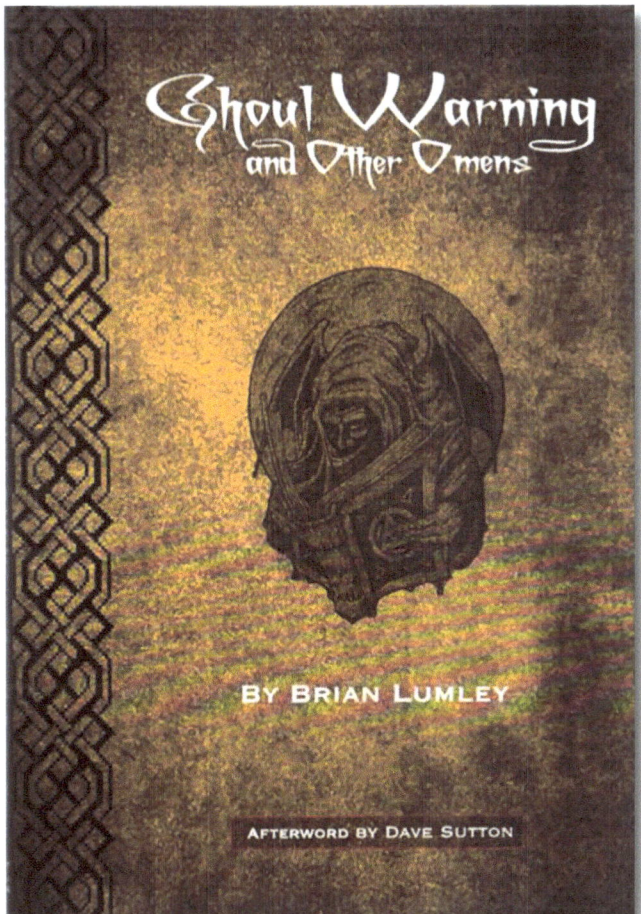

Ghoul Warning and Other Omens, a collection of poems by Brian Lumley - published by Stanza Press, a division of PS Publishing, 2012 Cover by Jim Pitts - repeated three times inside the book. Artwork originally used on the cover by Spectre Press in *Cthulhu 3*.

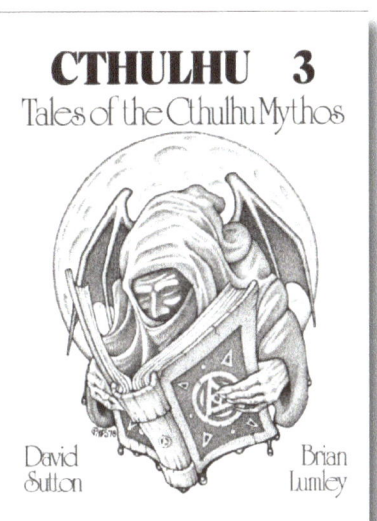

Original artwork for the back cover of *The Compleat Khash Volume Two: Sorcery in Shad*

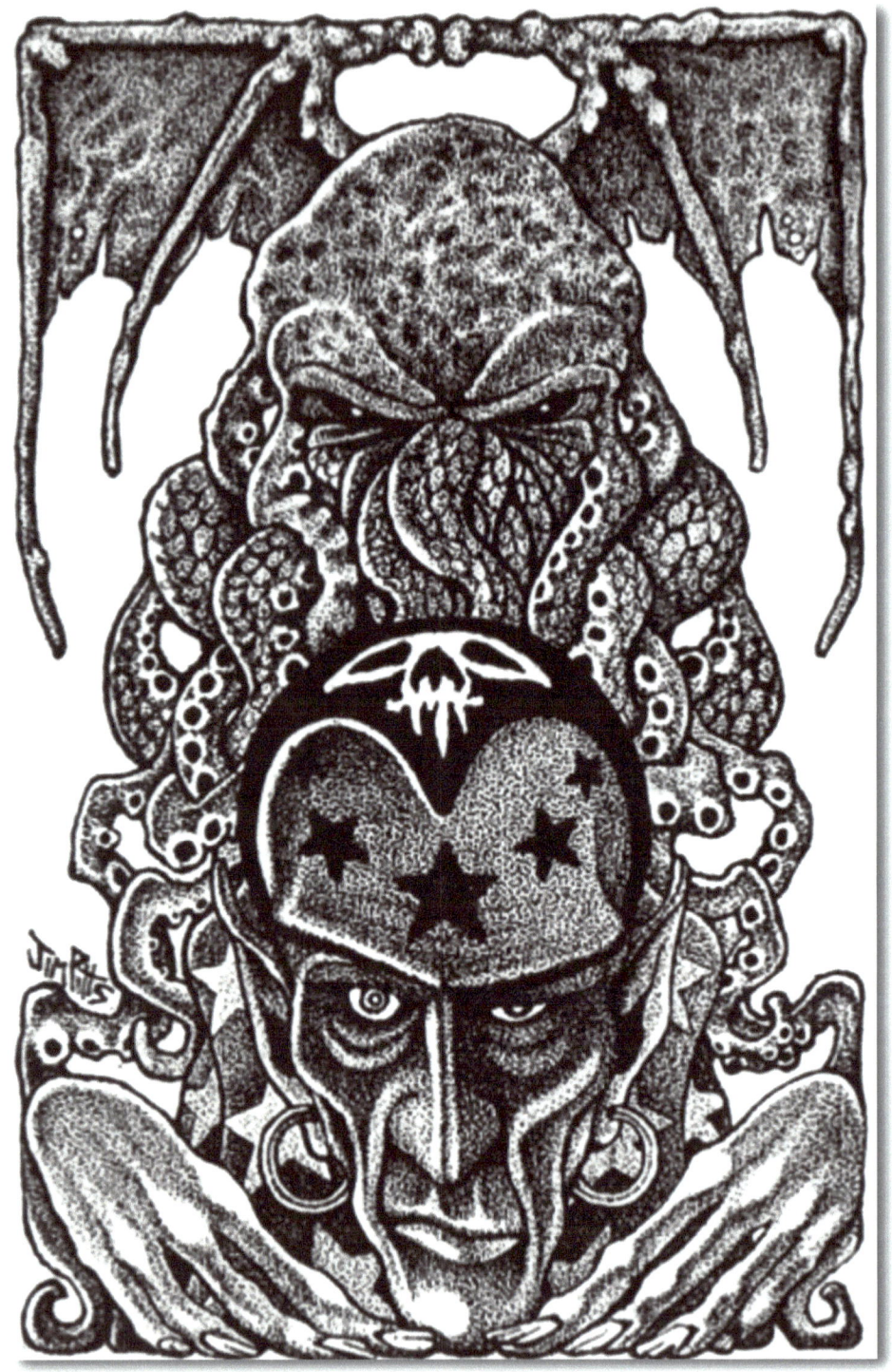

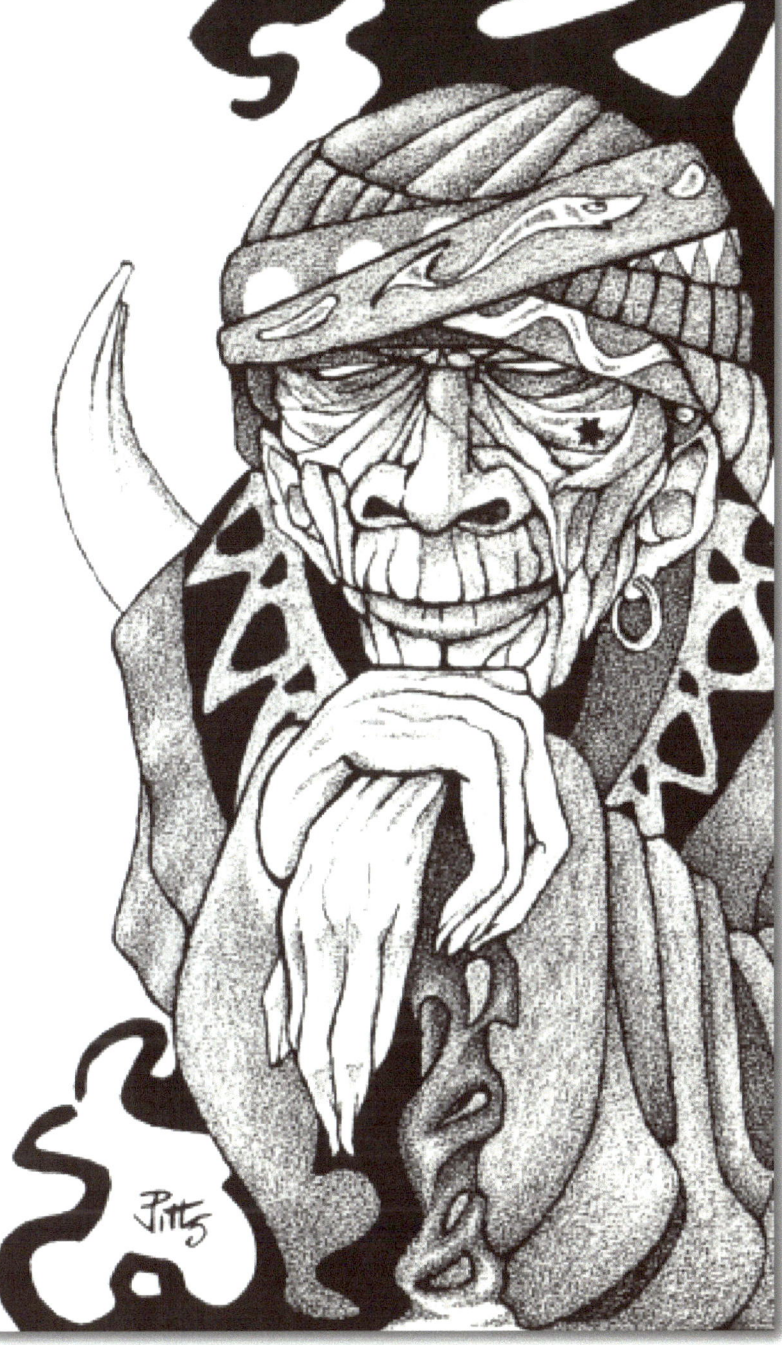

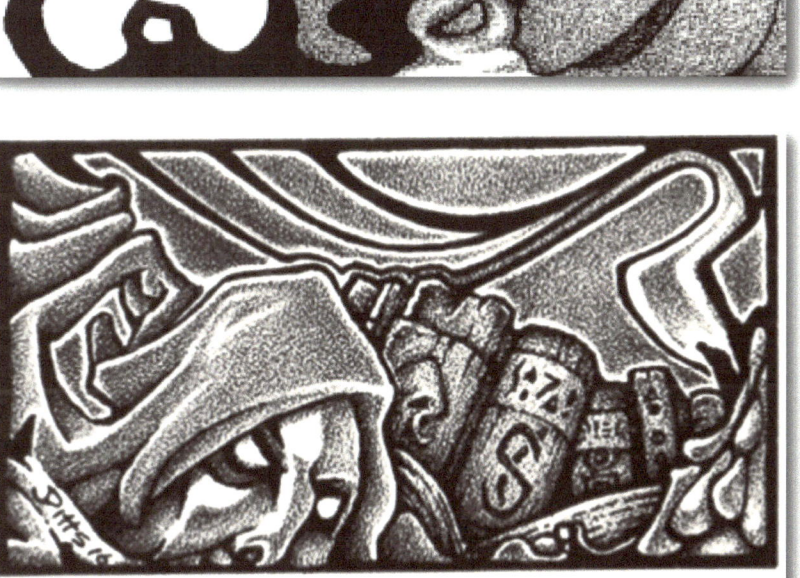

Picture to the left is an interior illustration in *The House of Cthulhu*

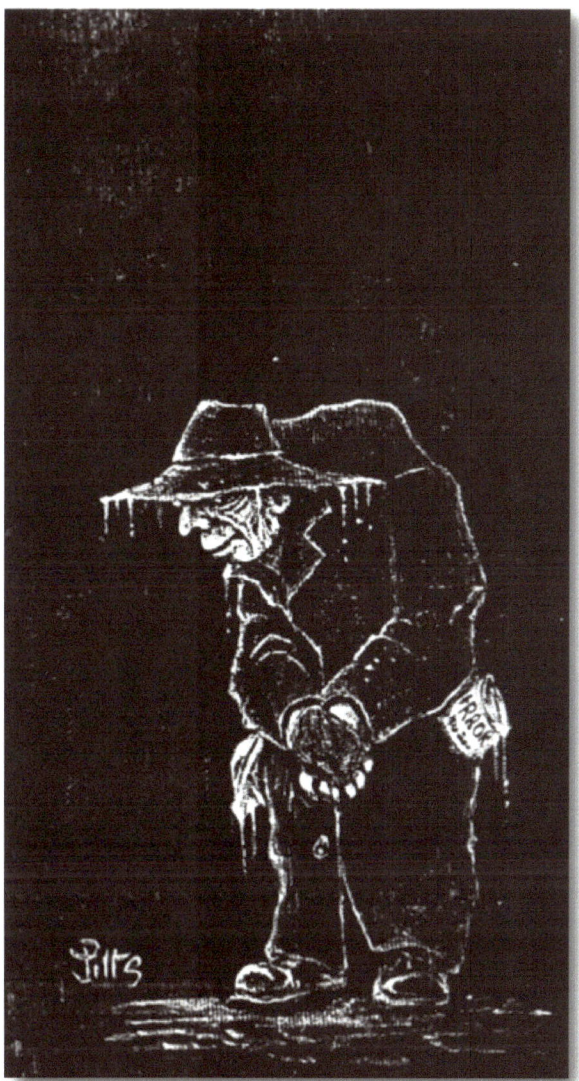

The above picture is from a Brian Lumley story called *The Whisperer*. "The little fellow" - a very ugly little man with a lopsided hump and dark or dirty features, like a gnomish gypsy. He was dressed in a floppy wide - brimmed hat that fell half over his face and a black overcoat longer than himself that trailed to the floor. - Acrylics. unsure of date or publication. probably about 1990.

To the left: interior art from *Earth, Air, Fire & Water*, 2017

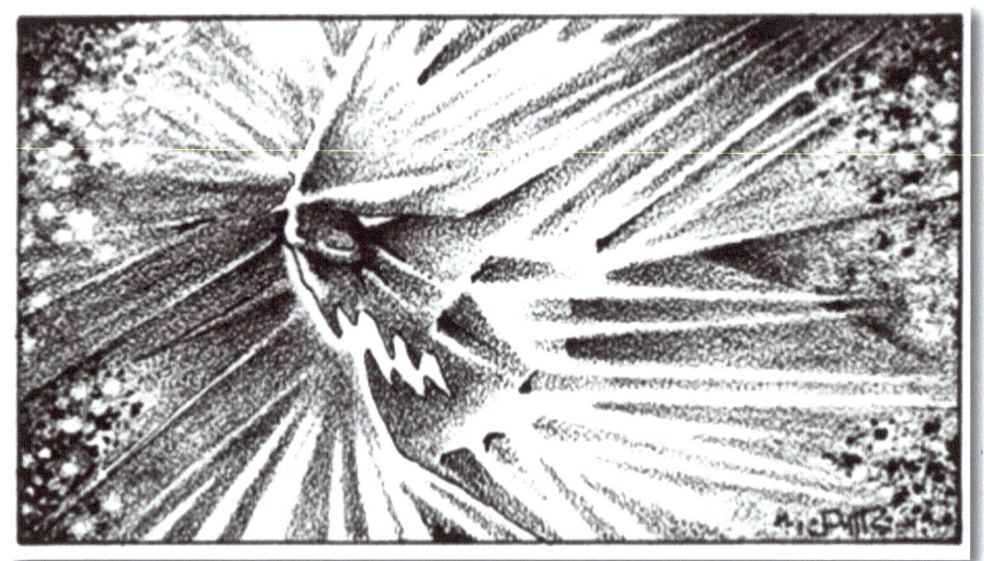
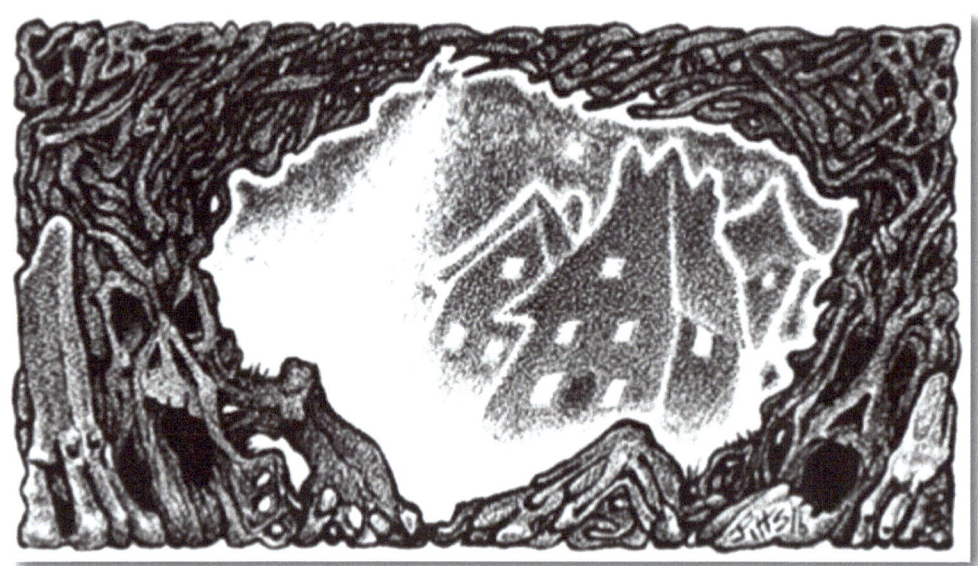
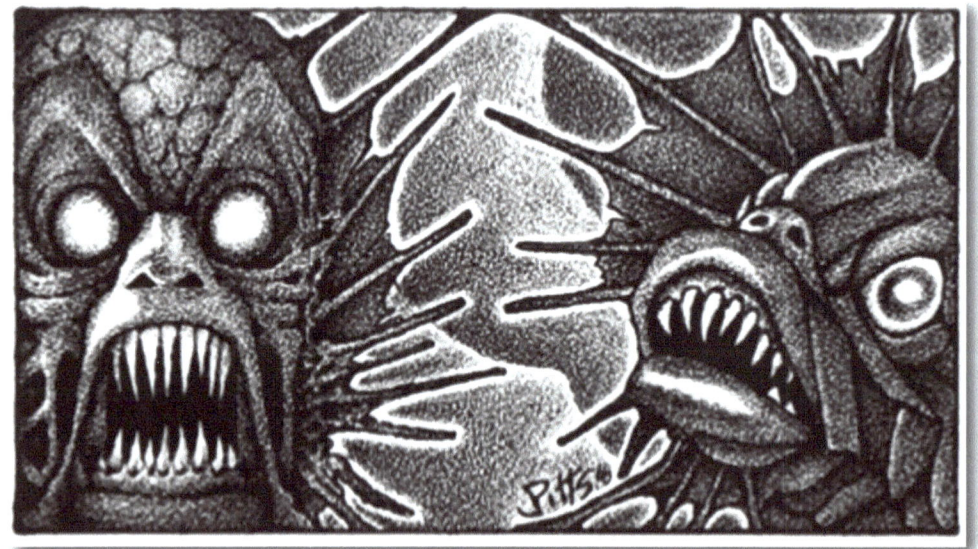

Above: three interior illustrations from *Earth, Air, Fire & Water* by Brian Lumley, 2017

Five interior illustrations for Brian Lumley's latest collection from Fedogan and Bremer: *Earth, Air, Fire and Water: Four Tales of Elemental Mythos Horror.*

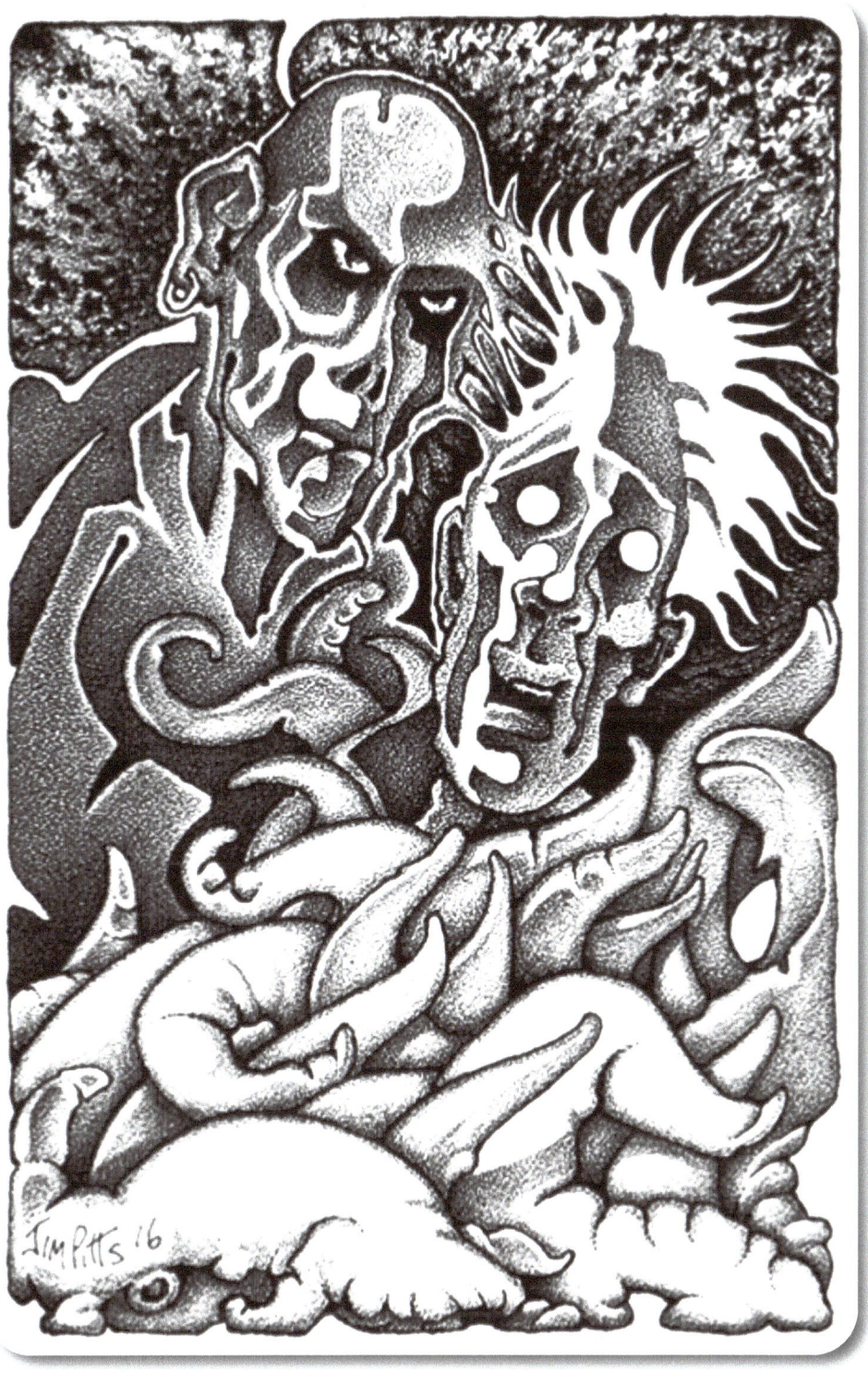

Illustration for the story *Lord of the Worms*

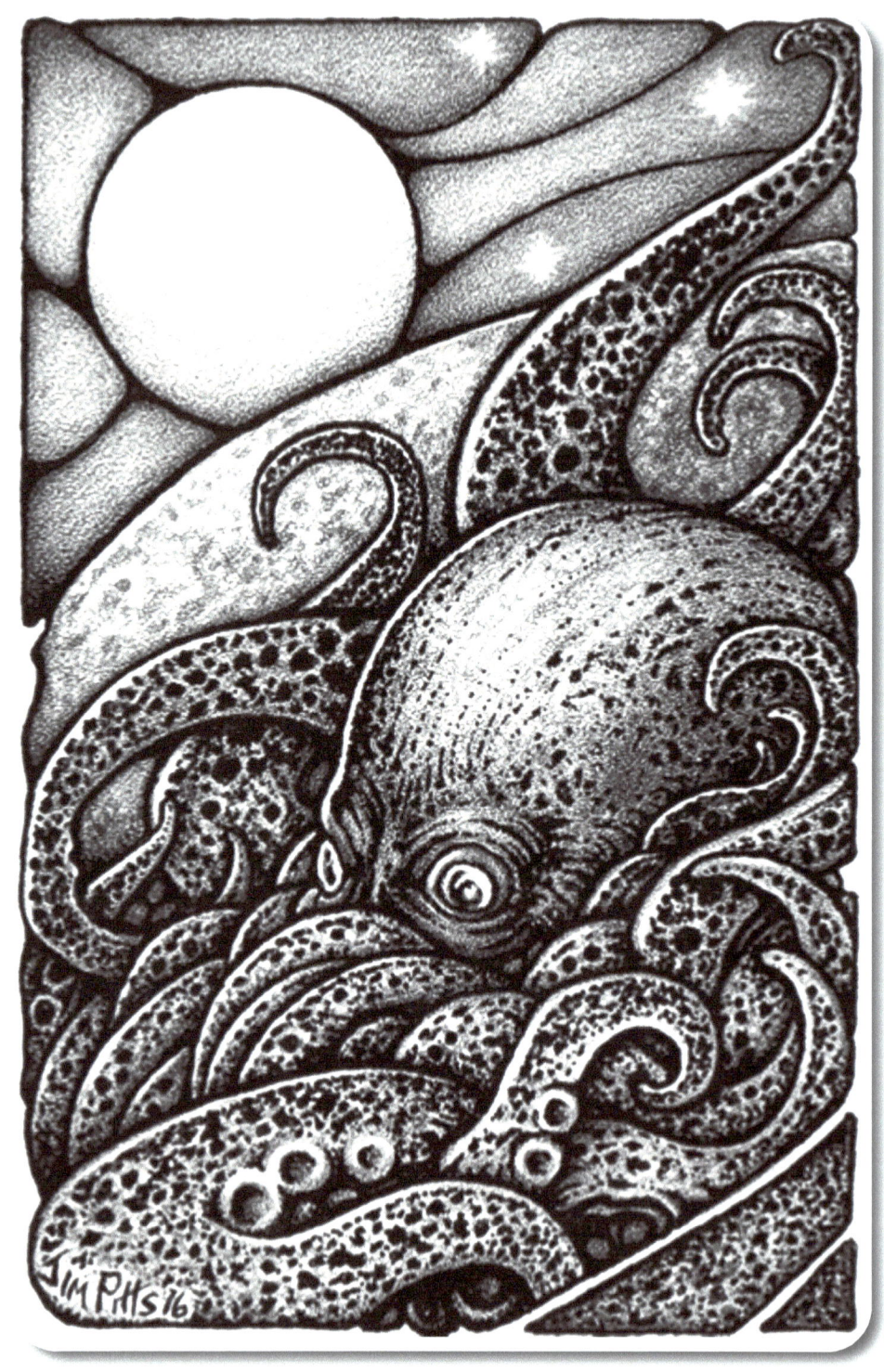

Illustration for the story *The Changeling*

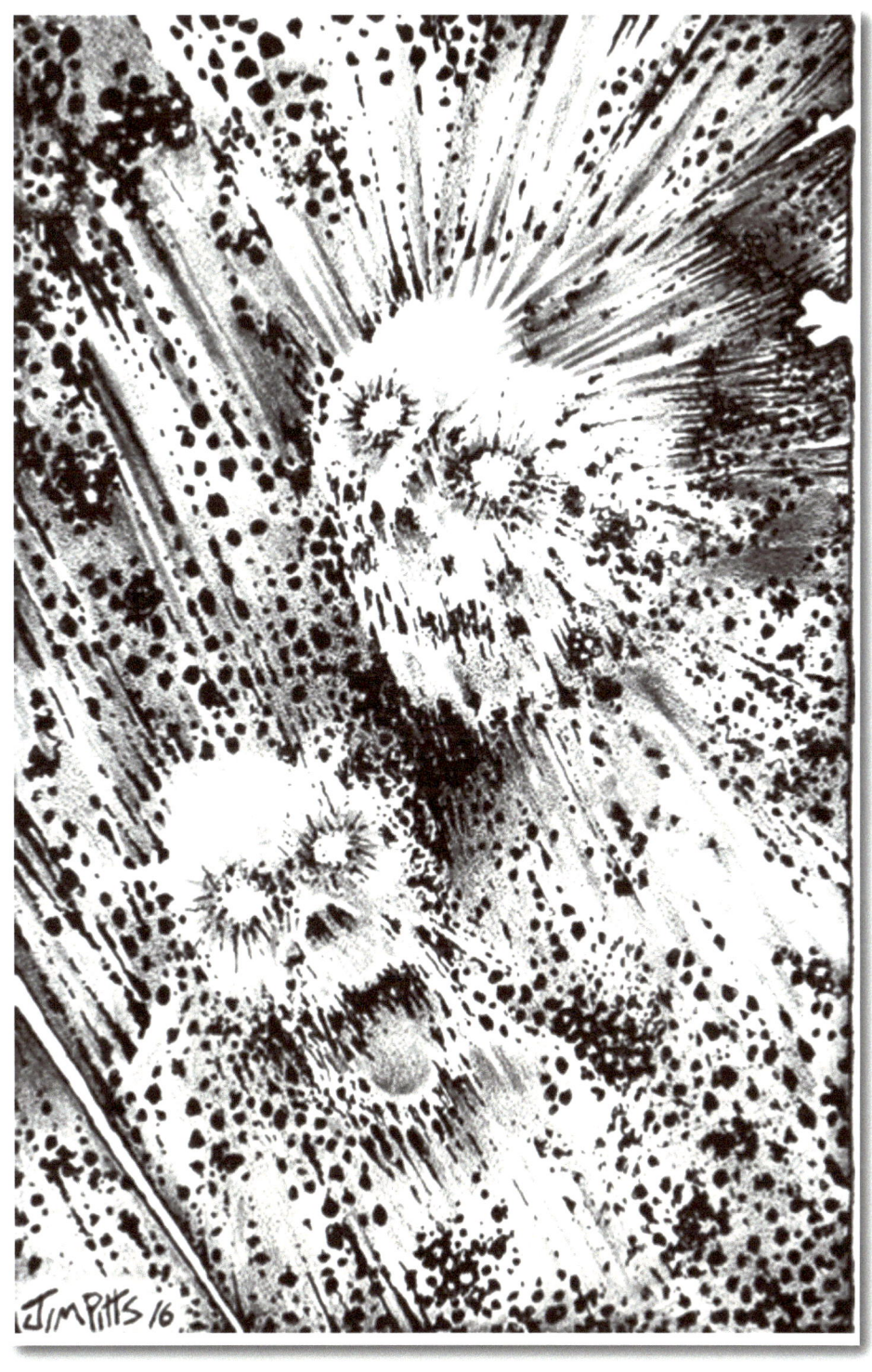

Illustration for the story *Born of the Winds*

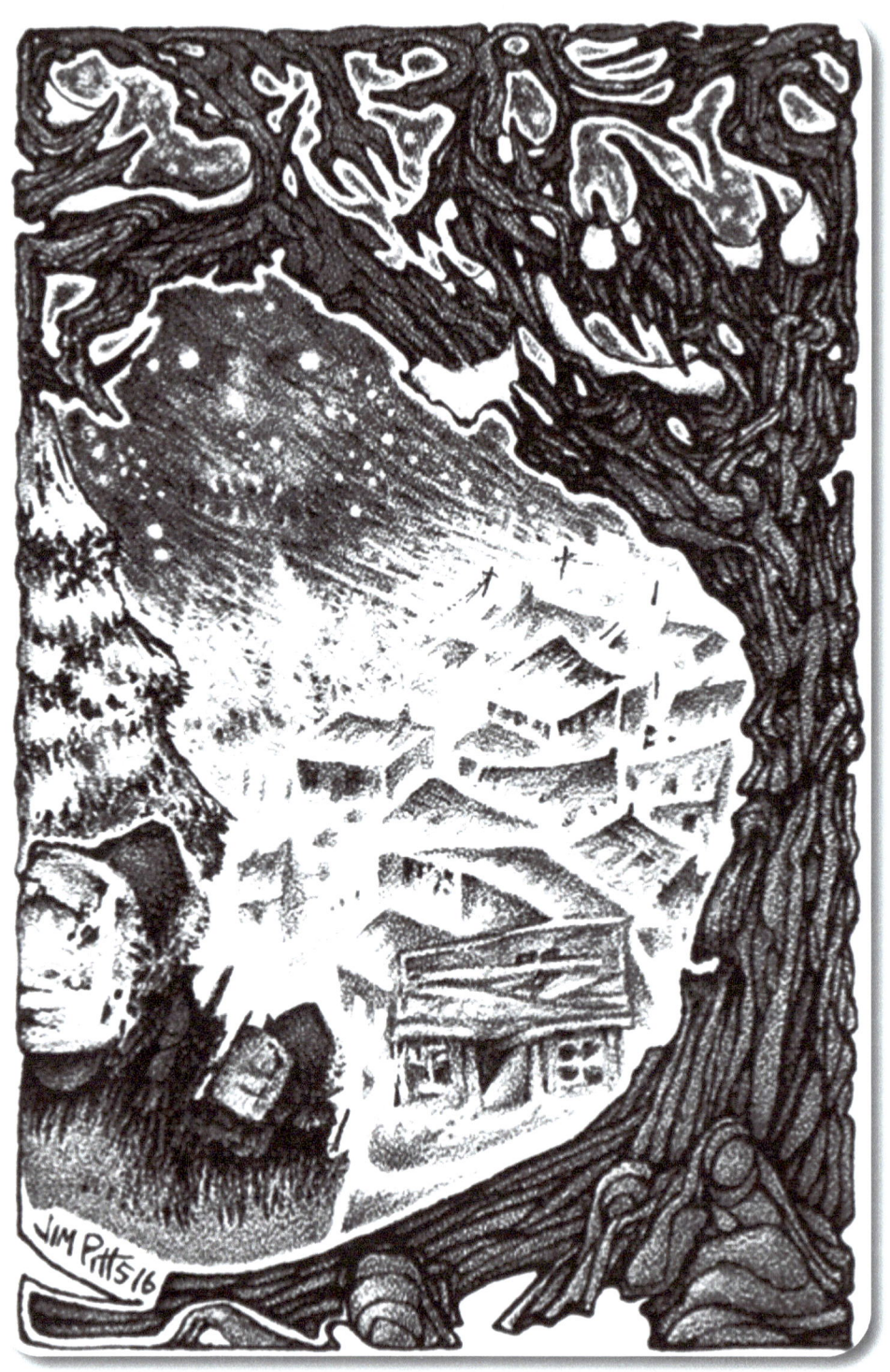

Illustration for the story *Born of the Winds*

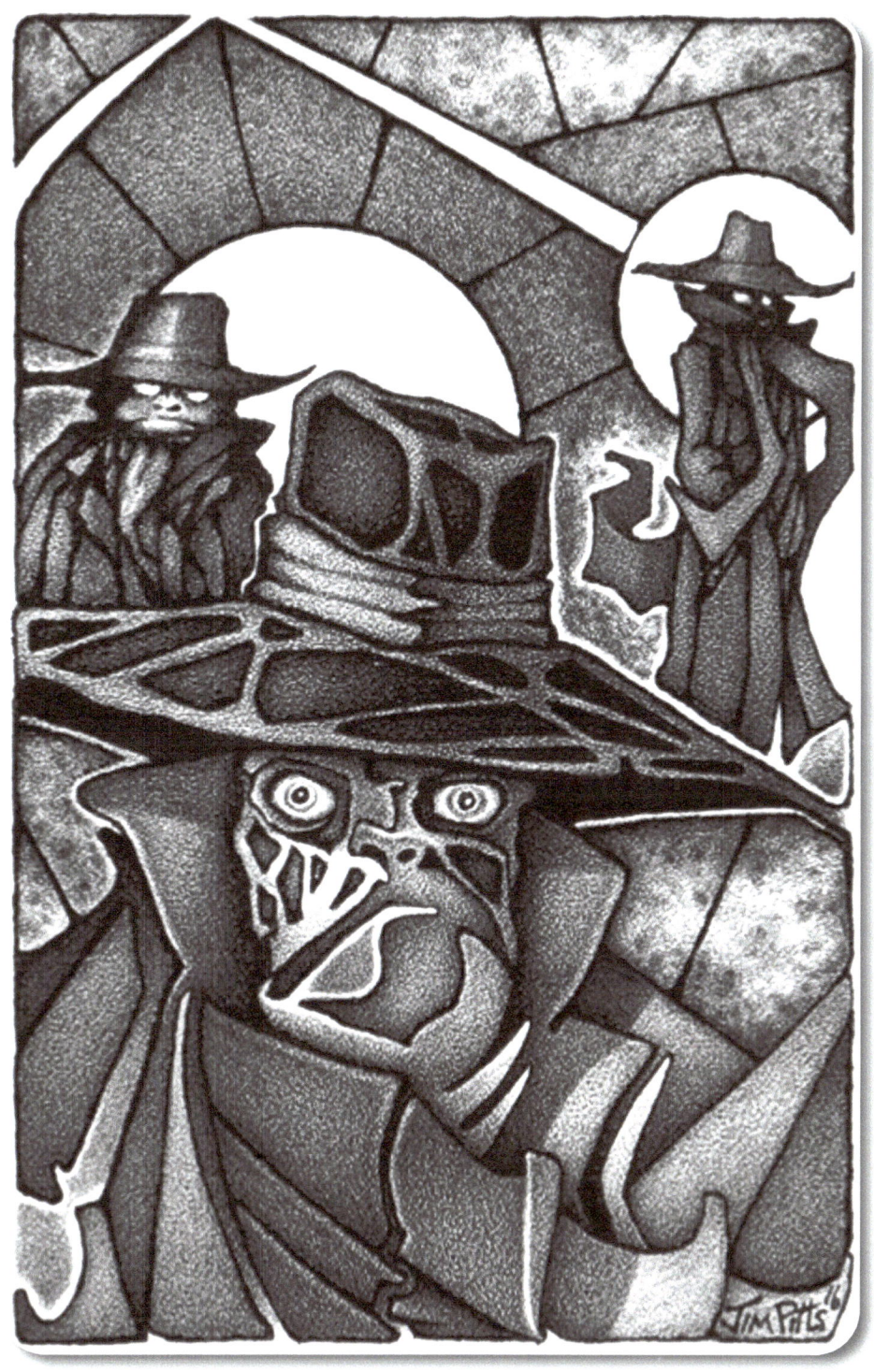

Illustration for the story *The Gathering*

The dust jacket and interior boards of *Earth, Air, Fire & Water* by Brian Lumley, Fedogan and Bremer, USA, 2017

Although the cover art is the work of artist Bob Eggleton, the black and white interior illustrations are by Jim Pitts, as is the design in gold against a black background on the boards.

The book was published in 2017 in two editions, a signed limited edition and a trade edition. The book contains four stories by Brian Lumley: *Lord of the Worms* (originally published in *Weirdbook 17*, 1983); *Born of the Winds* (*The Magazine of Fantasy & Science Fiction*, 1975); *The Gathering* (original to this book); and *The Changeling* (*Faerie Tales*, Jo Fletcher Books, 2013)

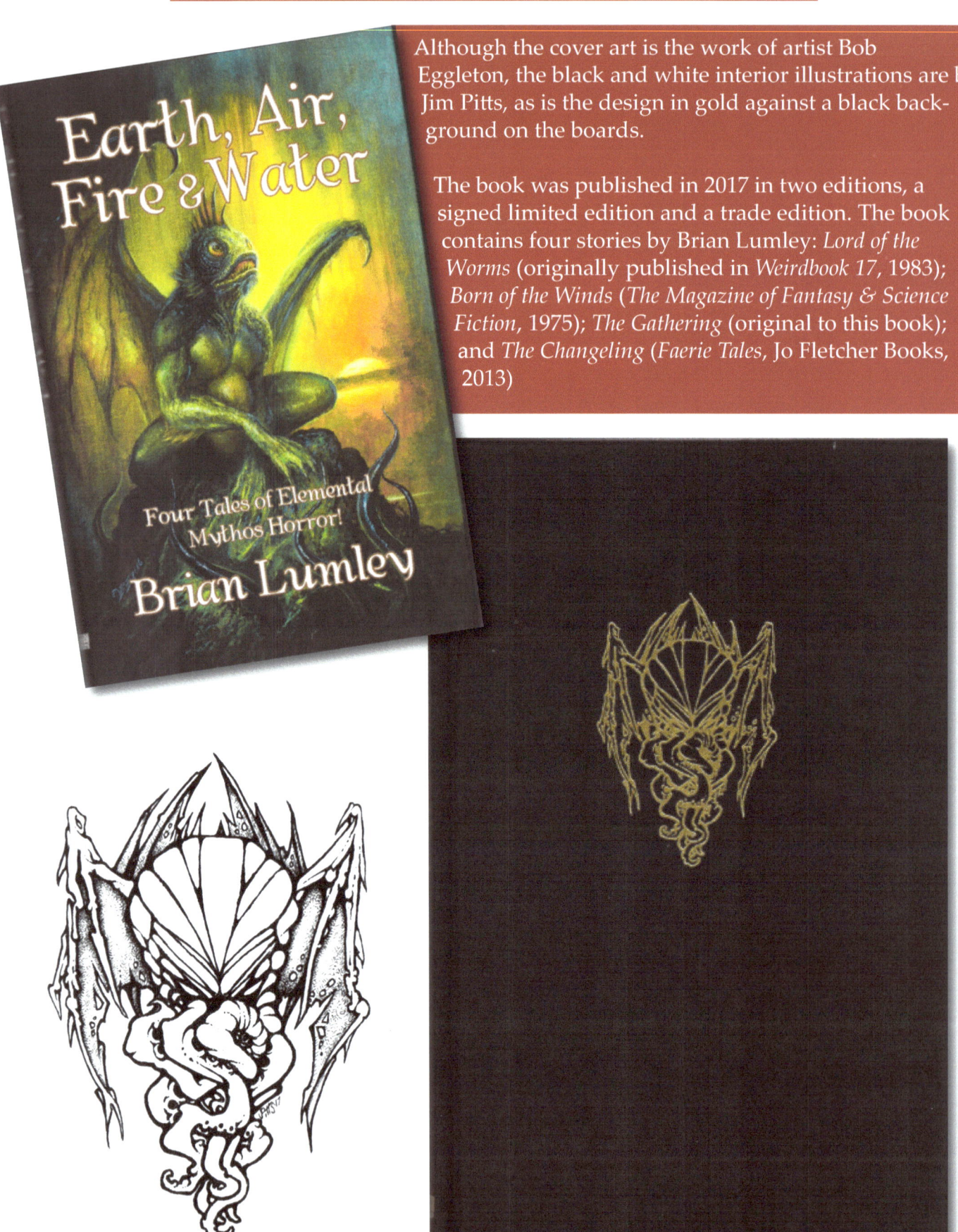

JIM PITTS
Society Gent and Artist
by Peter Coleborn

I first came across Jim Pitt's artwork in the British Fantasy Society publications of the 1970s. They appeared to be simple, stippled illustrations – but their complexity was limited by the then printing technology used by the Society. I pictured Jim (terrible pun. sorry) crouched over his desk meticulously dotting dots onto the paper until the image was complete. I even had a go myself and found it long-winded and much more difficult than it at first seemed to be. My awe of Jim's work went up a notch. Now, decades later, that awe is sky high.

After joining the BFS I discovered other small press magazines from the UK, including David Sutton's *Shadow* and Jon Harvey's *Balthus*. More examples of Jim's work unfolded. And in real life? Jim was one of the first artists I met in the flesh; the other two whom I met at early FantasyCons were colleagues and friends of Jim: Dave Carson and John Stewart. All of whom have left images of their artwork seared in my brain. And they all – especially Jim – helped define the overall look of the BFS over those early years. Jim even held various positions on the Society's committee, including co-editor of its *Newsletter* (with David A Riley).

Jim was a northerner and me, being from the south coast of Hampshire, was a tad concerned at meeting him at FantasyCon – you know, folk from up north being "hard men", not averse to a bit of argy-bargy. But there was no need. He was a perfect gent and soon he (along with many of the other people you'll see mentioned elsewhere in this publication – David A Sutton, Adrian Cole, Stephen Jones, Sandra Sutton, Jo Fletcher, Mike Chinn and so on) made me feel comfortable in this new and, at the time, alien environment.

Later, I'd moved to Nottingham and following a drink with BFS stalwart Jon Harvey I quickly found myself on the committee and – to cut a long story short, since this is about Jim Pitts and not me – in 1987 I started the ten-issue run of *Winter Chills* (aka *Chills* from issue five). I was quite nervous at the time, approaching writers such as R Chetwynd-Hayes and Ramsey Campbell for fiction. As for the art: Jim came up trumps with the superb illustration for Chetwynd-Hayes' "The Hanging Tree" (see page 18). Jim illustrated several of the stories in *Winter Chills/Chills* – and graced the cover with issue 9. Two of my all-time favourite Jim Pitts illustrations come from this era, artwork for "The Doll" by Guy N Smith (*Winter Chills* 2 – page 170, bottom left) and "The Pet Peeve" by Rick Kleffel (*Chills* 6). To be honest, however, it is very, very difficult to single out a favourite Jim Pitts drawing or painting. After all, they are all good and demonstrate Jim's growing expertise and confidence with his chosen artistic talent. Just look at the cover of *Beneath the Ground*, edited by Joel Lane, or his artwork for *Kadath* magazine. All sublime. And there's something else about his artwork: no matter the subject, no matter the dark elements therein, there is inevitably a sense of humour, it maybe sly, almost hidden, but I venture it's there.

And another thing: Jim has always been accommodating and willing to help out with the BFS and the projects created by his friends. Read David Sutton's essay, for example. For my part, when I needed an artist – pronto – for the chapbook *Birthday* by Mark Morris (page 102), and one for *Silver Rhapsody* (celebrating the first 25 years of the BFS, edited by Jan Edwards and John Carter – page 116), well, Jim came up trumps. As far as I recall, the cover of *Silver Rhapsody* featured one of Jim's first colour pieces for the BFS. Jim was the first artist highlighted for the BFS portfolio series, which I had the joy to produce: *Olde Horrors* featured six plates and appeared in 1989 (see page 121).

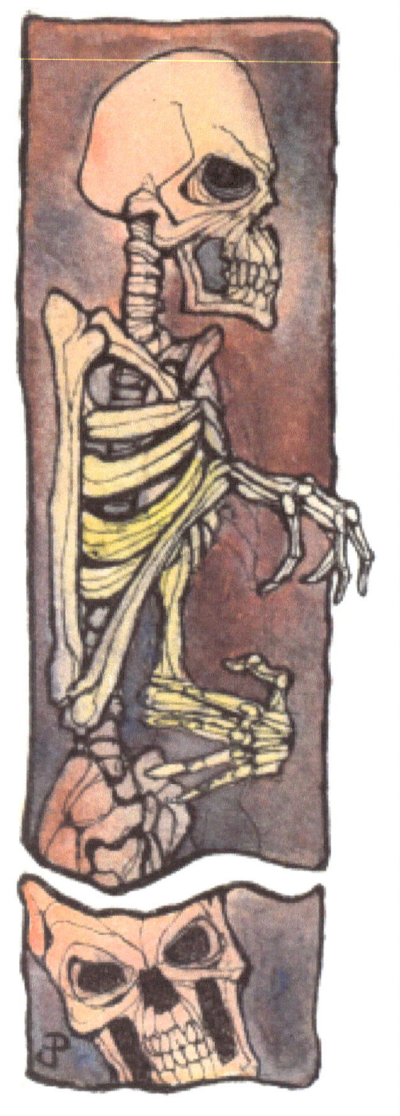

Towards the end of the Millennium I launched The Alchemy Press. Among its first publications was the aforementioned *Beneath the Ground*. Check out page 111 to view this stunning image. Jim contributed two full-pages to the Press' *Swords of the Millennium* edited by Mike Chinn. These two perfectly illustrate Jim's ability to embrace heroic (albeit strange) fantasy (for Adrian Cole's Dark "Destroyer") and weird fantasy (for Joel Lane's Clark Ashton Smith-inspired "The Hunger of the Leaves"). They also reflect different styles: pen and ink and wash for the former, pen and ink for the latter.

After an initial flurry, the Press took a sabbatical and in the first few years of the 21st century there seemed to be little in artwork in the BFS and other UK fanzines. Luckily, along came POD (although some may say "unluckily" but that's an argument for another day), and with it a revival of "fan" art. Jim's art has since appeared and enhanced publications from David Riley's Parallel Universe Publications, Jon Harvey's *Worlds of the Unknown*, as well as *Dead Water* by David Sutton (page 112) and the magnificent frontispiece for *Nick Nightmare Investigates* by Adrian Cole (both The Alchemy Press), and others.

If there is just one wish I could have for Jim – but alas one can't change past events – it's that I wish Jim had made that BIG break into professionalism. His expertise, his craft and quality deserve it. I've known Jim Pitts for over 40 years and I am pleased to call him friend. I am equally delighted to witness the evolving techniques, from simple stipple to pen and ink, to wash, to water colours and coloured inks. I hear he continues to experiment with other styles (just glance at the sweep of artwork herein). Long may that continue.

Peter Coleborn

The above illustration was carried out using ink and water colour.

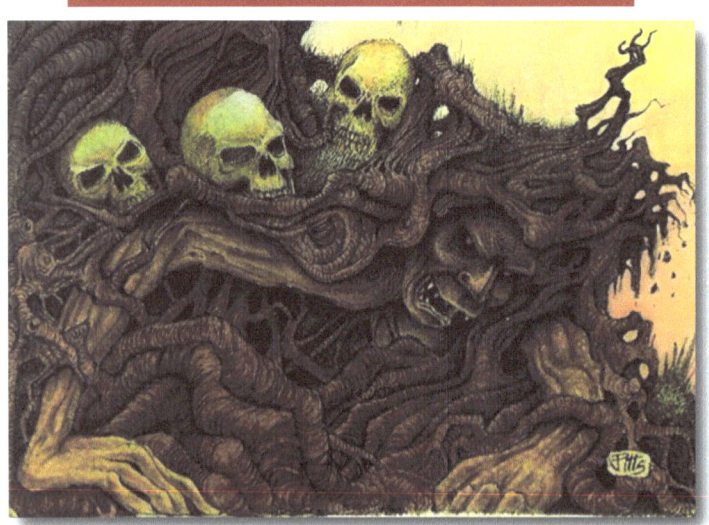

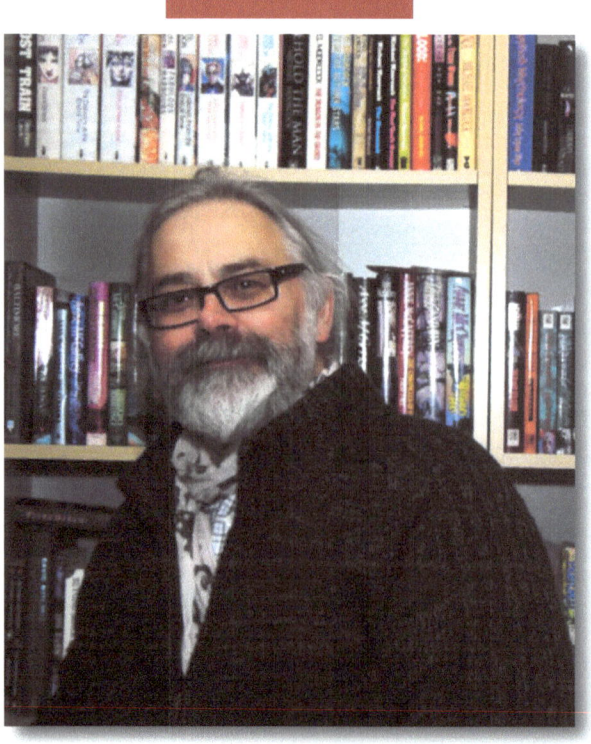

"Samathiel's Summons" by Ian Watson published in *Winter Chills* # 1

"The Real Wolf" by Thomas Ligotti published in *Winter Chills* # 2

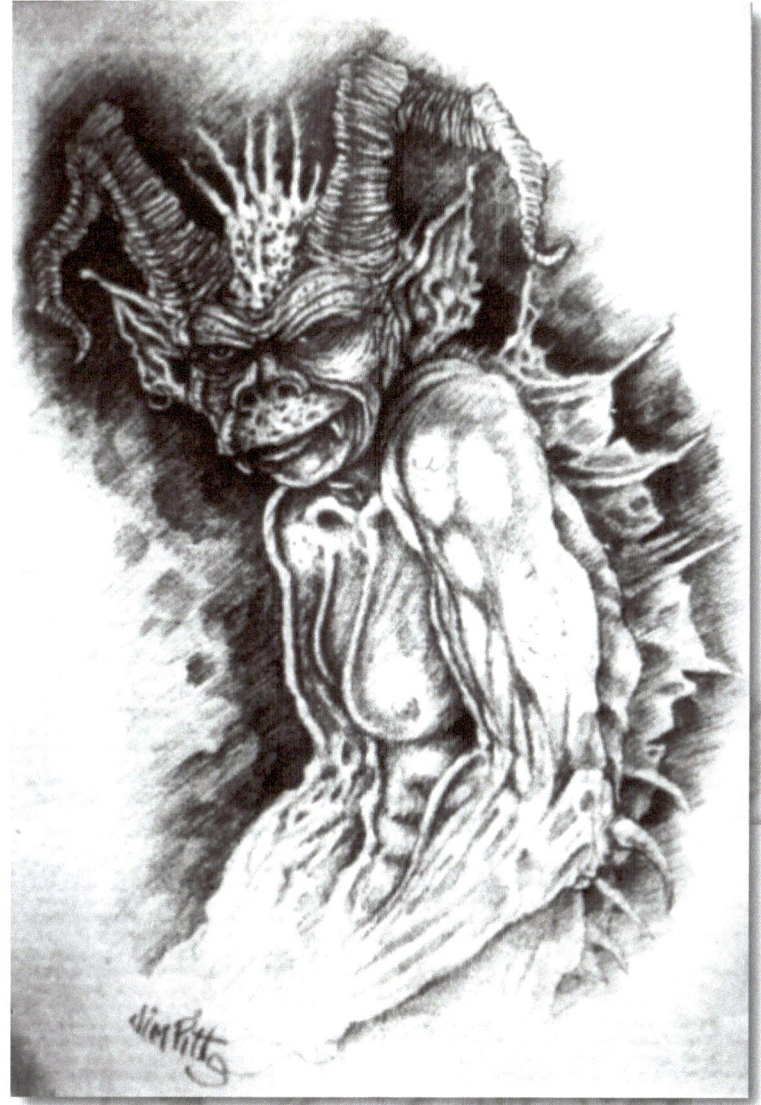

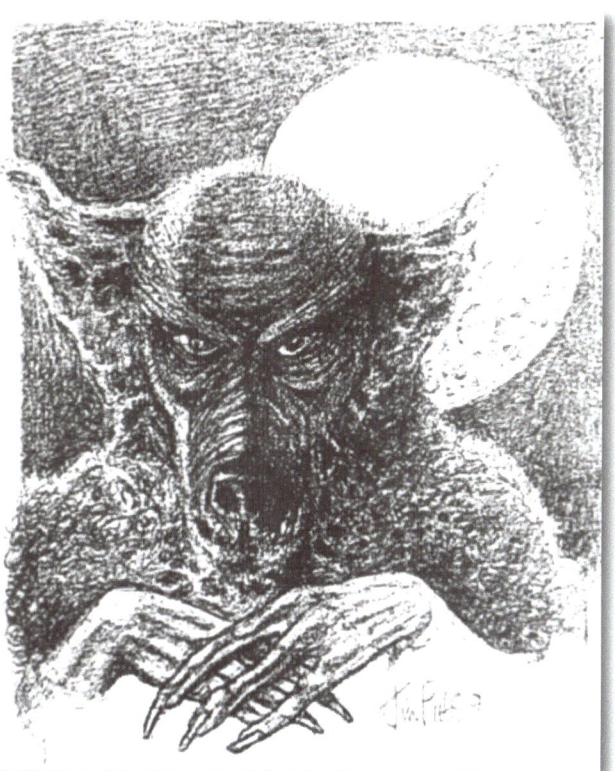

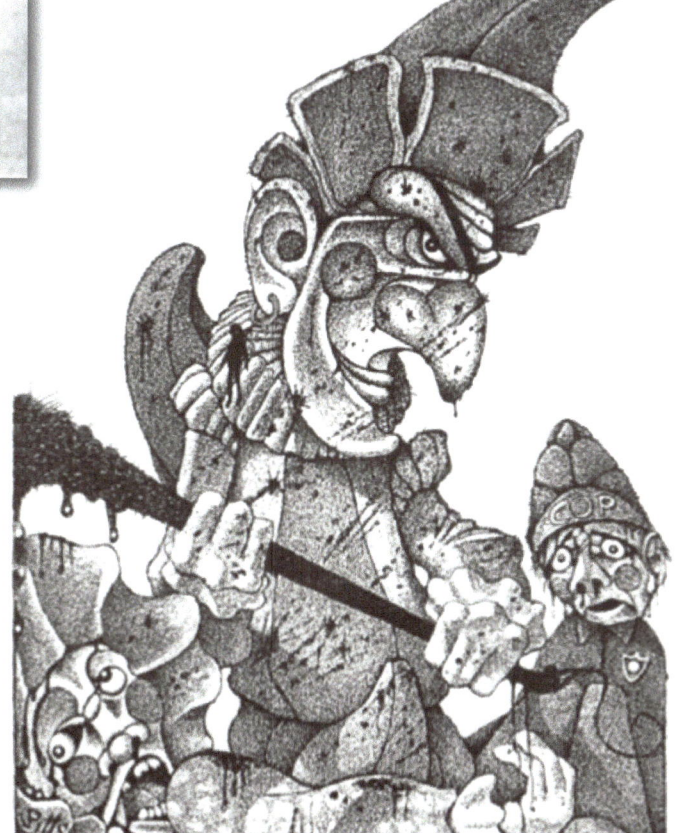

"The Doll" by Guy N. Smith published in *Winter Chills* # 4

"The Pet Peeve" by Rick Kleffel published in *Winter Chills* # 5

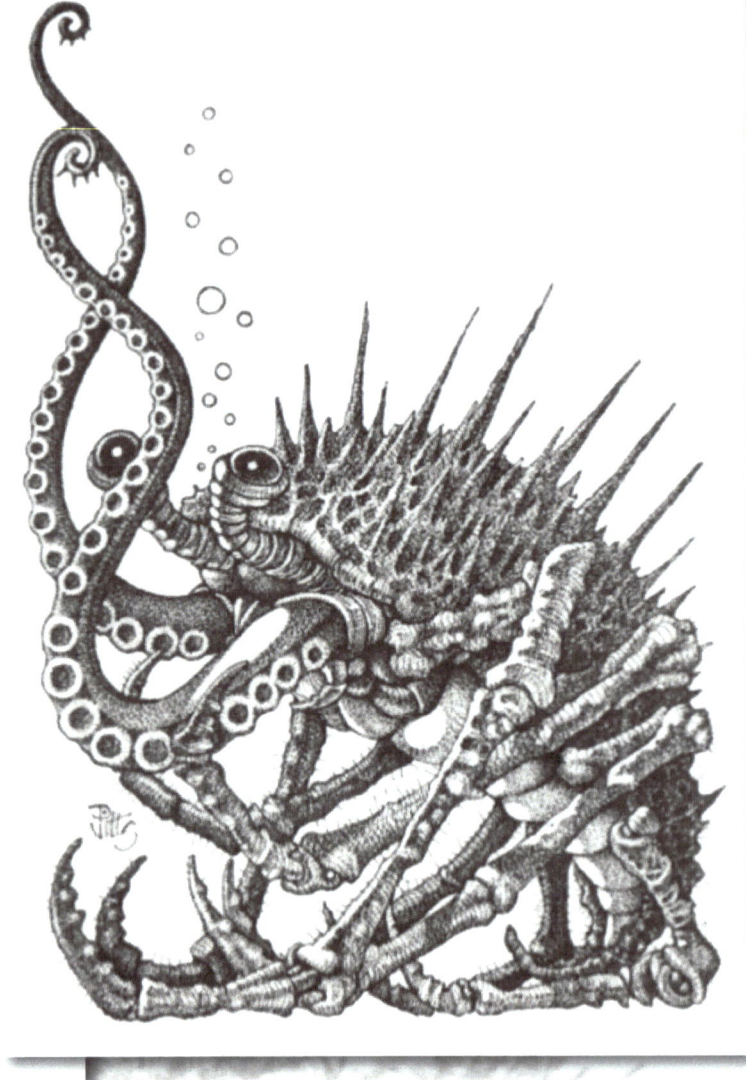

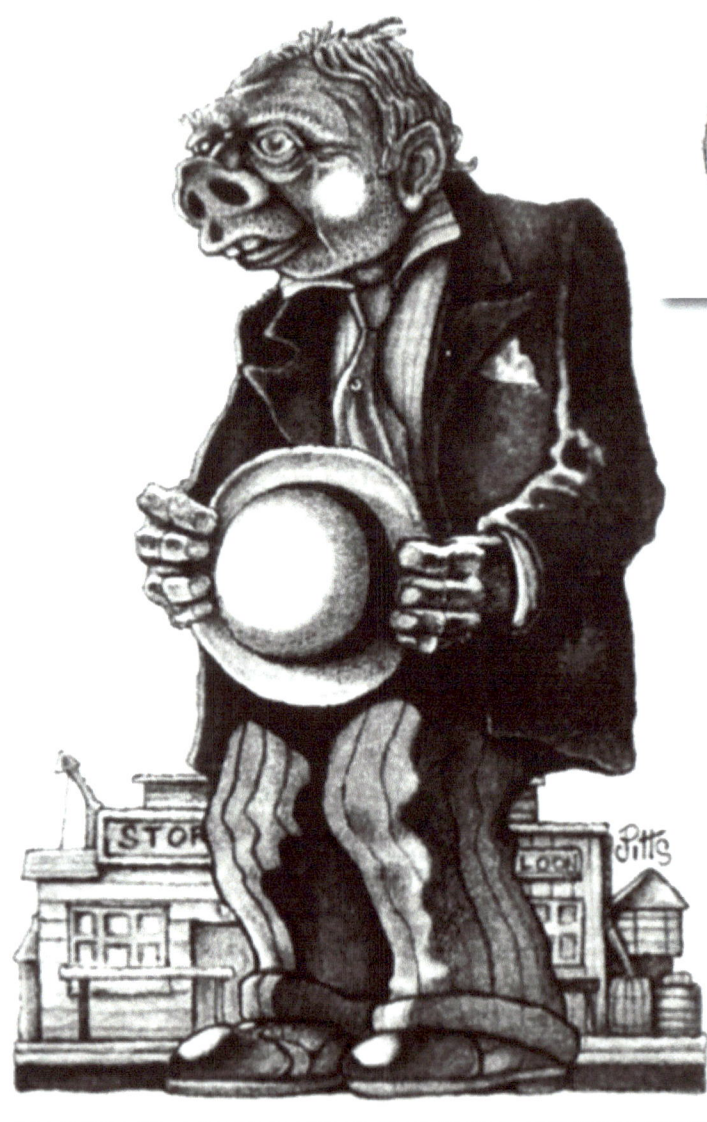

"A Date with the Hangman's Daughter" by Tia Travis published in *Winter Chills* # 3

BENEATH THE GROUND
edited by Joel Lane

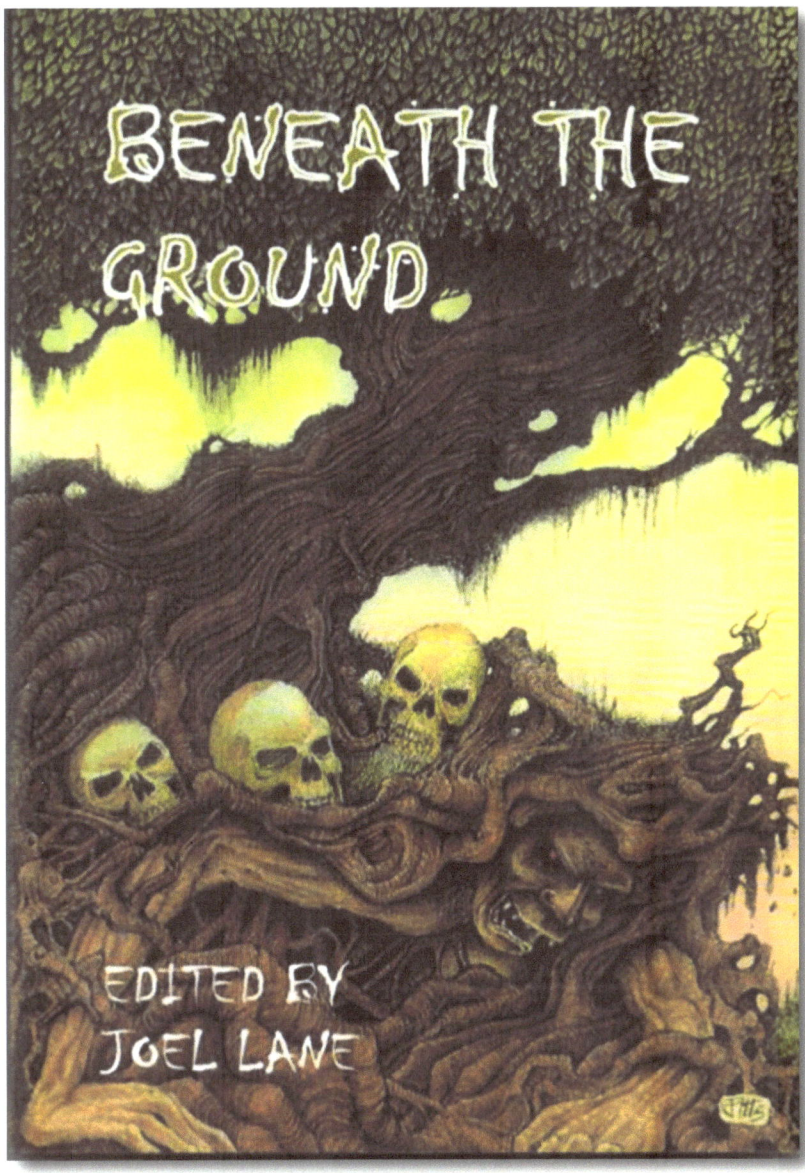

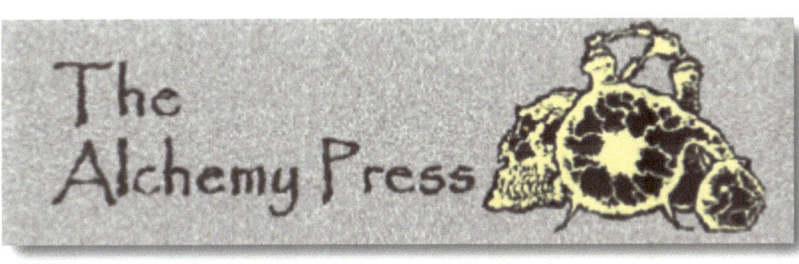

Beneath the Ground, edited by Joel Lane, was published by Alchemy Press in 2003. It included 13 stories:
No Map and No Guide by Joel Lane
The End of a Summer's Day by Ramsey Campbell
In the Tunnels by Pauline E Dungate
Tomb of the Janissaries by David Sutton
The Empty Room by Tim Lebbon
'Where Once I Did My Love Beguile' by John Howard
Going Underground by Mike McKeown
Lost and Found by Simon Avery
Grendel's Lair by Paul Finch
From the Hearth by D F Lewis
Nights at the Regal by Jason Gould
Empty Stations by Nicholas Royle
The Stone Man by Derek Fox
To Walk in Midnight's Realm by Simon Bestwick

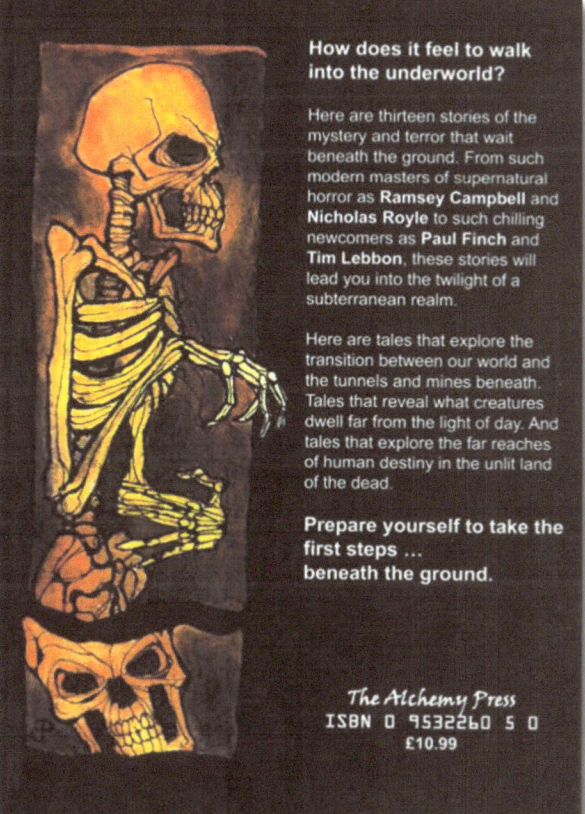

How does it feel to walk into the underworld?

Here are thirteen stories of the mystery and terror that wait beneath the ground. From such modern masters of supernatural horror as **Ramsey Campbell** and **Nicholas Royle** to such chilling newcomers as **Paul Finch** and **Tim Lebbon**, these stories will lead you into the twilight of a subterranean realm.

Here are tales that explore the transition between our world and the tunnels and mines beneath. Tales that reveal what creatures dwell far from the light of day. And tales that explore the far reaches of human destiny in the unlit land of the dead.

**Prepare yourself to take the first steps ...
beneath the ground.**

The Alchemy Press
ISBN 0 9532260 5 0
£10.99

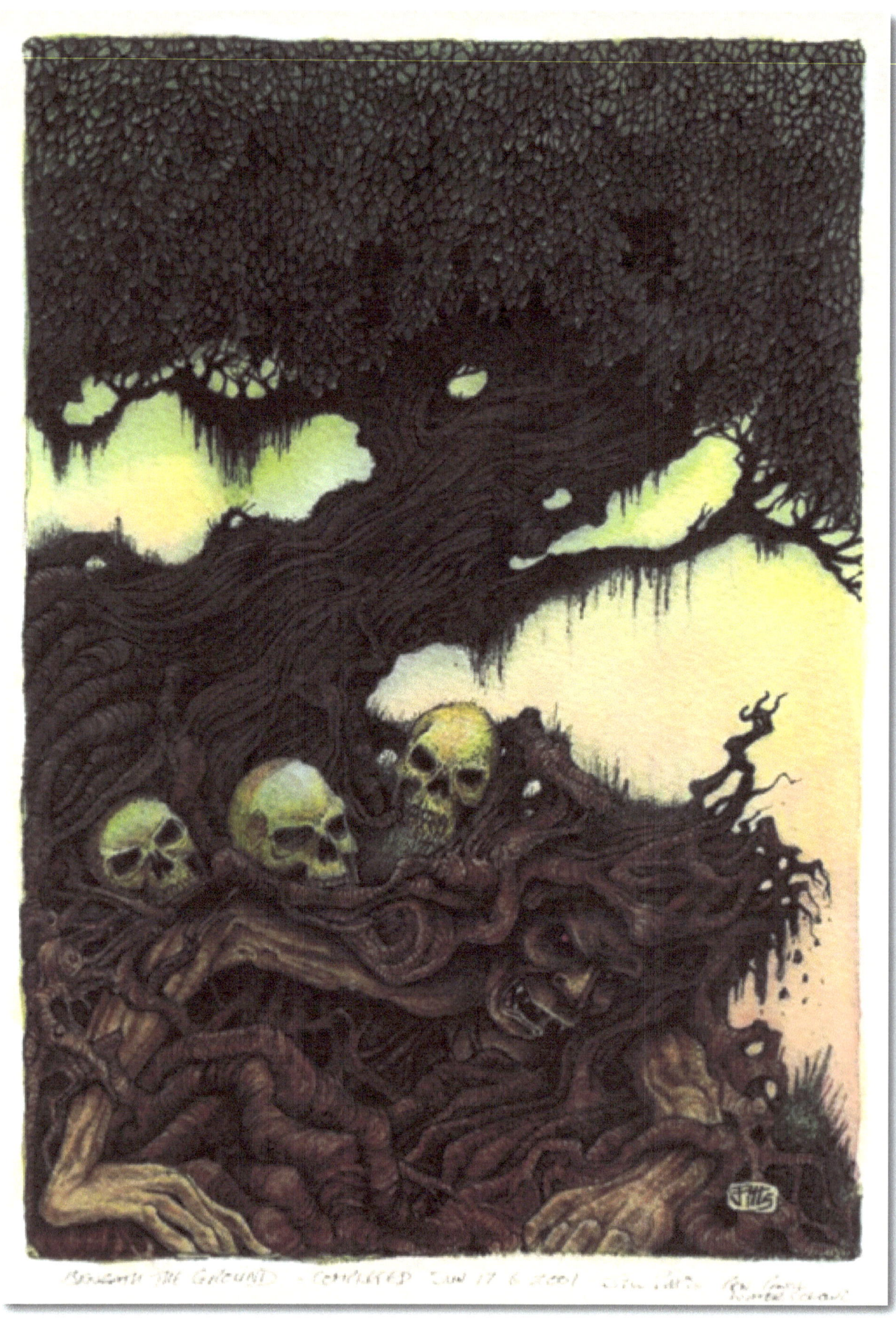

DEAD WATER
by David A. Sutton

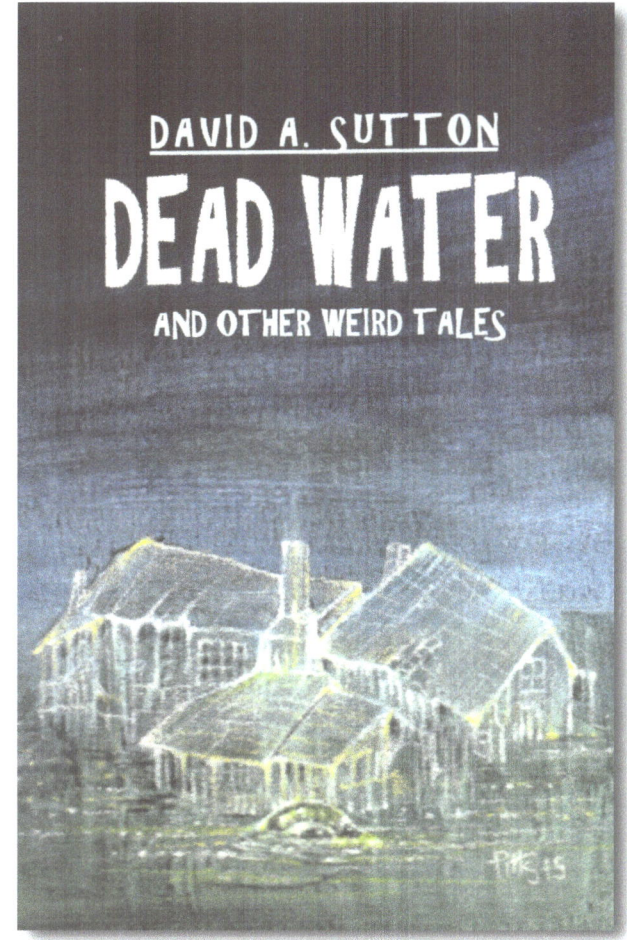

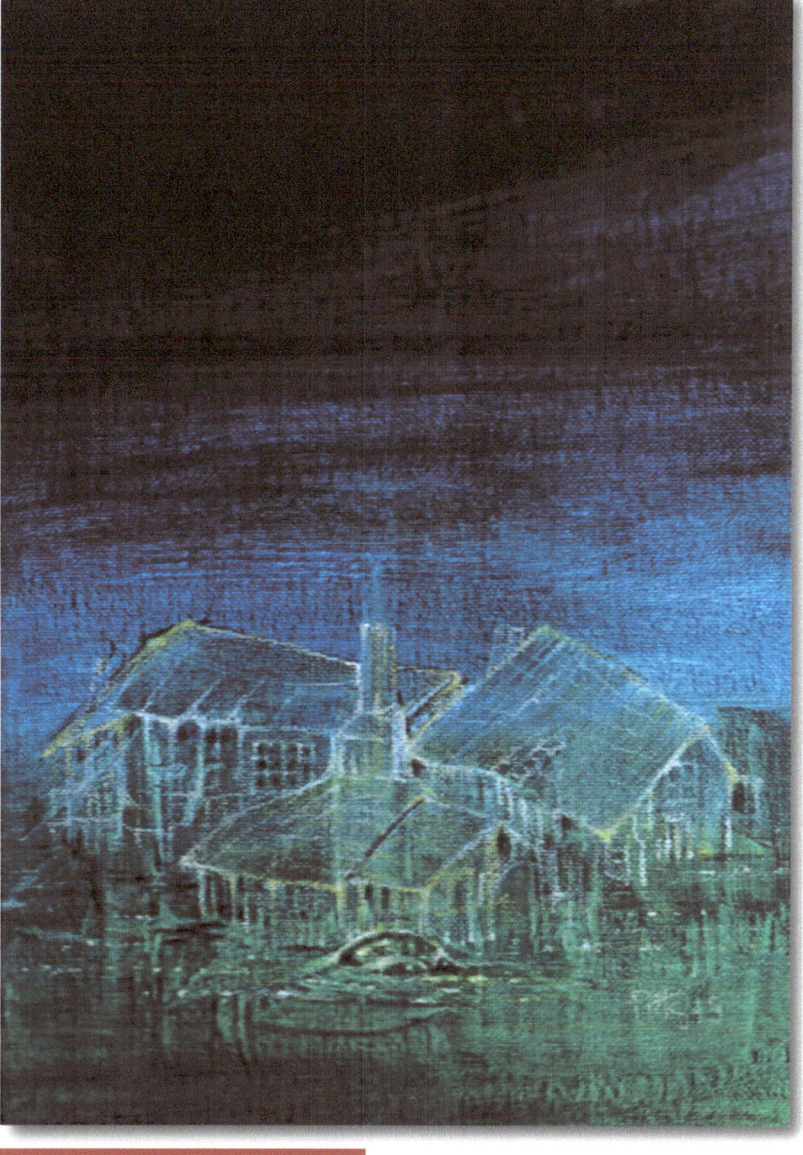

The original artwork was acrylic paint and pencil/pastel.

Front cover of *Dead Water and Other Weird Tales* by David A. Sutton, published by Alchemy Press, 2015.

Silver Rhapsody was edited for the British Fantasy Society by Jan Edwards and John Carter

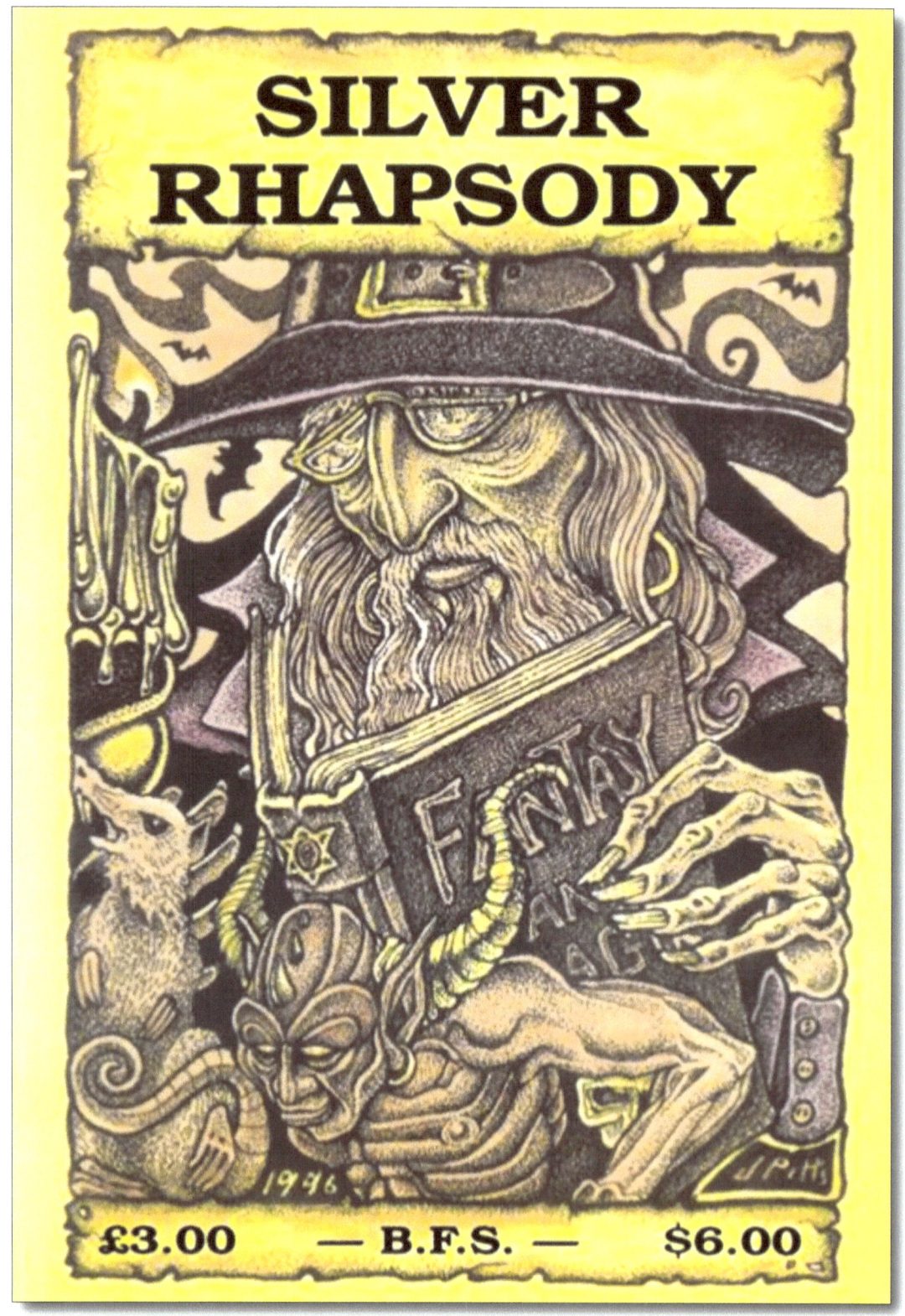

Two illustrations from *Swords Against the Millenium*, published by Alchemy Press. The first illustration is from Adrian Cole's *Dark Destroyer*. The second is from Joel Lane's *The Hunger of the Leaves*.

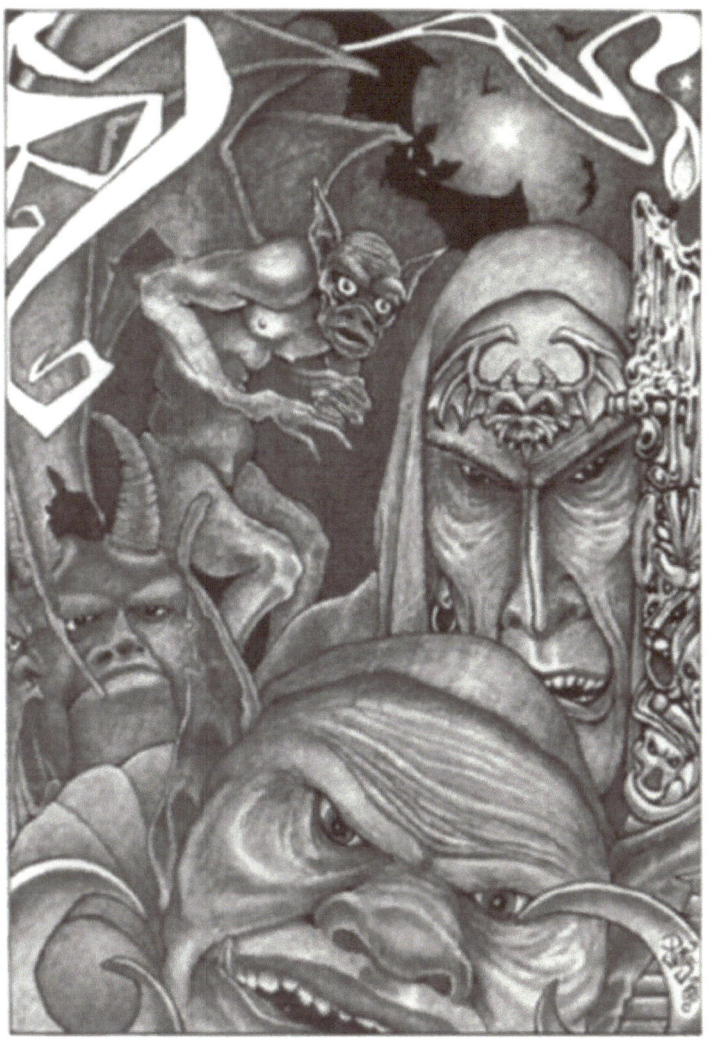

DARK DESTROYER

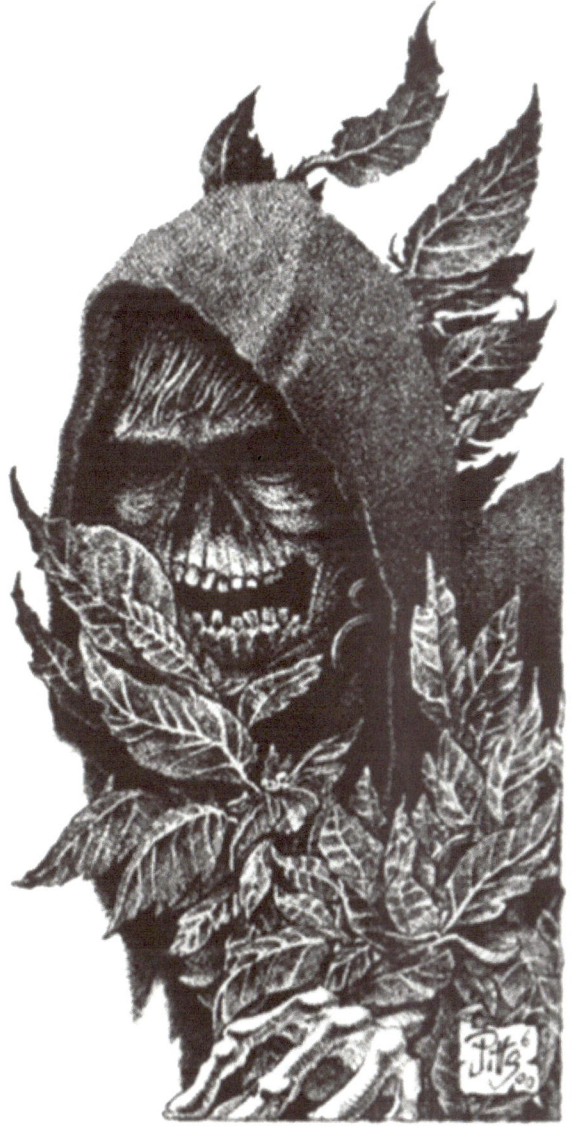

THE HUNGER OF THE LEAVES

An interpretation of H. P. Lovecraft's *The Strange High House in the Mist*. Carbon pencil on stipple board.

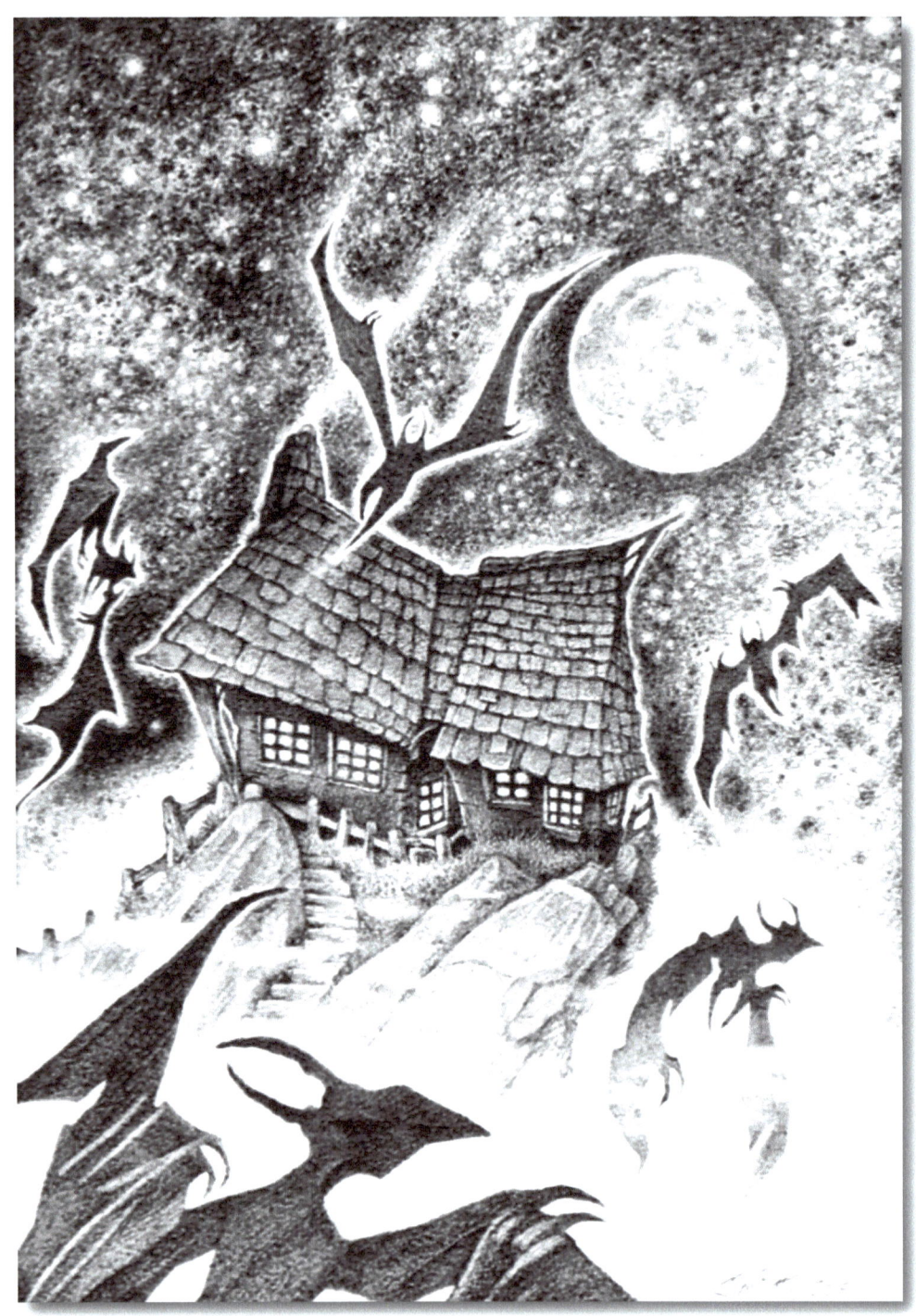

Frontispiece to David A. Sutton's collection *Dead Water and Other Weird Tales*, published by Alchemy Press in 2016. This was drawn in ballpoint pen on watercolour paper. It's a depiction of the "very Deep Ones". It was also published as a quality print by Spectre Press in 2014.

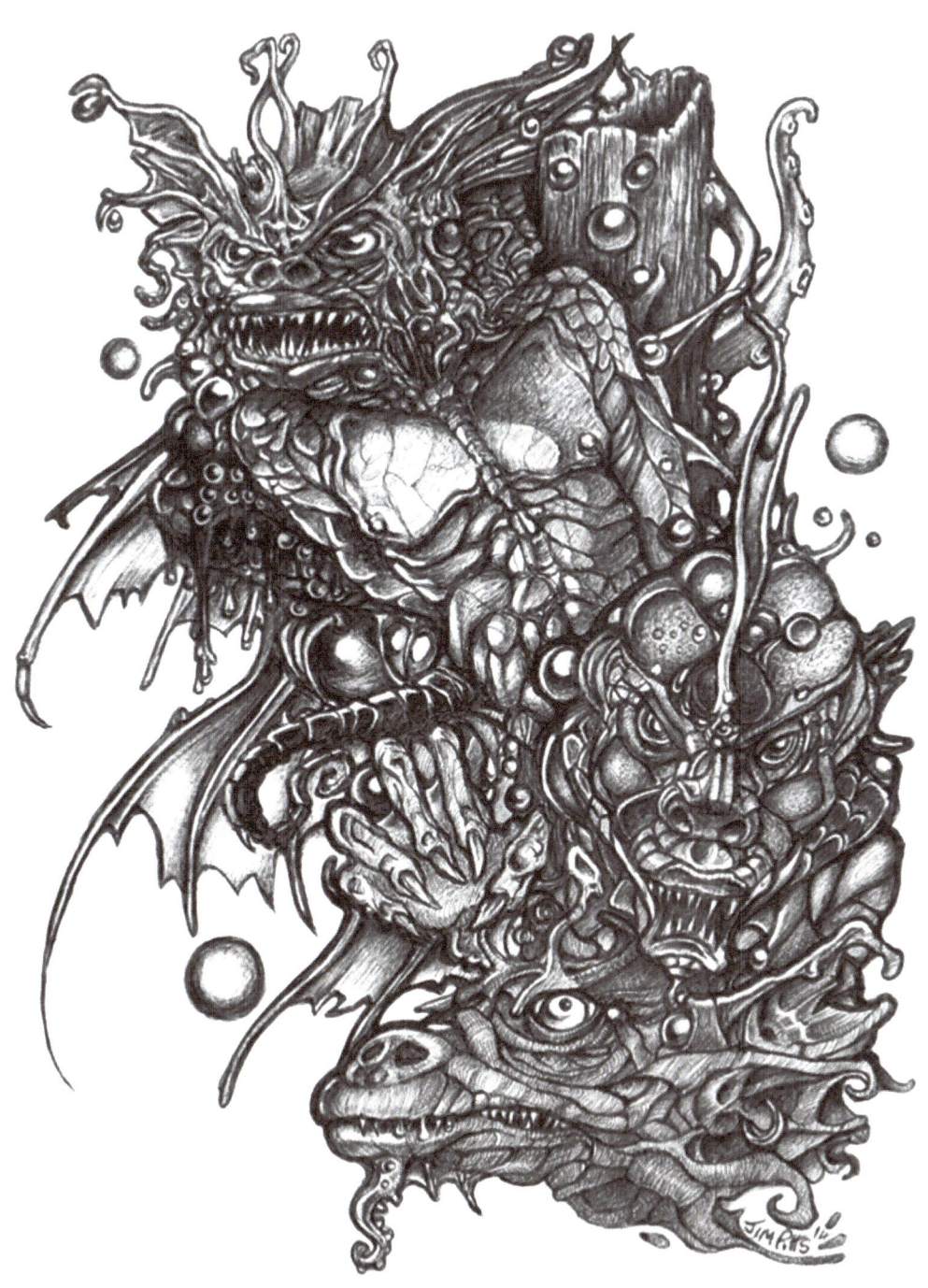

SKELETON CREW 1991 Article about Jim Pitts

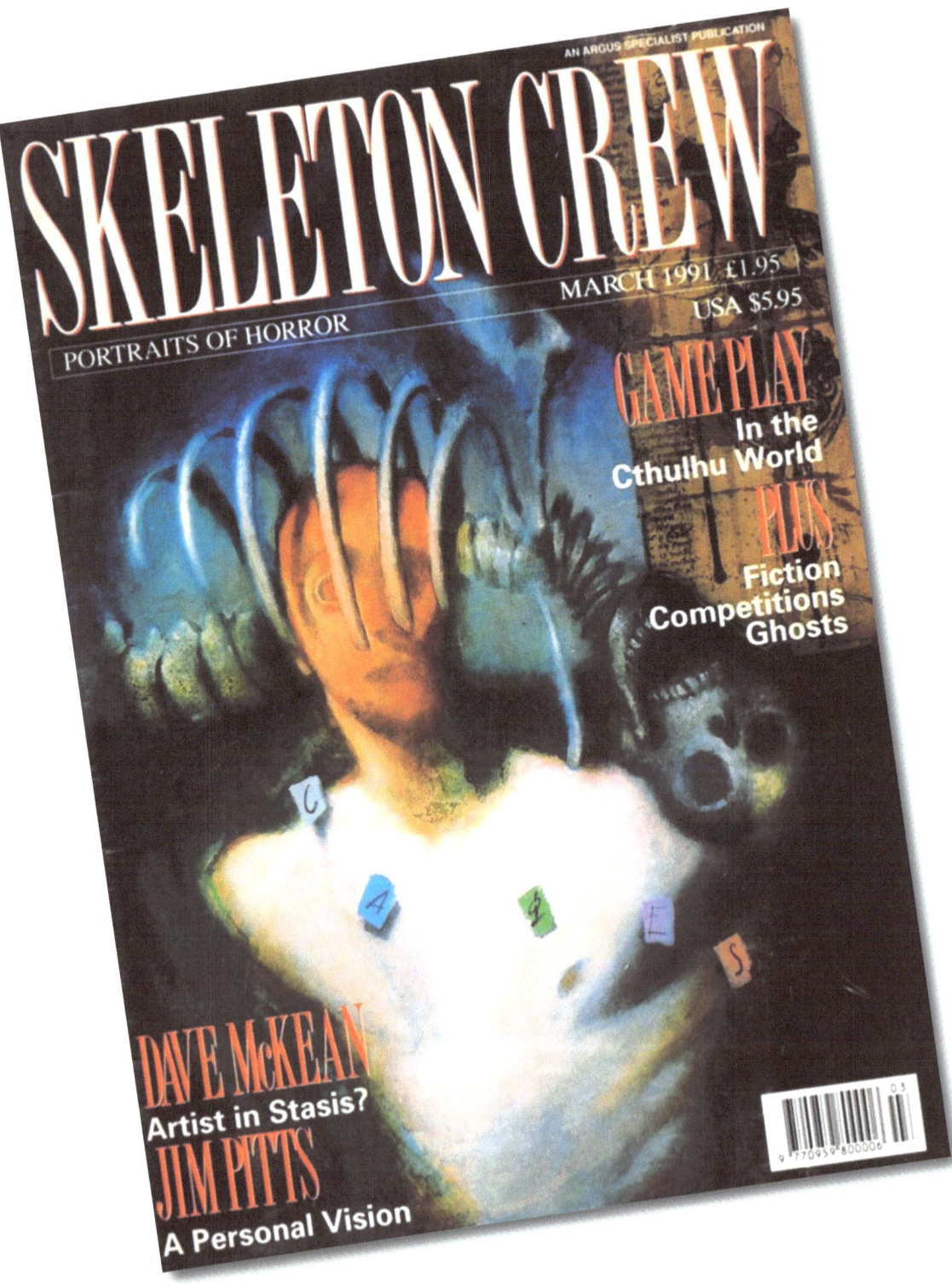

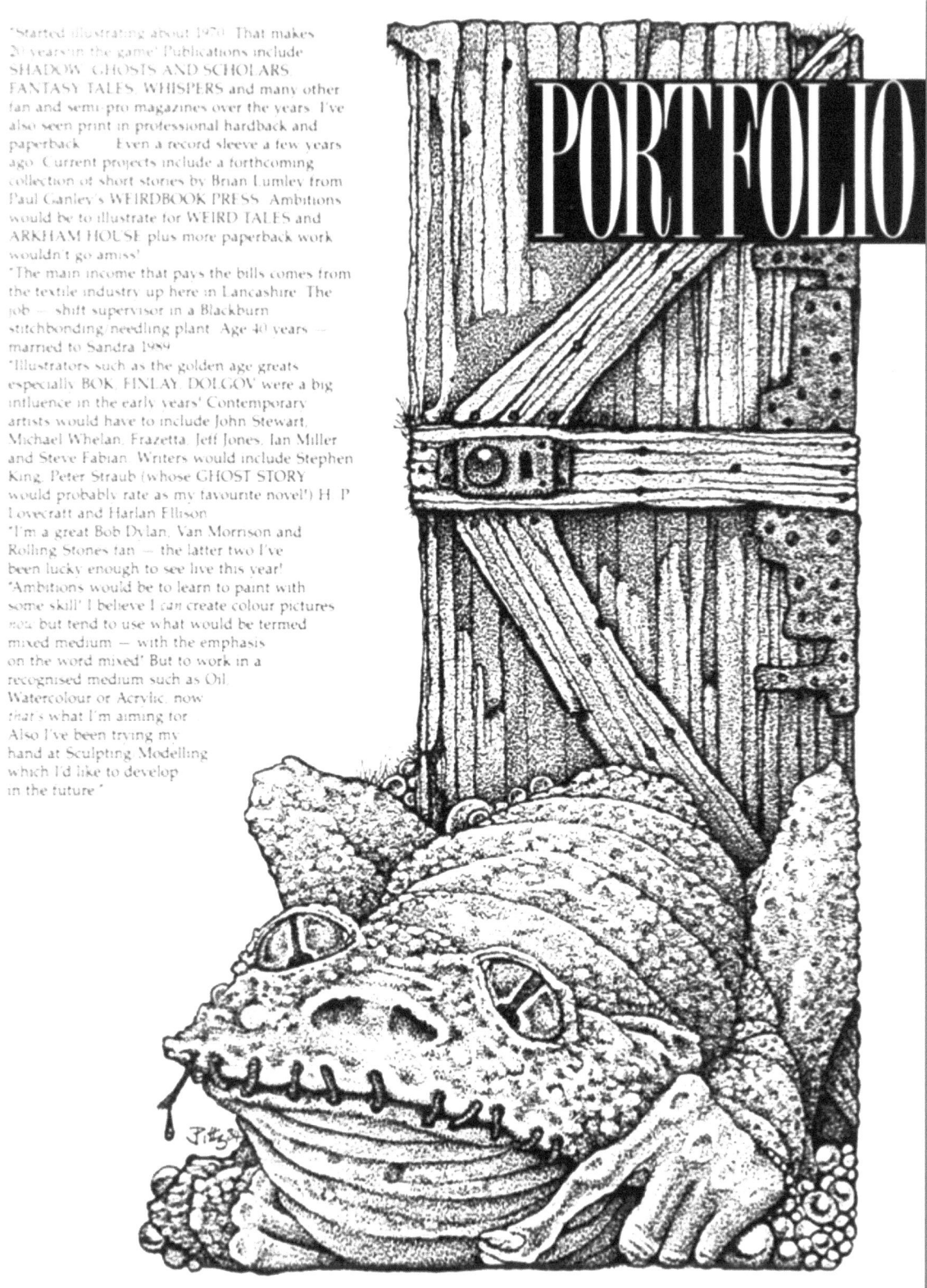

'Started illustrating about 1970. That makes 20 years in the game! Publications include SHADOW, GHOSTS AND SCHOLARS, FANTASY TALES, WHISPERS and many other fan and semi-pro magazines over the years. I've also seen print in professional hardback and paperback. Even a record sleeve a few years ago. Current projects include a forthcoming collection of short stories by Brian Lumley from Paul Ganley's WEIRDBOOK PRESS. Ambitions would be to illustrate for WEIRD TALES and ARKHAM HOUSE plus more paperback work wouldn't go amiss!

'The main income that pays the bills comes from the textile industry up here in Lancashire. The job — shift supervisor in a Blackburn stitchbonding/needling plant. Age 40 years — married to Sandra 1989.

'Illustrators such as the golden age greats especially BOK, FINLAY, DOLGOV were a big influence in the early years! Contemporary artists would have to include John Stewart, Michael Whelan, Frazetta, Jeff Jones, Ian Miller and Steve Fabian. Writers would include Stephen King, Peter Straub (whose GHOST STORY would probably rate as my favourite novel!) H. P. Lovecraft and Harlan Ellison.

'I'm a great Bob Dylan, Van Morrison and Rolling Stones fan — the latter two I've been lucky enough to see live this year!

'Ambitions would be to learn to paint with some skill! I believe I *can* create colour pictures *now*, but tend to use what would be termed mixed medium — with the emphasis on the word mixed! But to work in a recognised medium such as Oil, Watercolour or Acrylic, now *that's* what I'm aiming for. Also I've been trying my hand at Sculpting/Modelling which I'd like to develop in the future.'

Skeleton Crew, March 1991

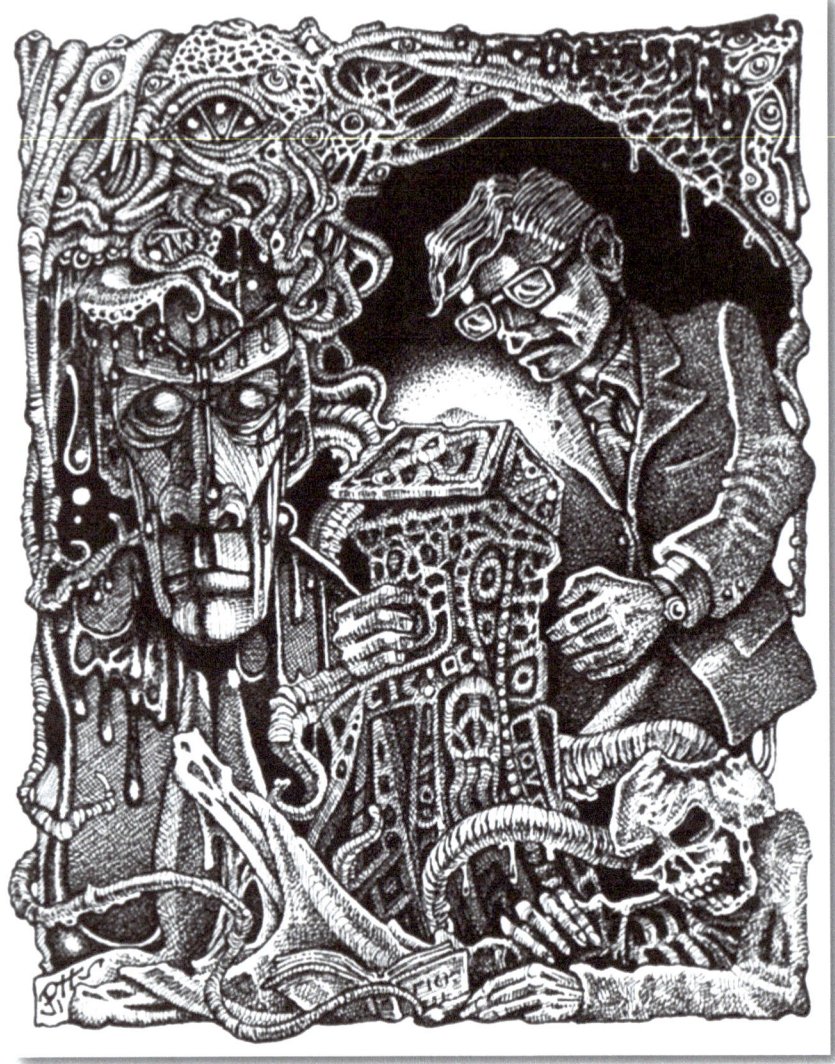

Skeleton Crew was a semi-prozine British horror/fantasy magazine from the early 90s, edited by Dave Reeder. The above illustration is for H. P. Lovecraft's *The Haunter of the Dark*.

The picture to the right was an exercise in stippling and cross-hatch.

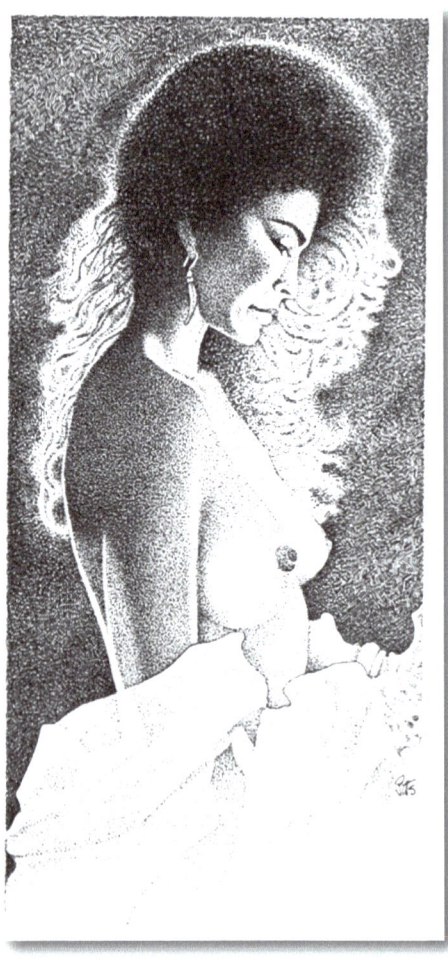

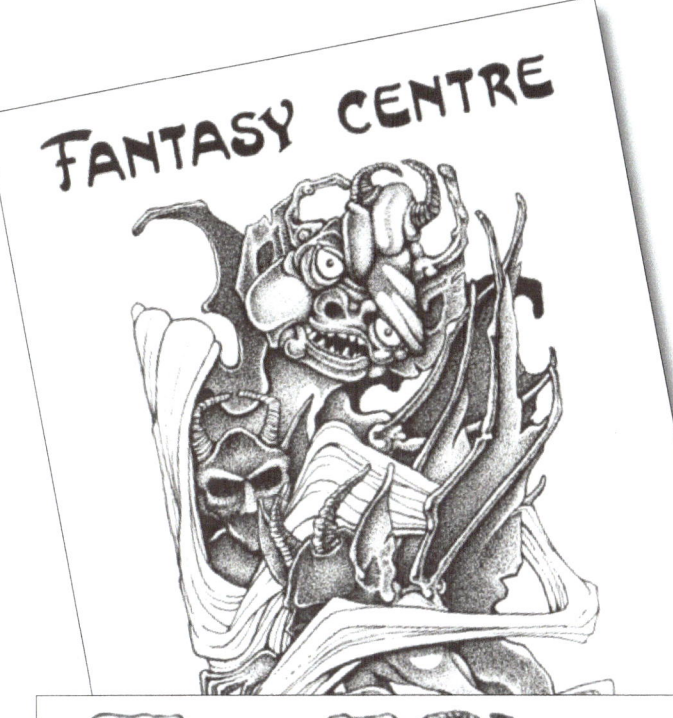
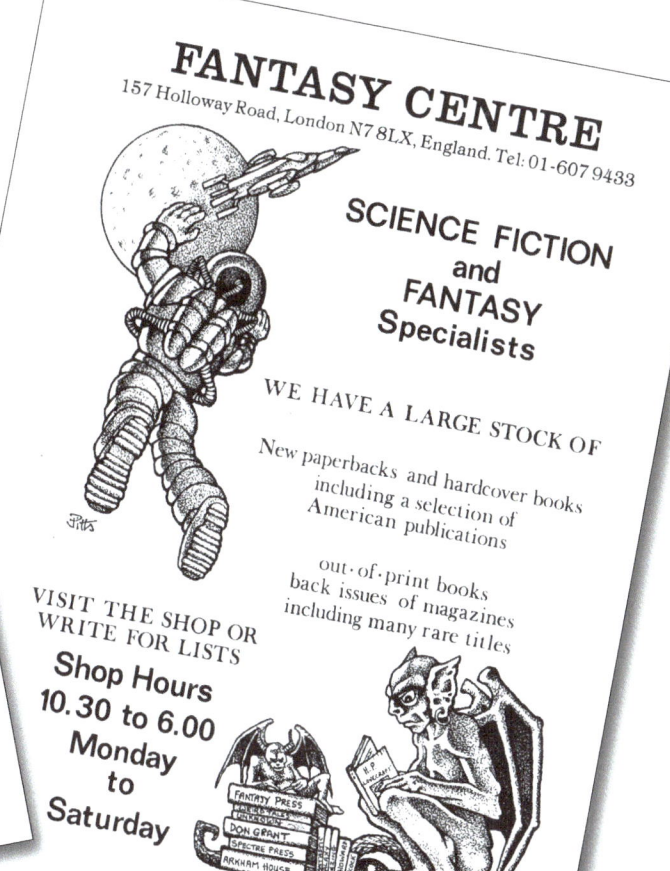

Some of the artwork Jim provided for *Fantasy Centre's* ads and catalogues.

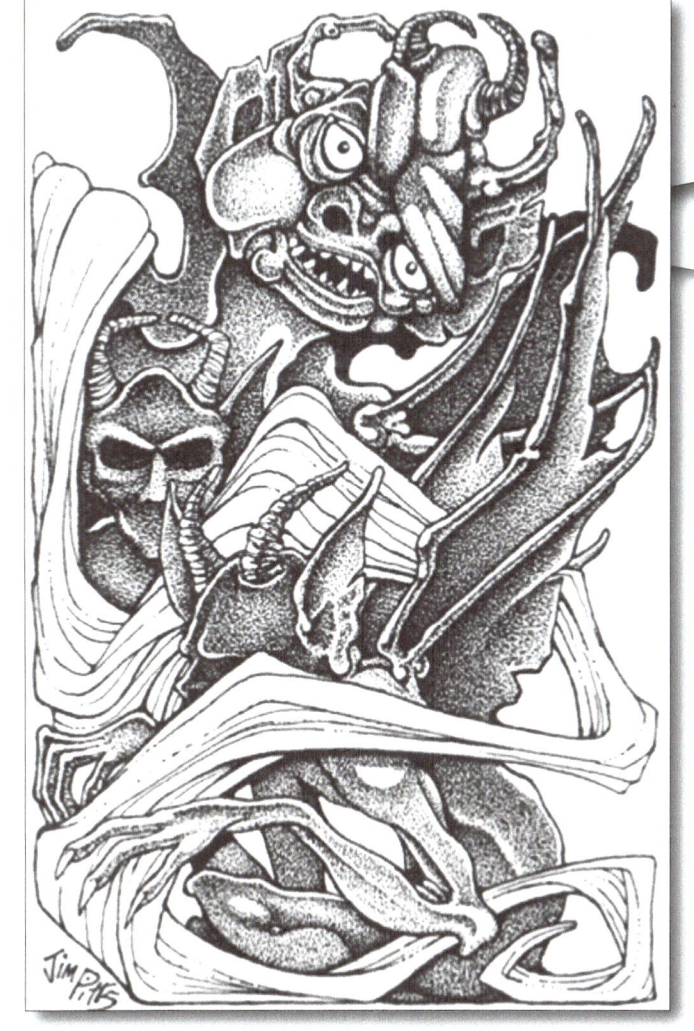

Included in *Phantasmagoria Books Catalogue 9*, September 1974.

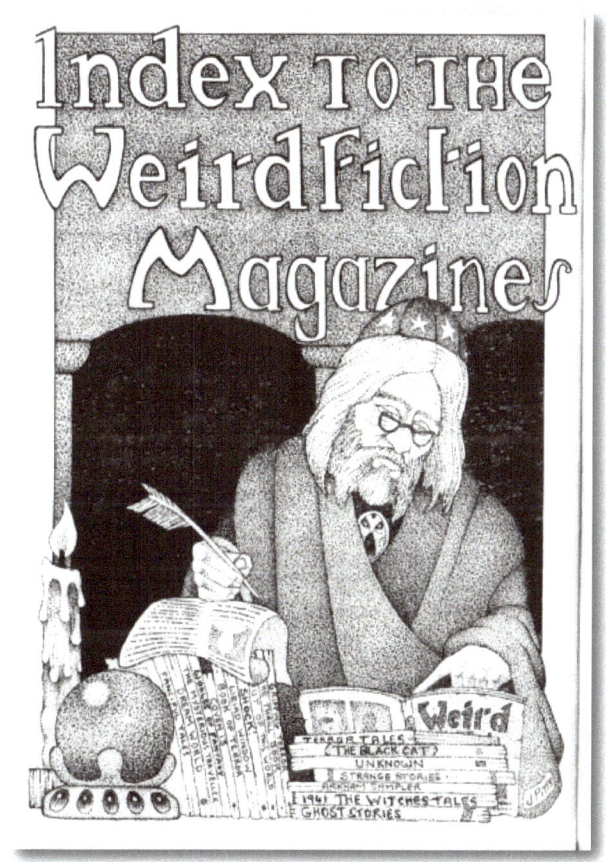

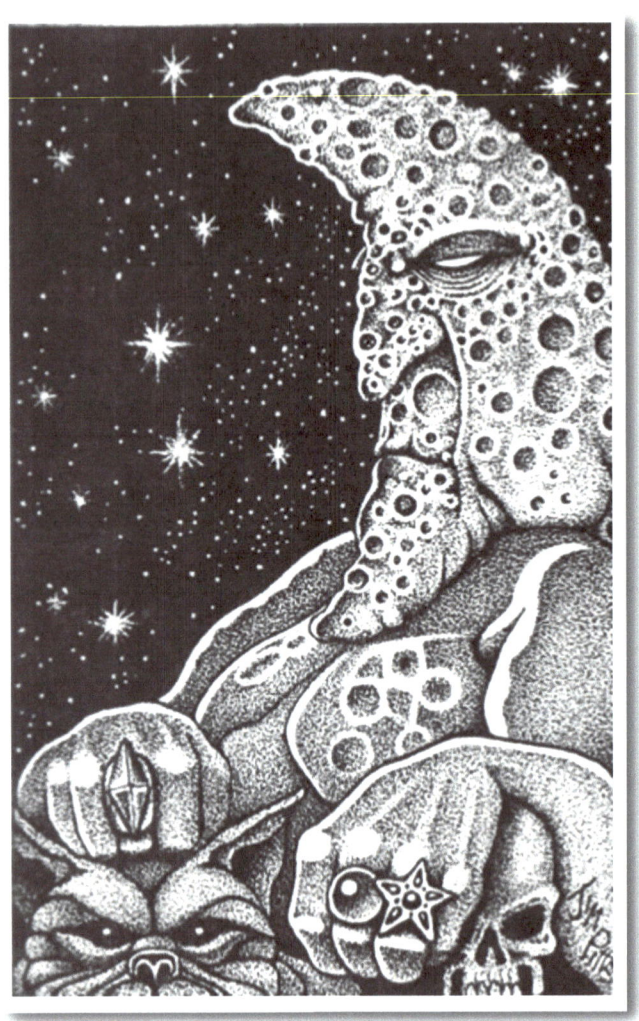
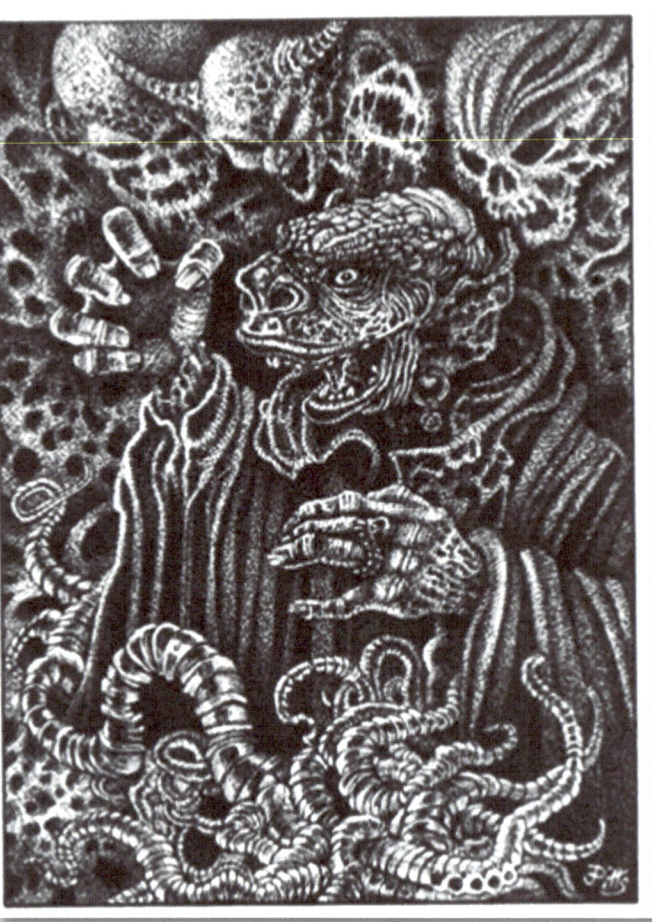
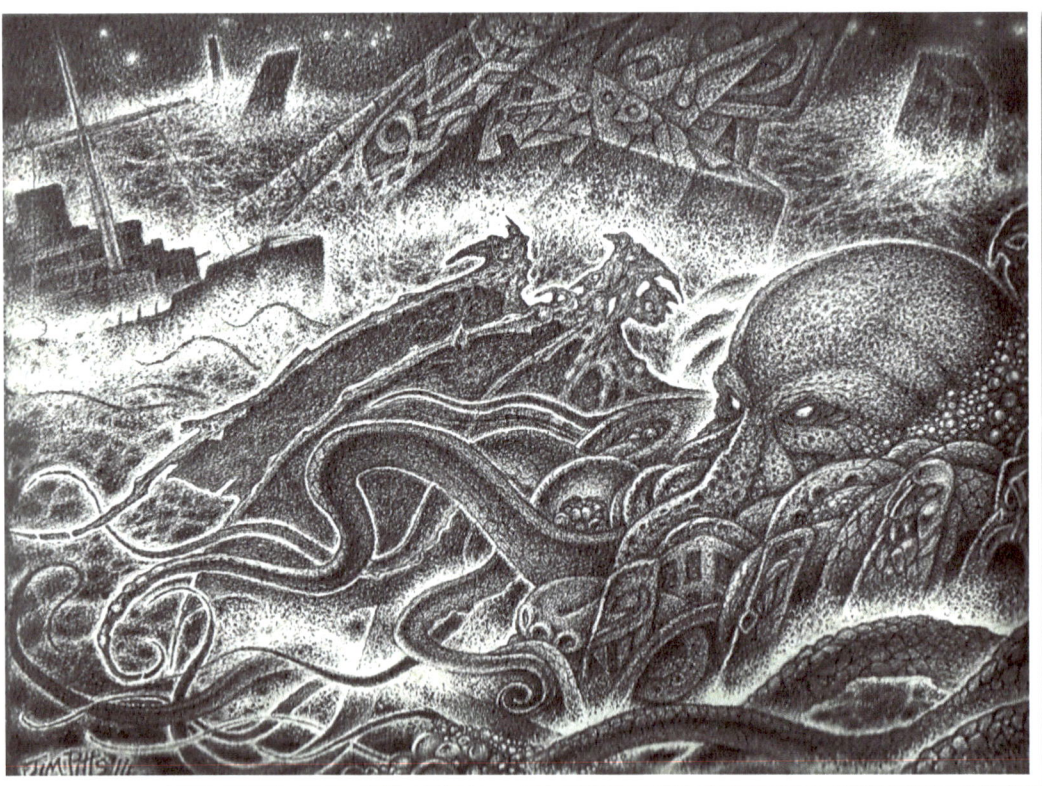

Top left: from *The Compleat Khash Vol Two: Sorcery in Shad* by Brian Lumley

Top right: *from The Compleat Khash Vol Two: Never a Backward Glance* by Brian Lumley

Bottom: *The Call of Cthulhu* by H. P. Lovecraft - carbon pencil on rough watercolour paper

Robert W. Chambers' *The King in Yellow*
"At last I was king, king by my right in Hastur."

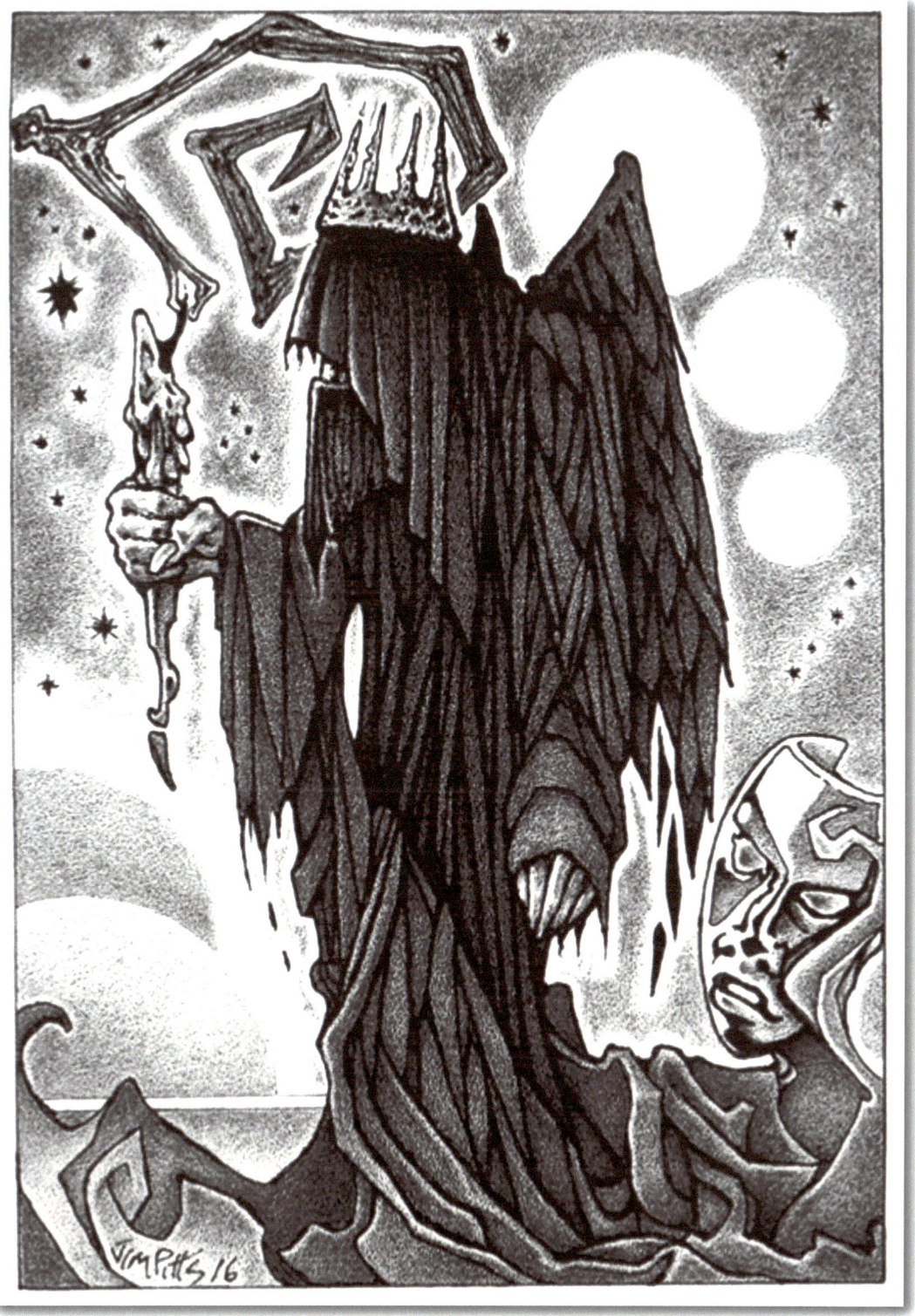

Robert W. Chambers' "The Mask" from *The King in Yellow* Act i, Scene 2
Camilla: You, sir, should unmask.
Stranger: Indeed?
Cassilda: Indeed it's time. We have all laid disguise but you.
Stranger: I wear no mask.
Camilla: (terrified, aside to Cassilda) No mask? No mask!

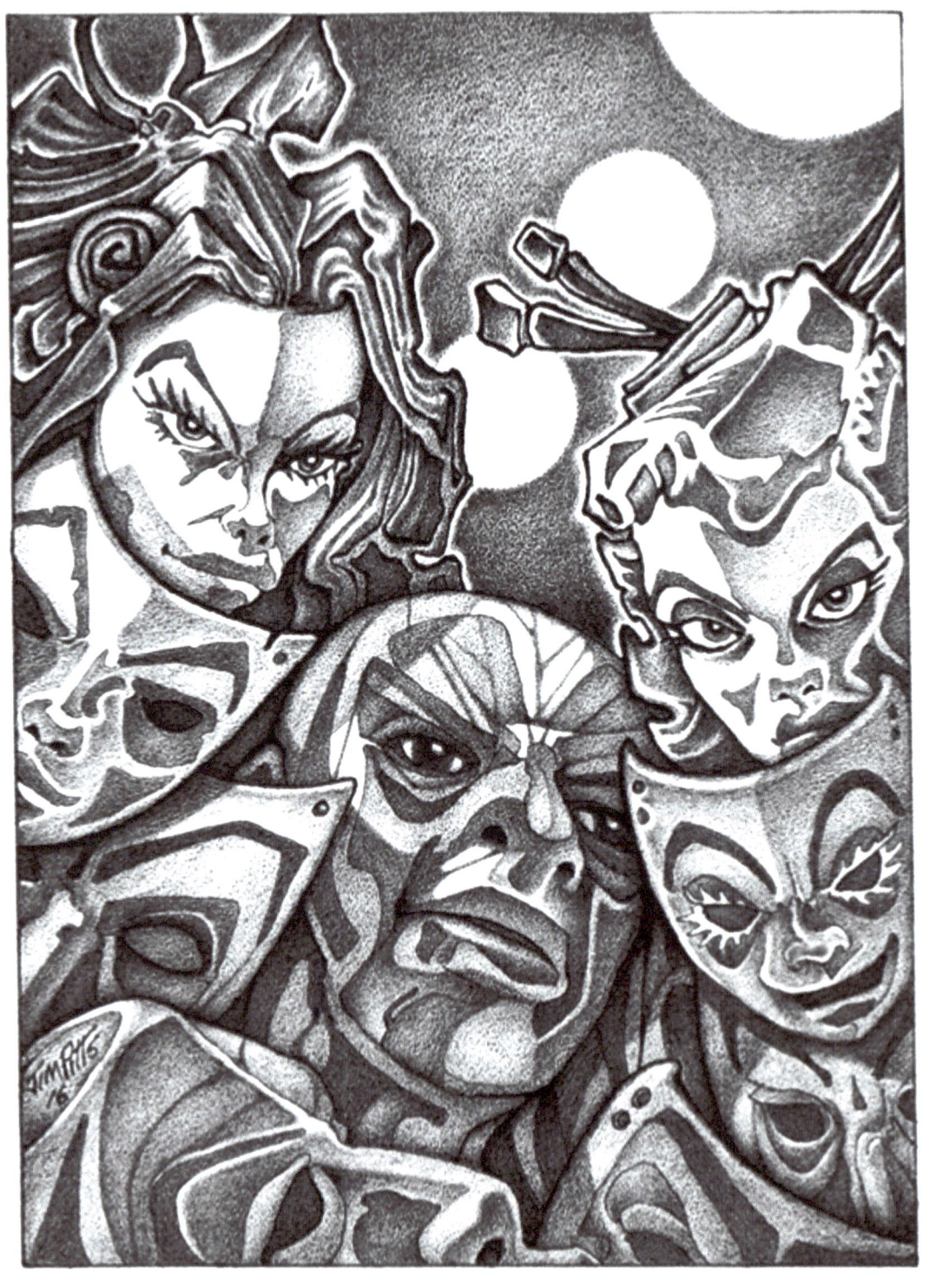

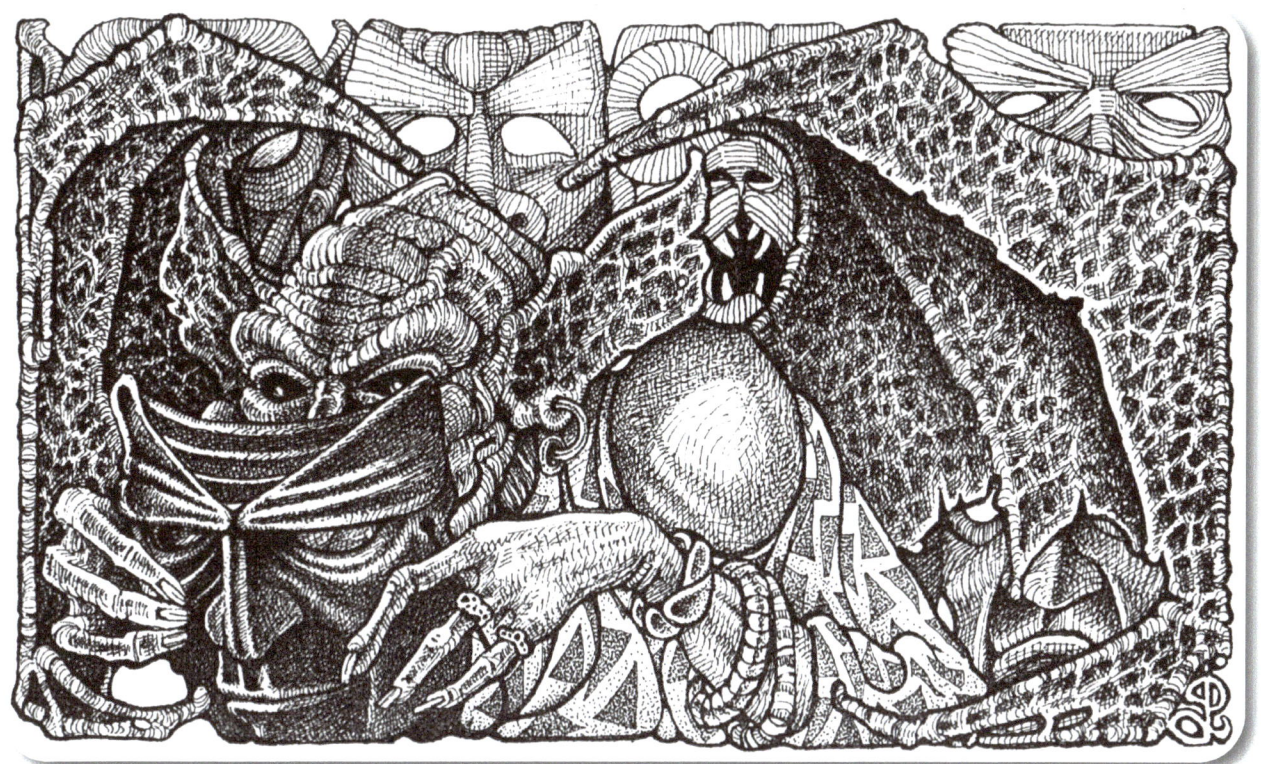

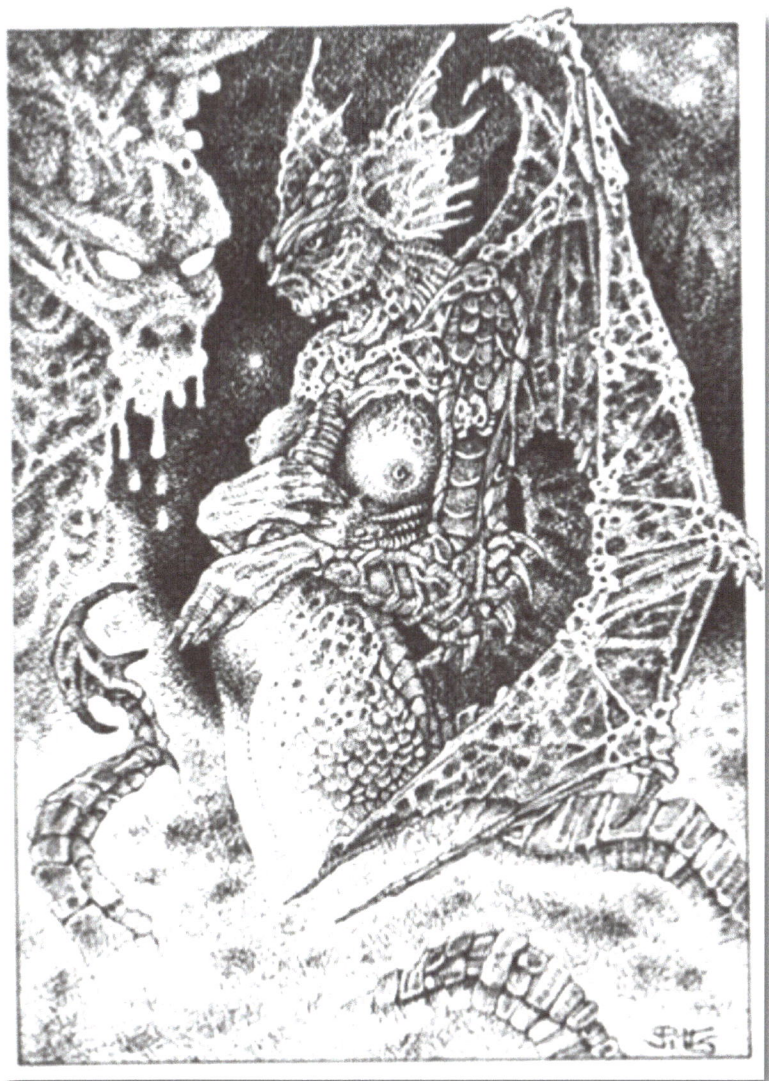

Top: illustration "Masks" - ink

Bottom: *The Compleat Khash Vol One: Never a Backward Glance* by Brian Lumley

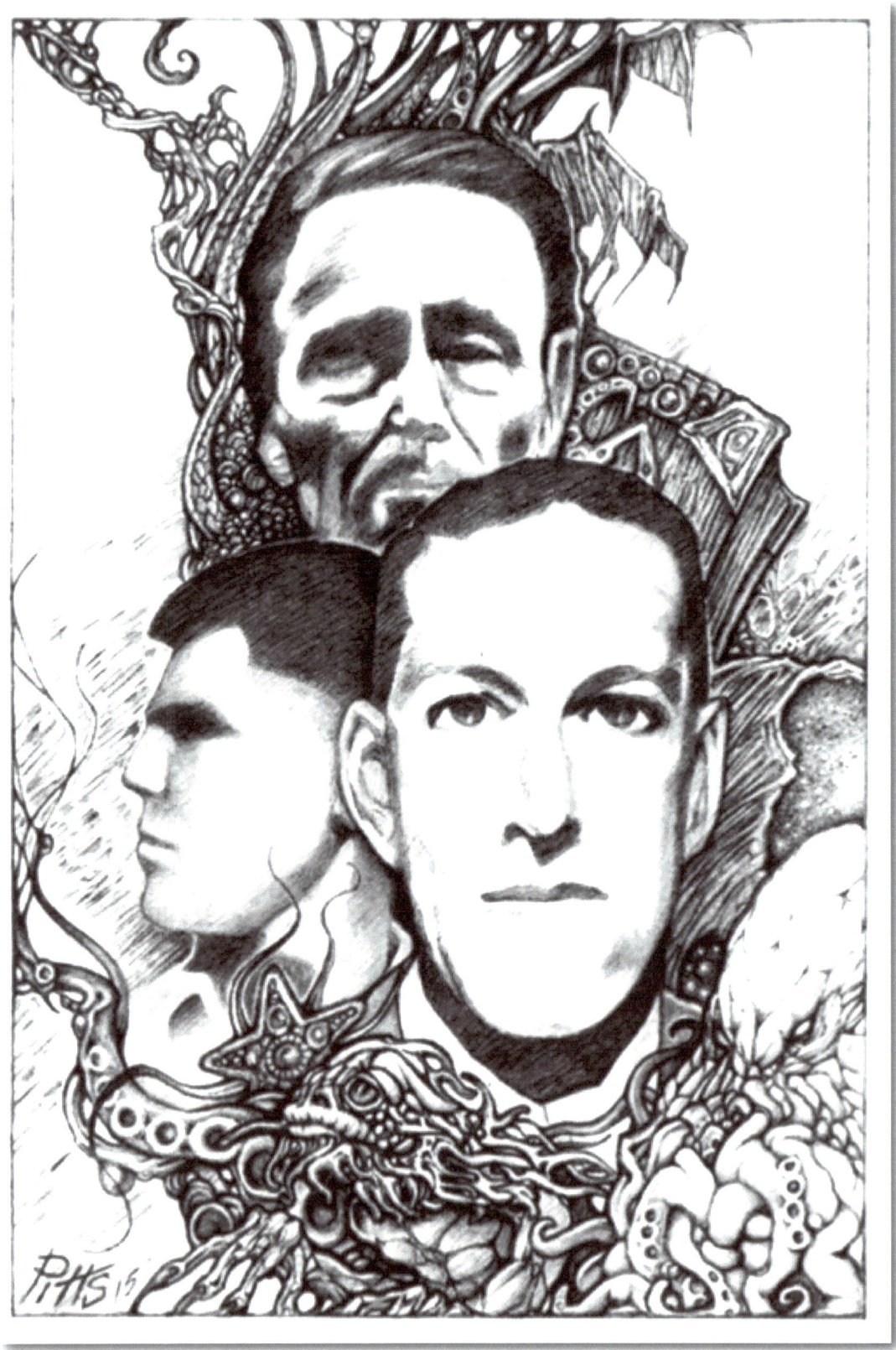

Clark Ashton Smith, Robert E. Howard and H. P. Lovecraft
Carbon pencil on water colour paper.

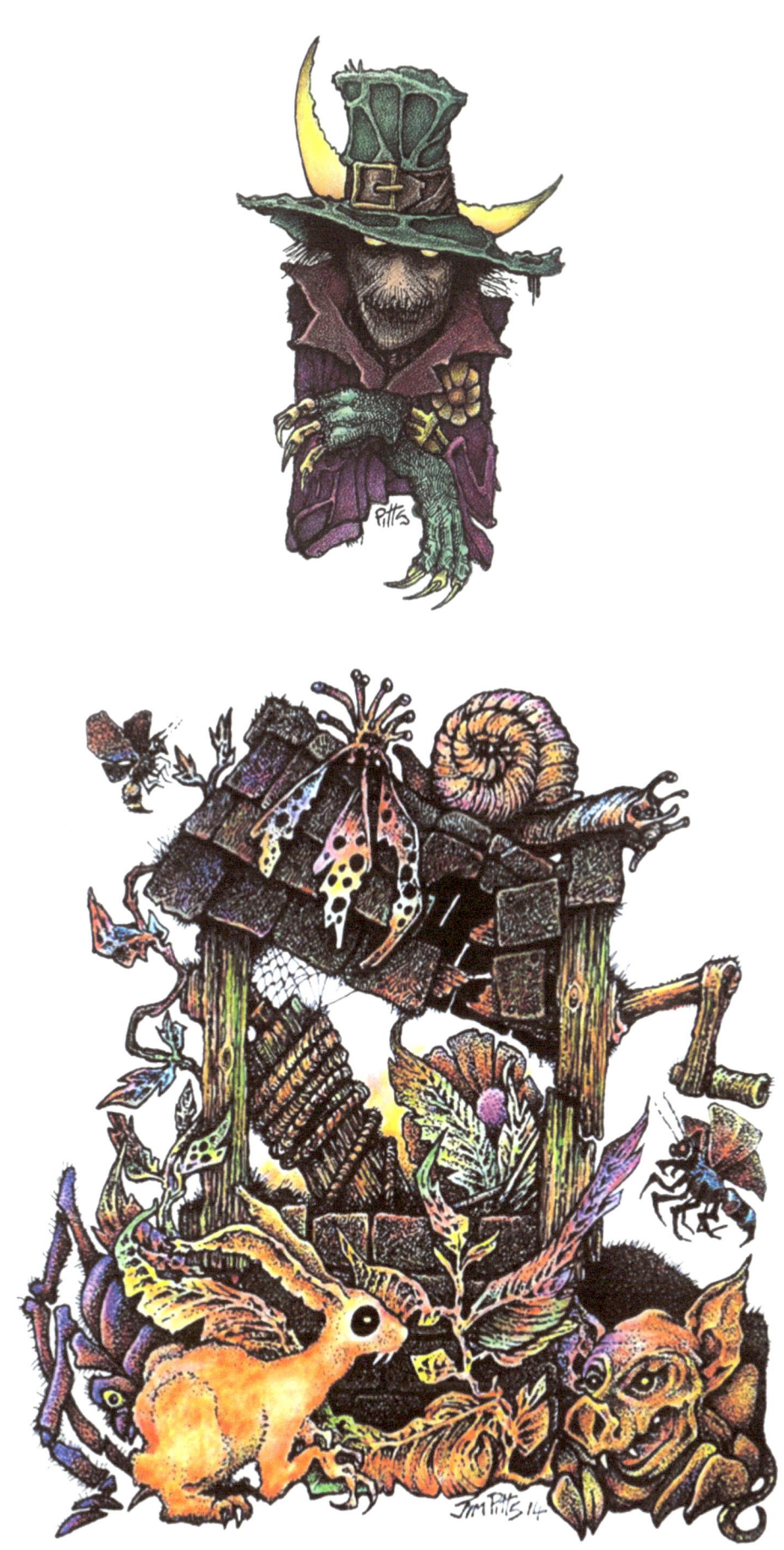

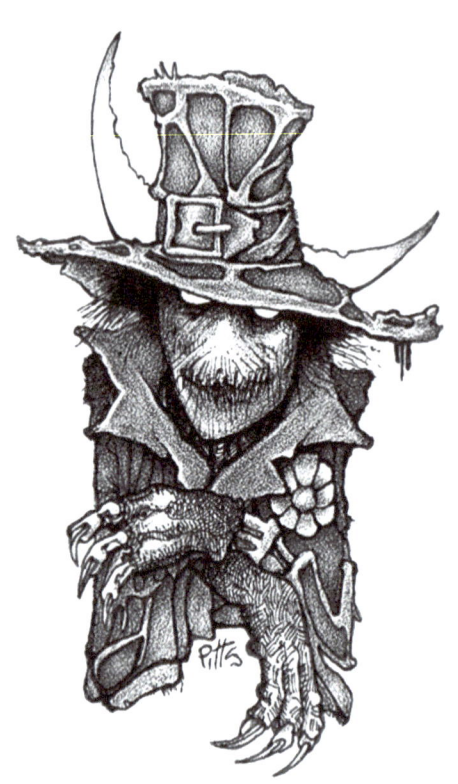

Original black and white artwork. Facing page: hand tinted with coloured pencils.

The top figure is "Mr October" from an original idea.

The illustration below is from *The Colour Out of Space* by H. P. Lovecraft

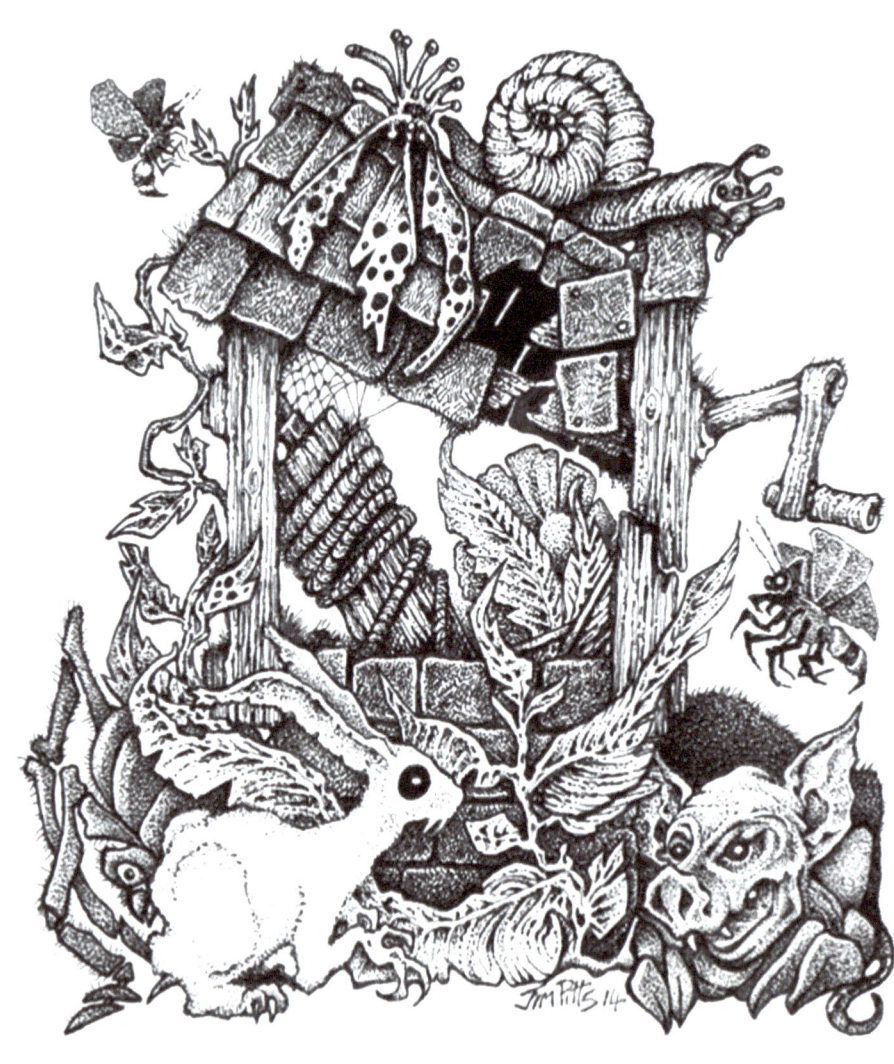

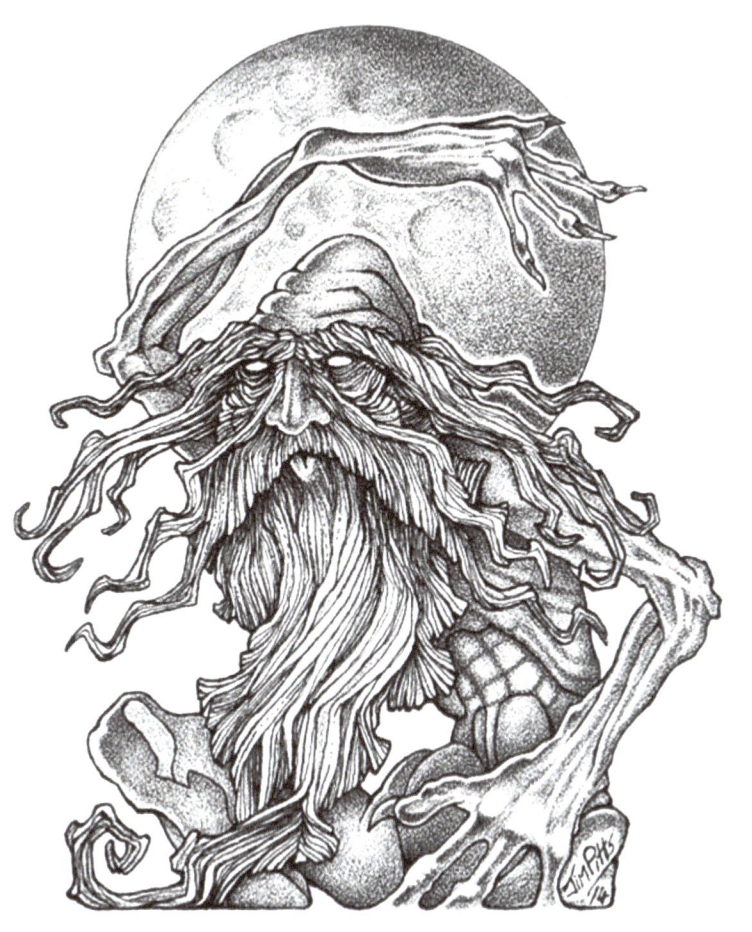

The illustration to the left was used as the front cover for *Cthulhu 7*.

The illustration below was used as the wraparound cover for the BFS chapbook, produced by Peter Coleborn - Mark Morris's *Birthday*.

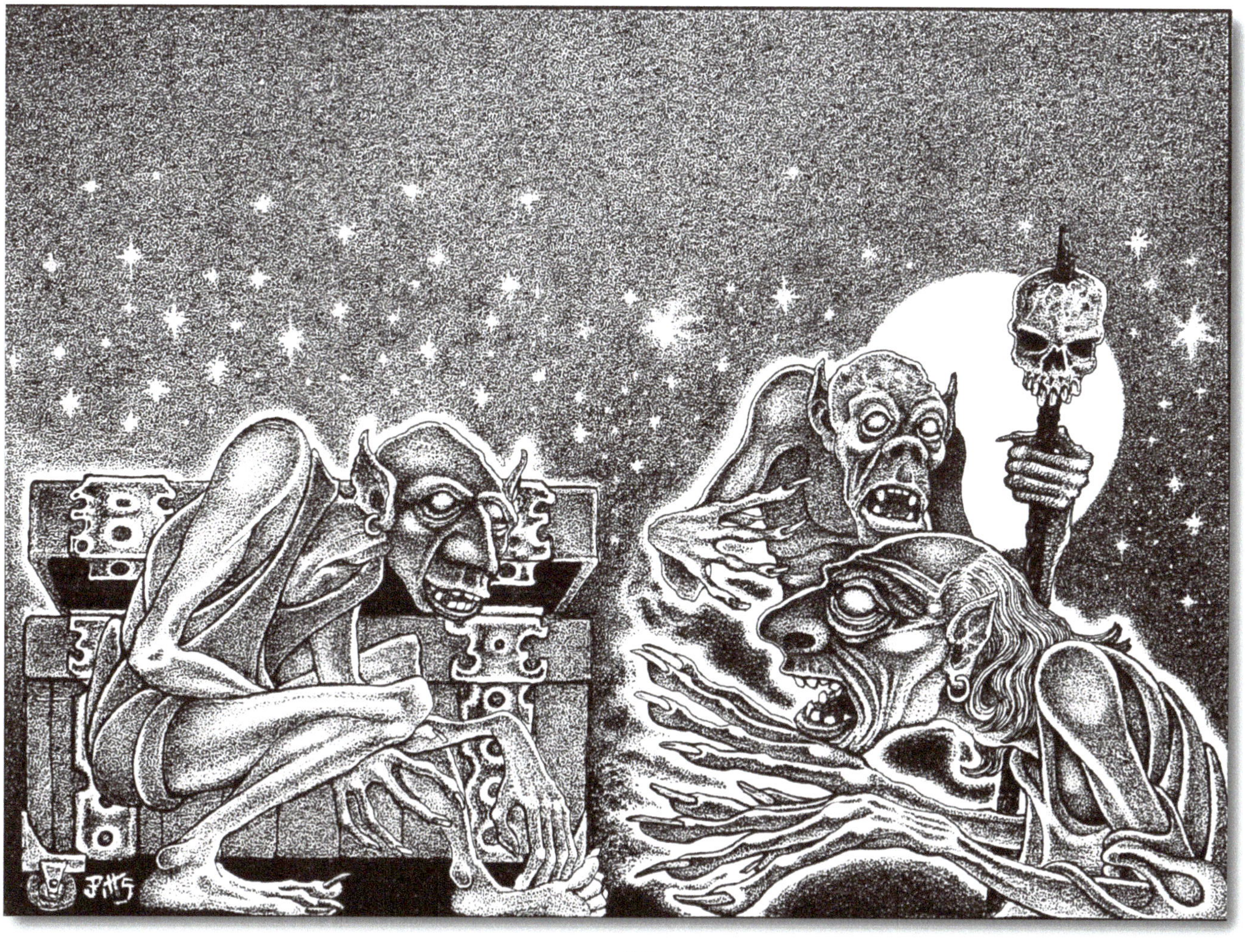

"Cthulhu" design - ink and pencil crayon

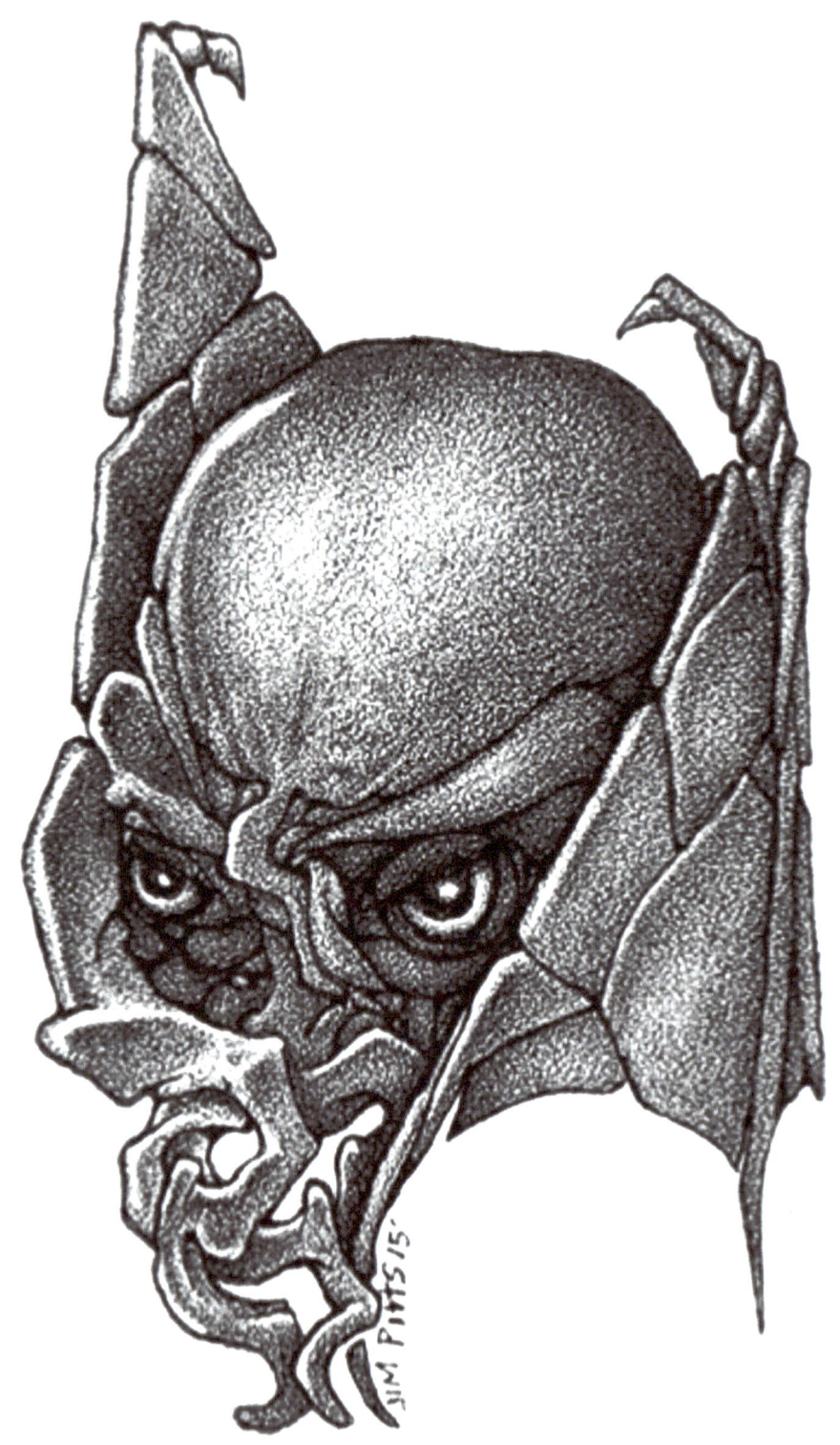

Necromancy in Naat by Clark Ashton Smith

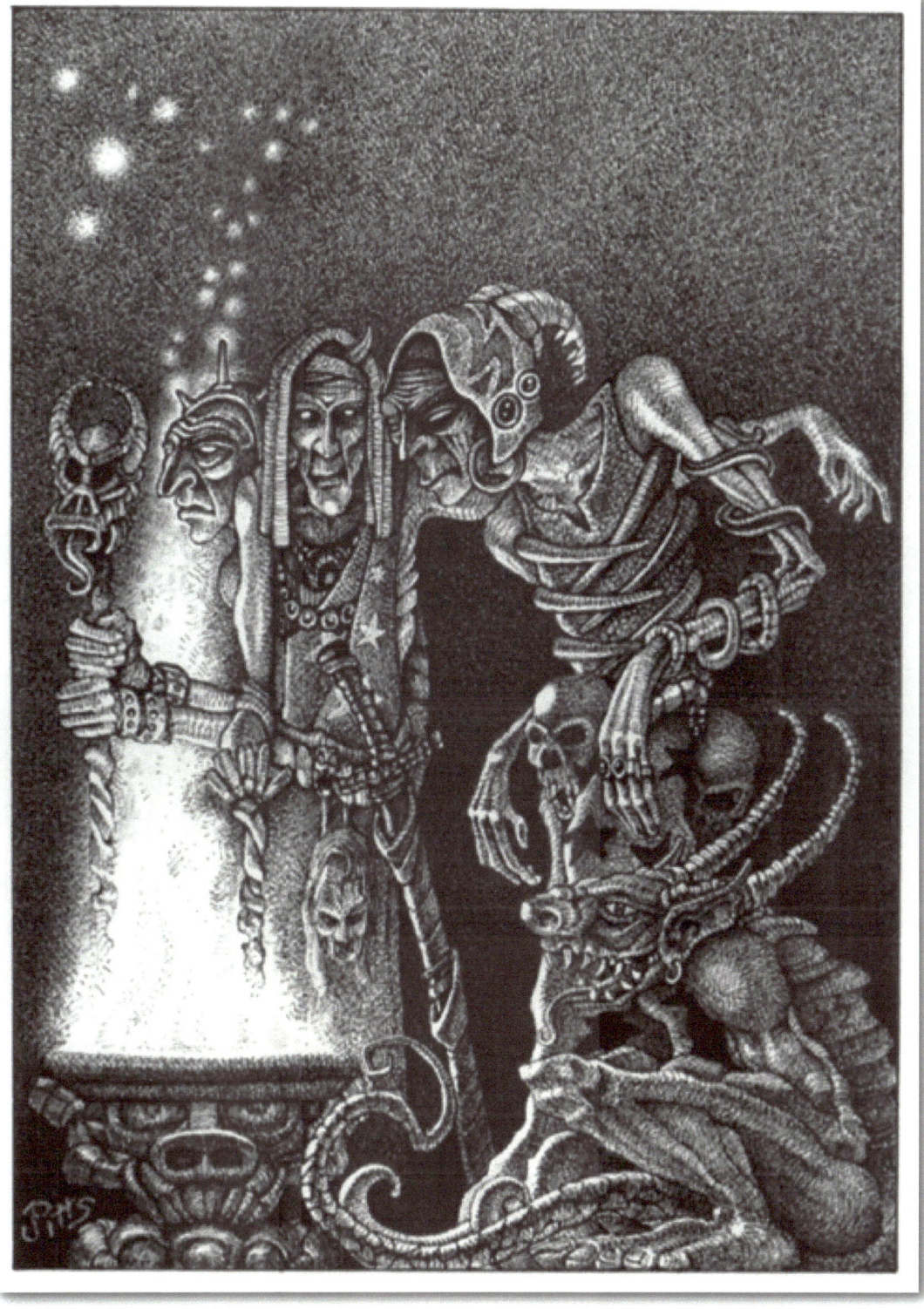

Inspired by M. R. James' *Casting of the Runes*
From the collection of Stephen Jones

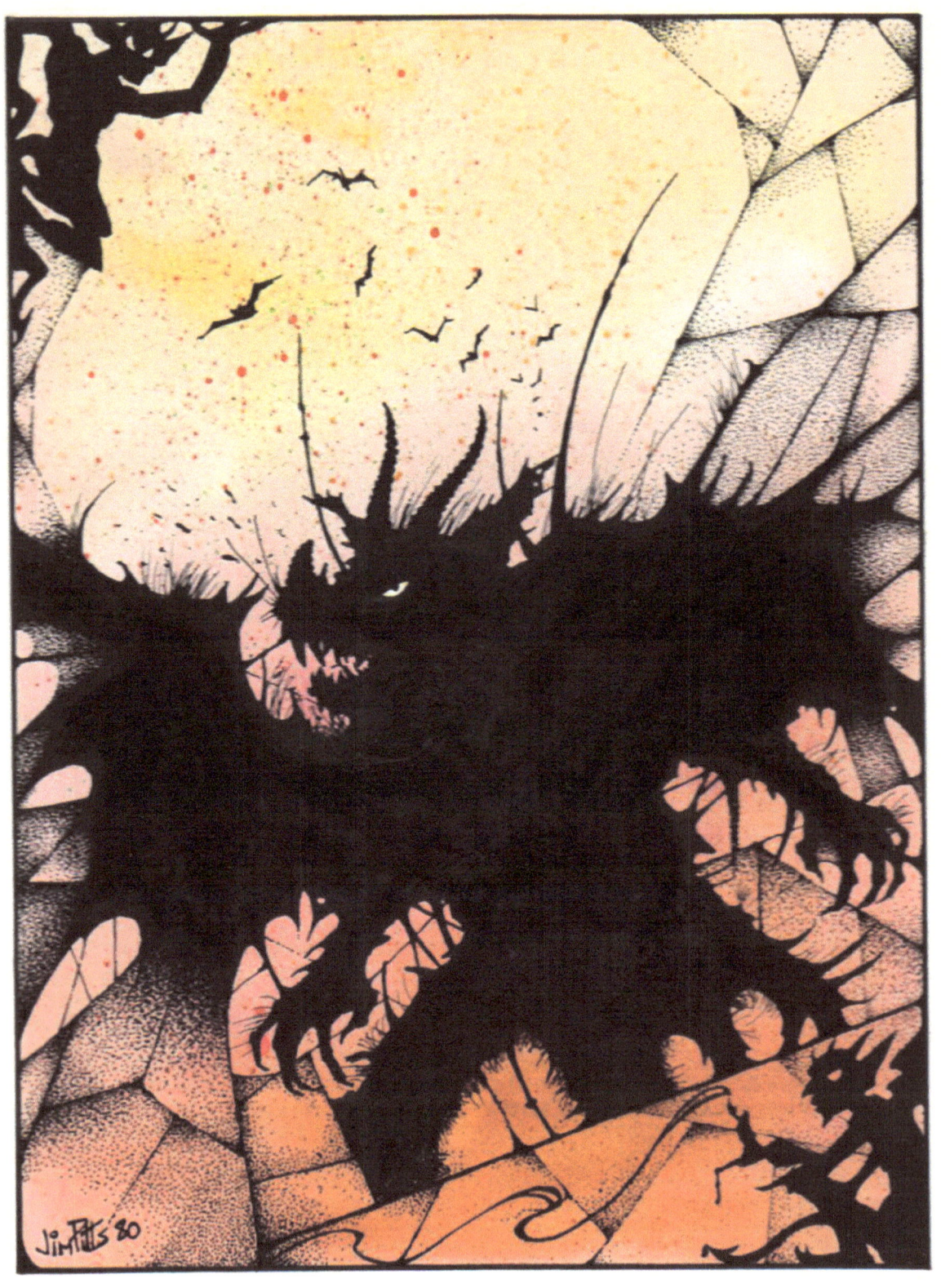

NORTHERN CHILLS
edited by Graeme Hurry

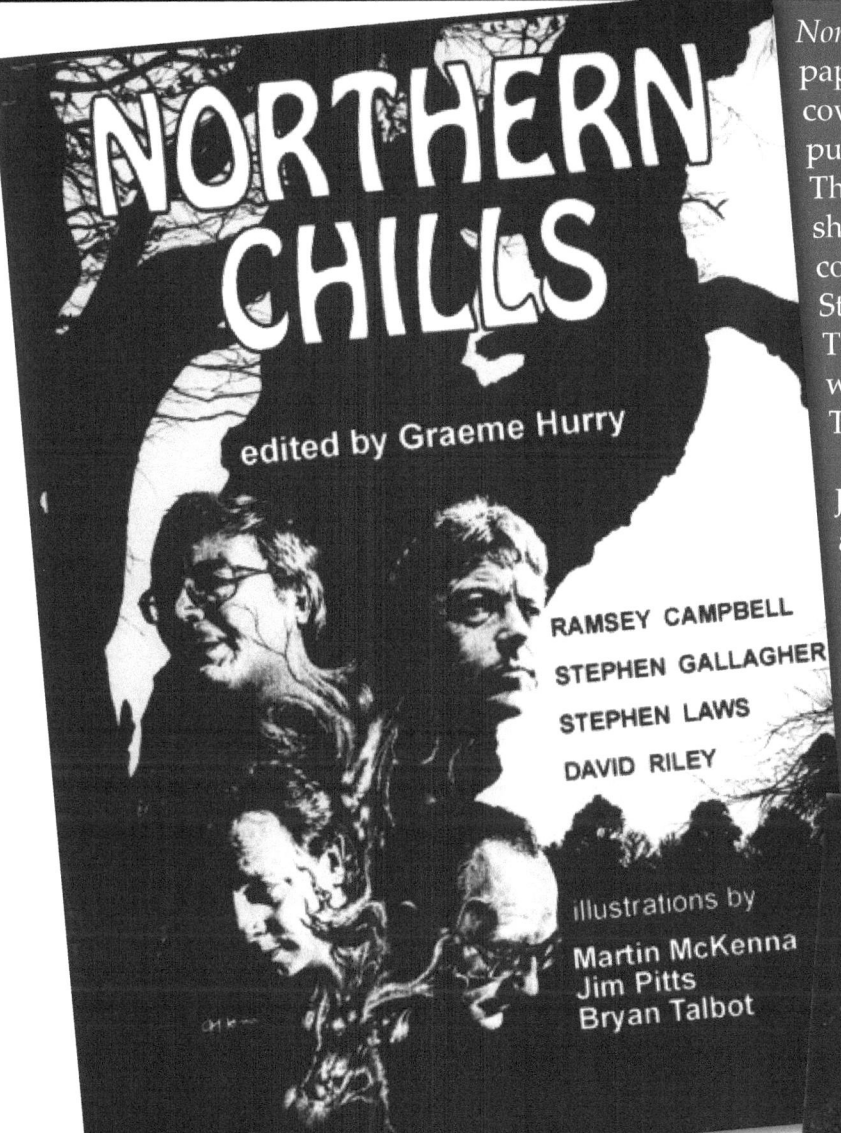

Northern Chills was published as a trade paperback and a limited edition hard cover by Graeme Hurry, a Preston-based publisher (Kimota Press), in 1994. The 100-page anthology contained five short stories by Ramsey Campbell (who contributed two), Stephen Gallagher, Stephen Laws and David A. Riley. The stories were illustrated in black and white by artists Martin McKenna, Bryan Talbot and Jim Pitts.

Jim Pitts illustrated *Mackintosh Willy* and *Above the World* by Ramsey Campbell (see pages 103 and 103), and also *Writer's Cramp* by David A. Riley. The book was launched at Fantasycon in September 1994, where all of the authors and artists were present to sign copies.

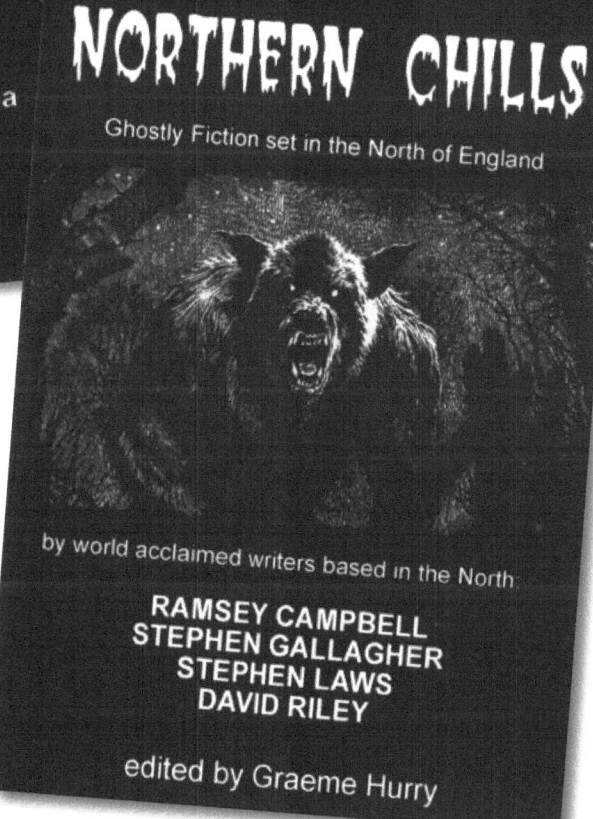

Cover illustrations for both the hard cover and paperback versions were by Martin McKenna. Above is the hard cover, with the faces of all four writers growing from a tree: top left: Ramsey Campbell; top right: Stephen Gallagher; bottom left: Stephen Laws; and bottom right: David A. Riley.

See pages 102 and 103 for Jim's illustrations for Ramsey Campbell's *Above the World* and *Mackintosh Willy*.

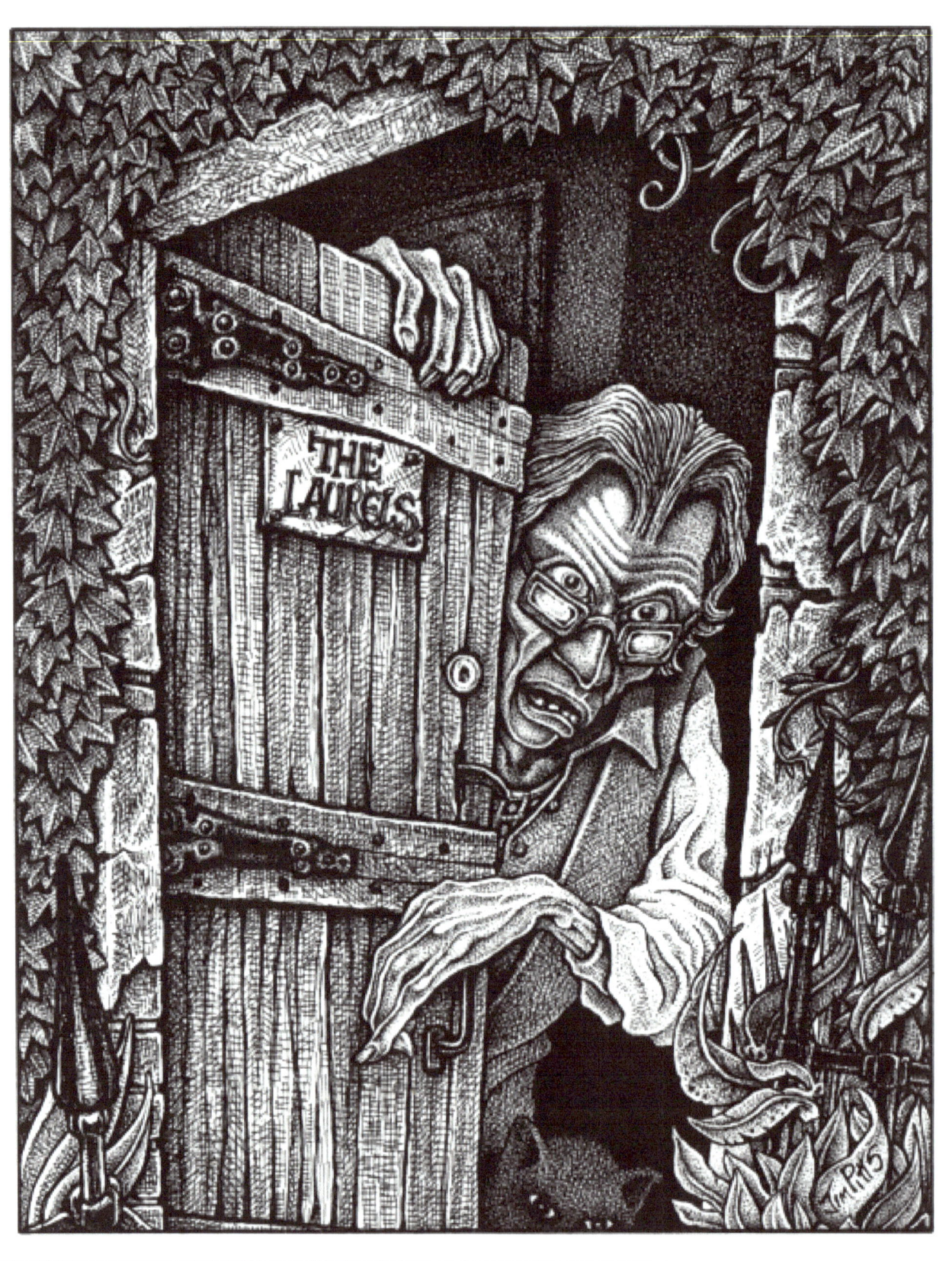

Writer's Cramp by David A. Riley

EXPERIMENTS IN COLOUR

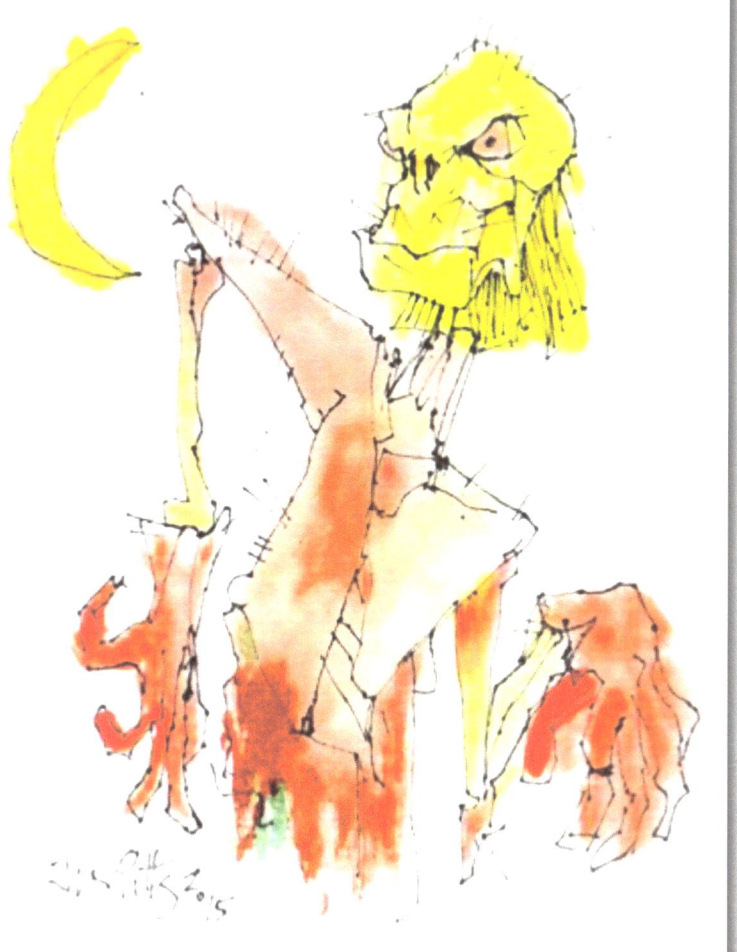

Halloween-inspired scarecrow

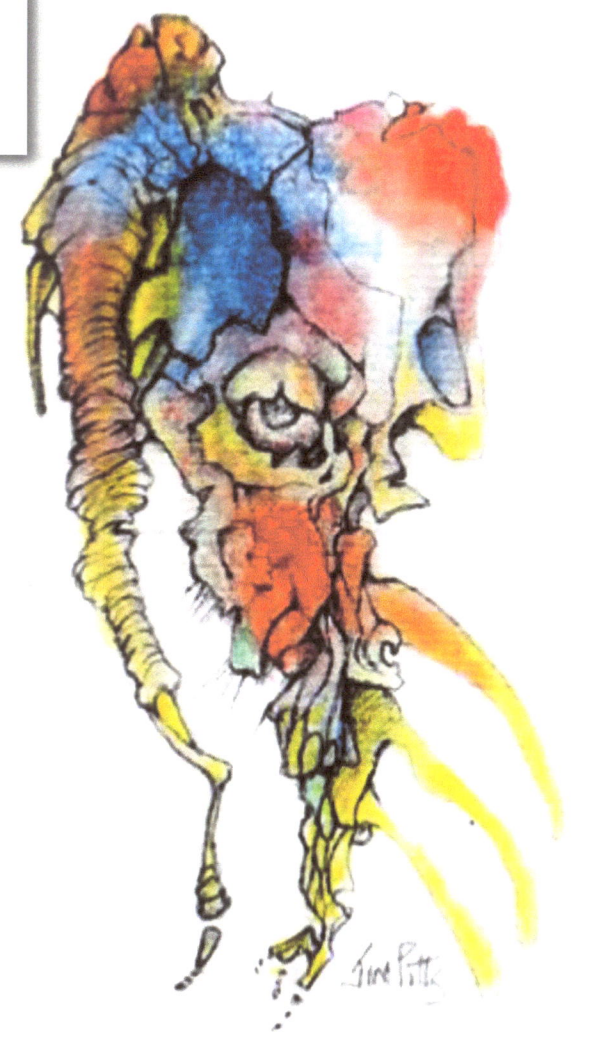

Coloured ink drawing inspired by skull found on Southport beach

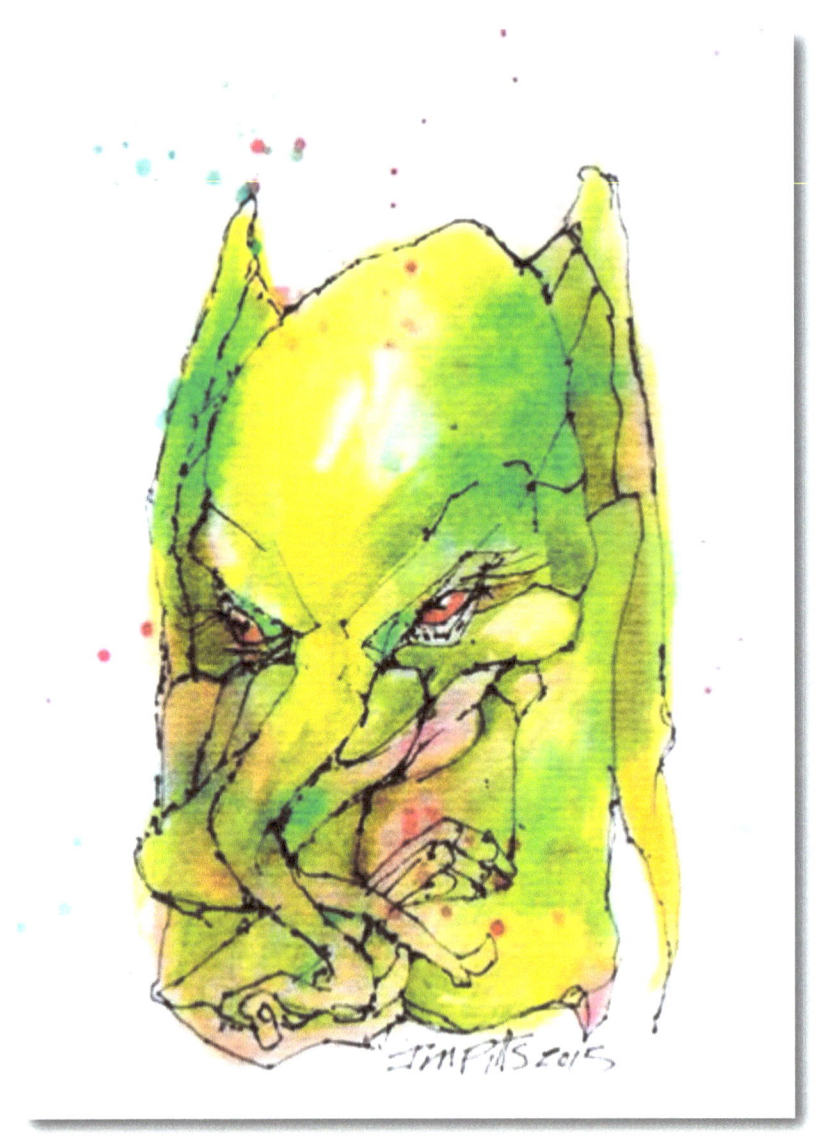

Early work for the cover of Adrian Cole's collection from Parallel Universe Publications, *Tough Guys*.

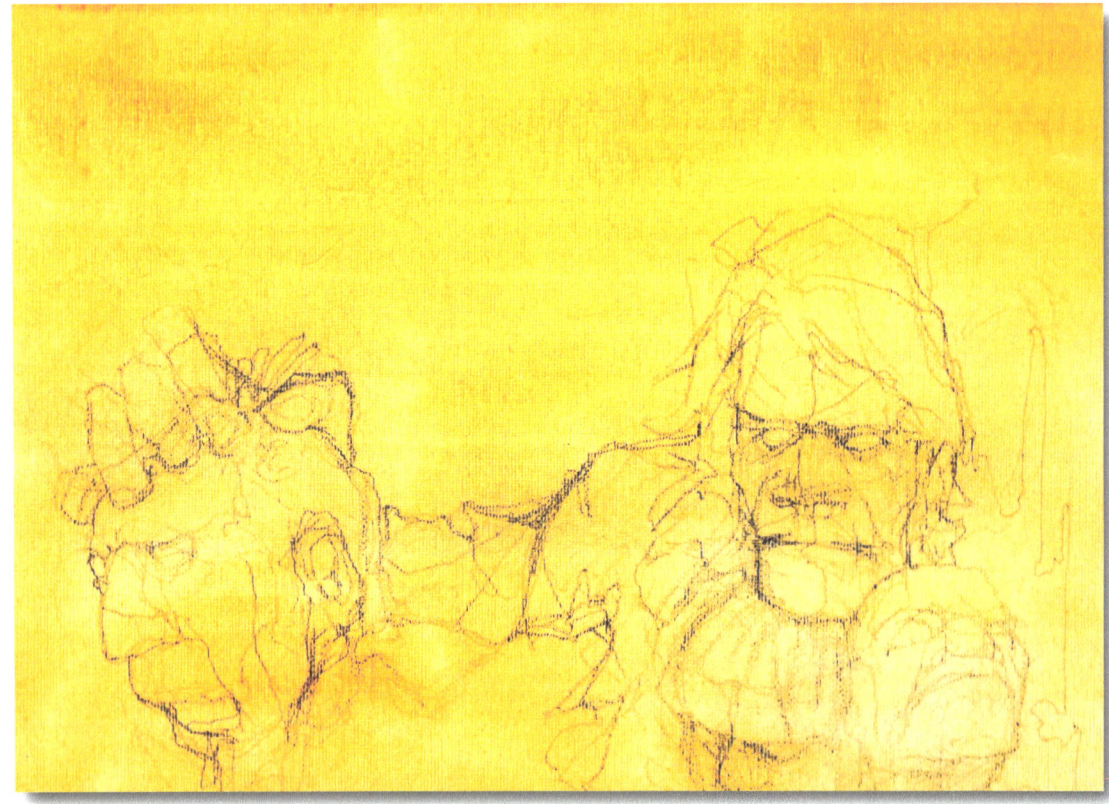

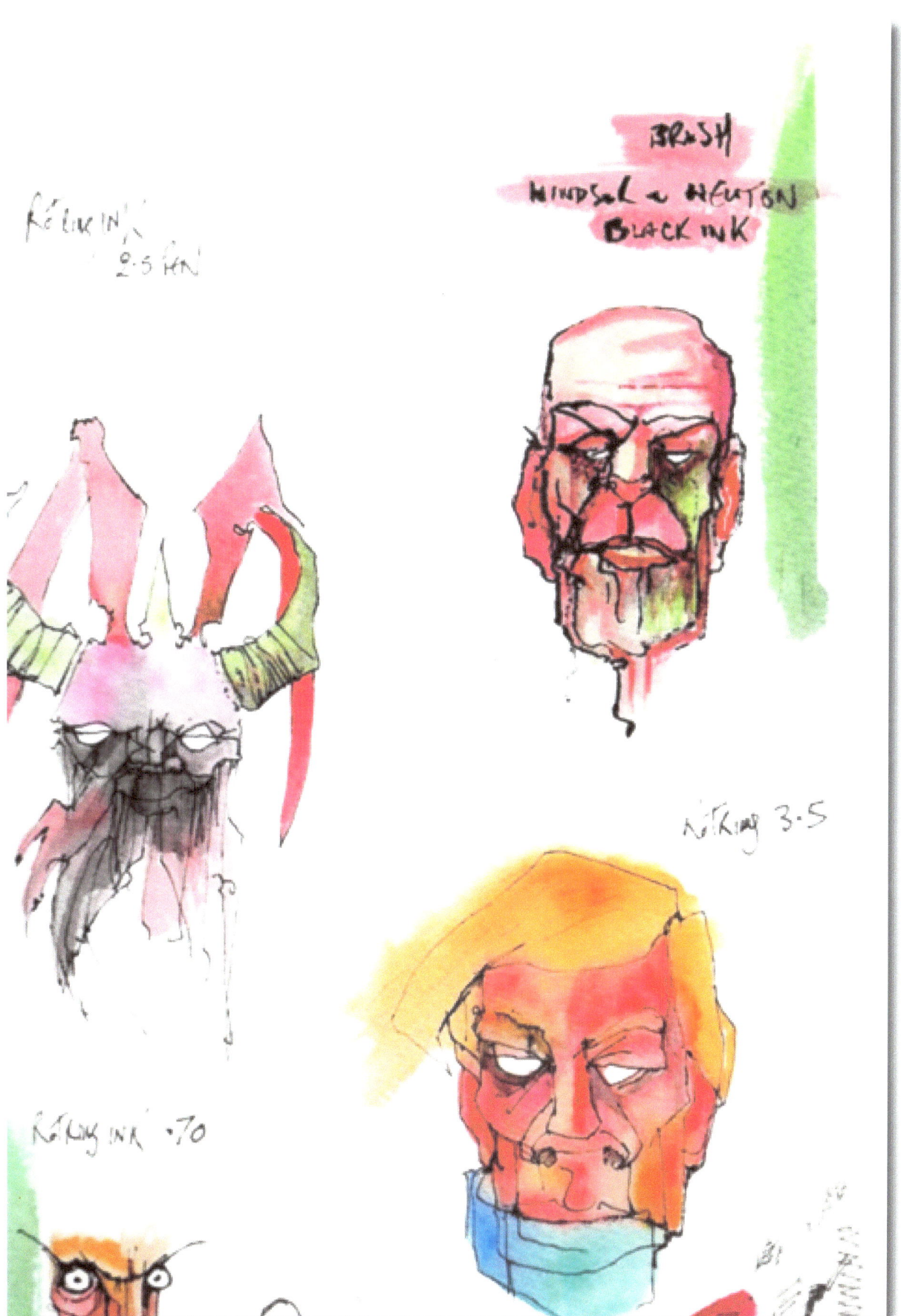

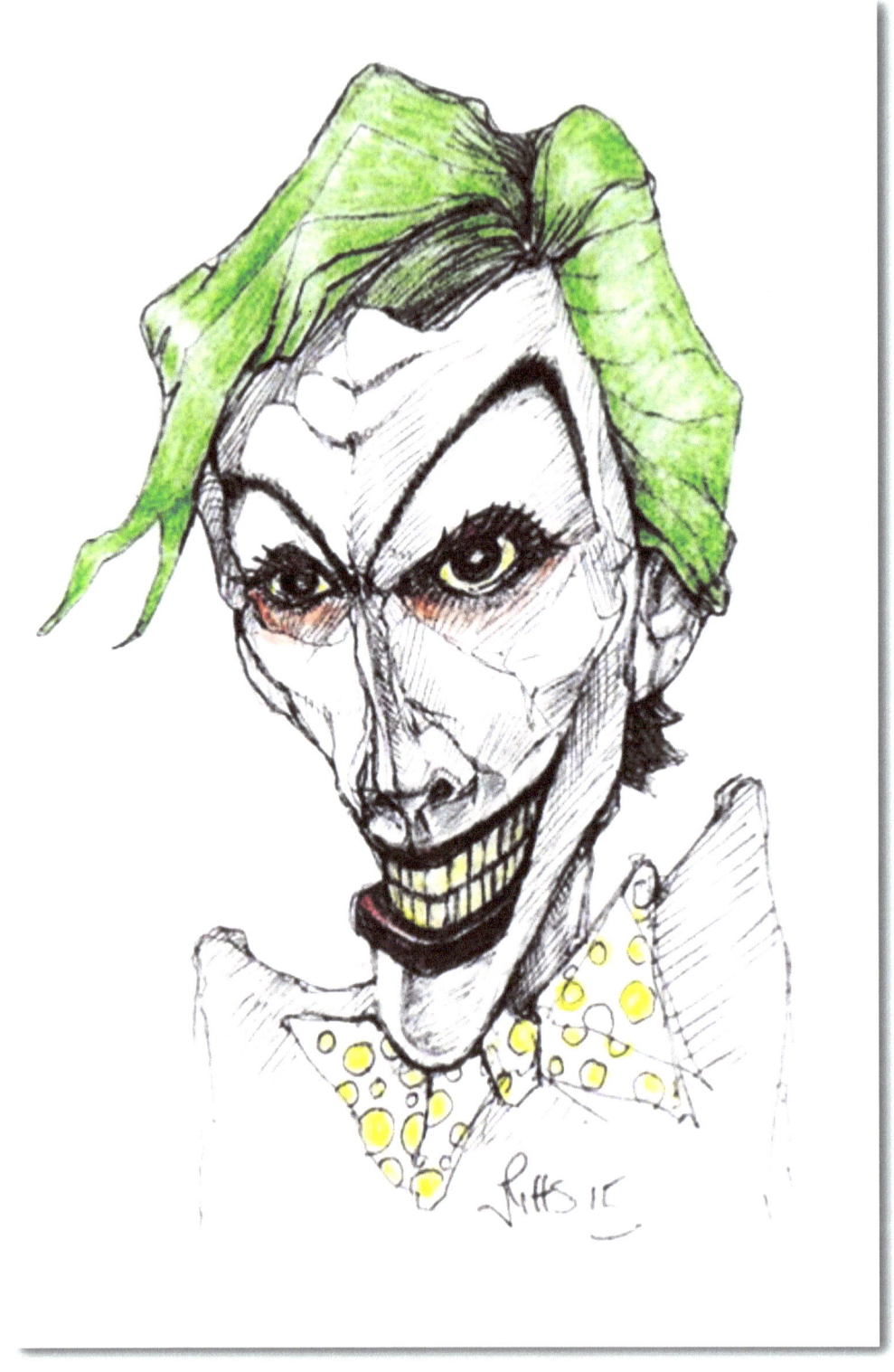

Sketch for "The Joker"

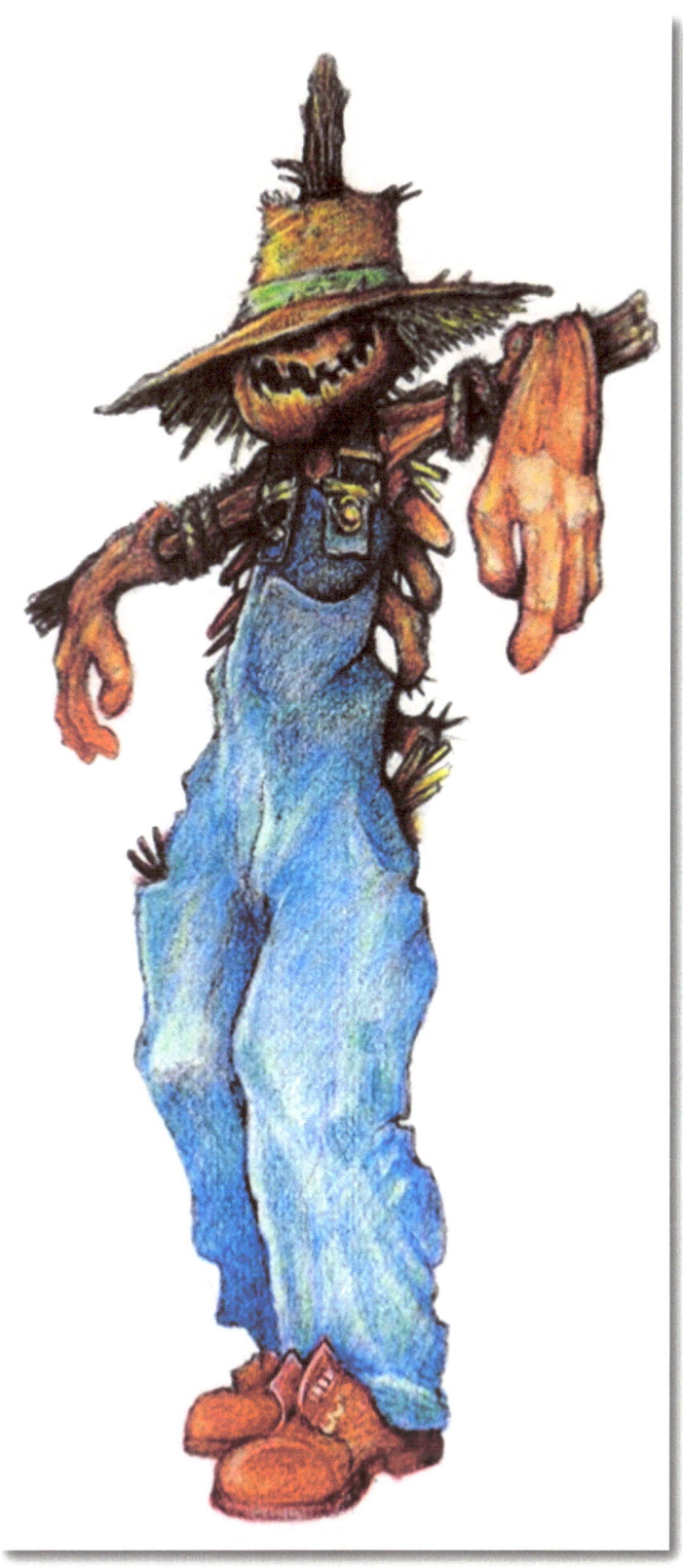

Halloween Scarecrow - colour pencil drawing.

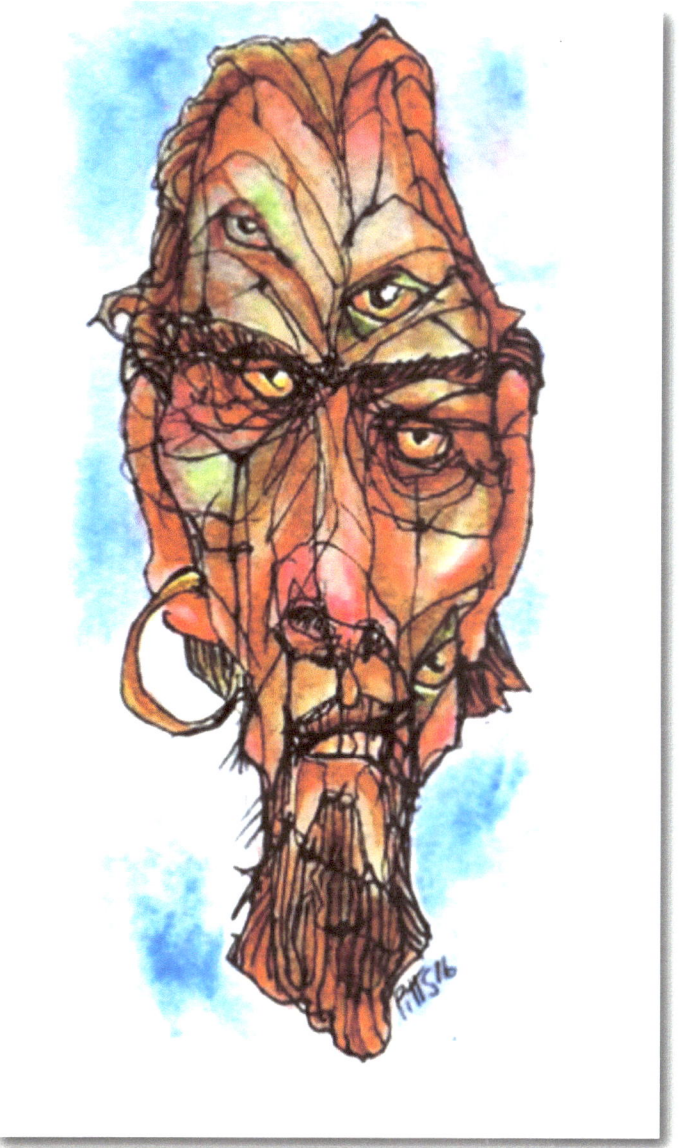

Inspired by Robert McCammon's *Swansong*.
Ink and watercolour.

"Tsathoggua" - Clark Ashton Smith's Cthulhu Mythos contribution to the pantheon of H. P. Lovecraft

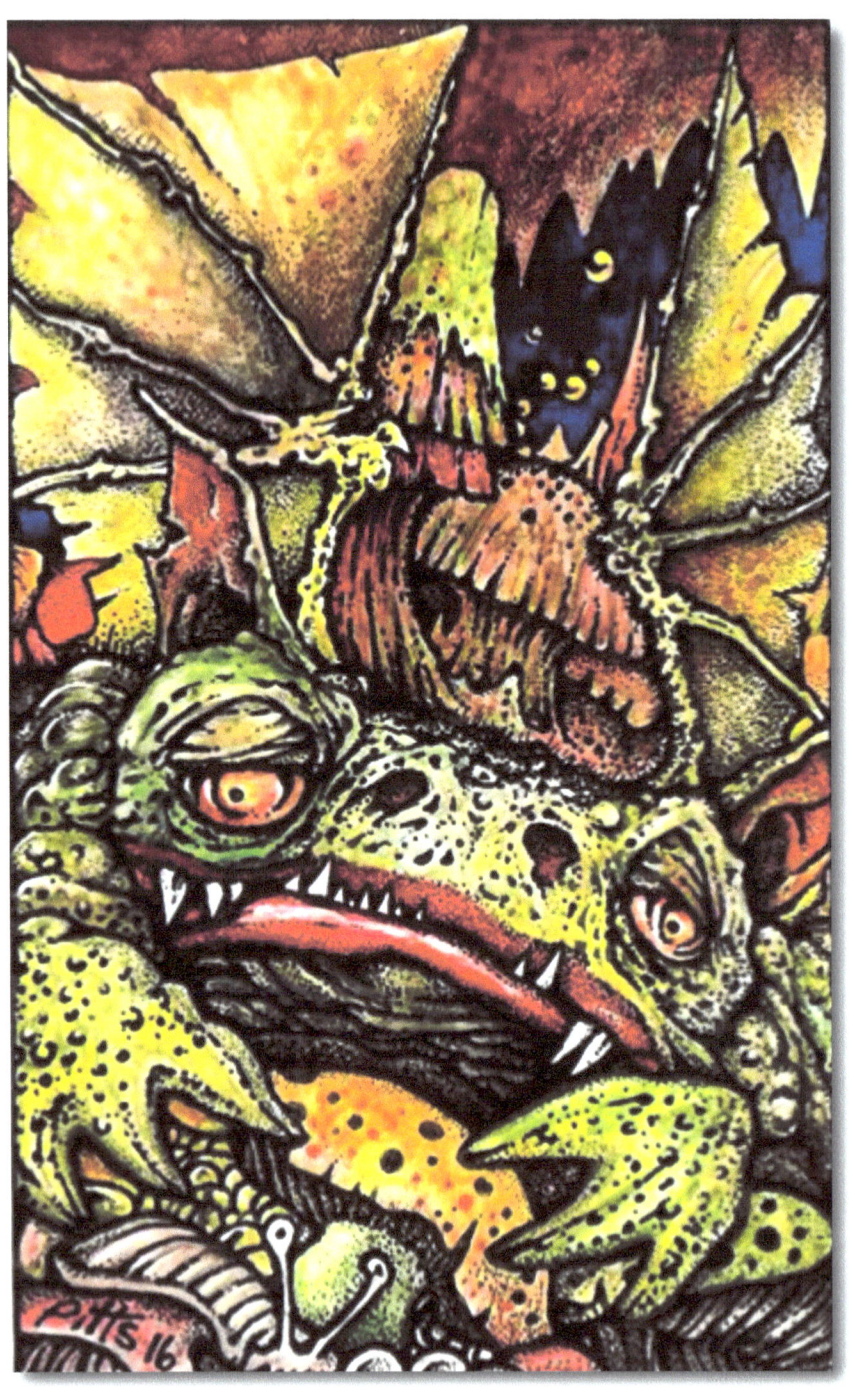

Frontispiece to Peter Coleborn's Alchemy Press award winning collection
Nick Nightmare Investigates by Adrian Cole

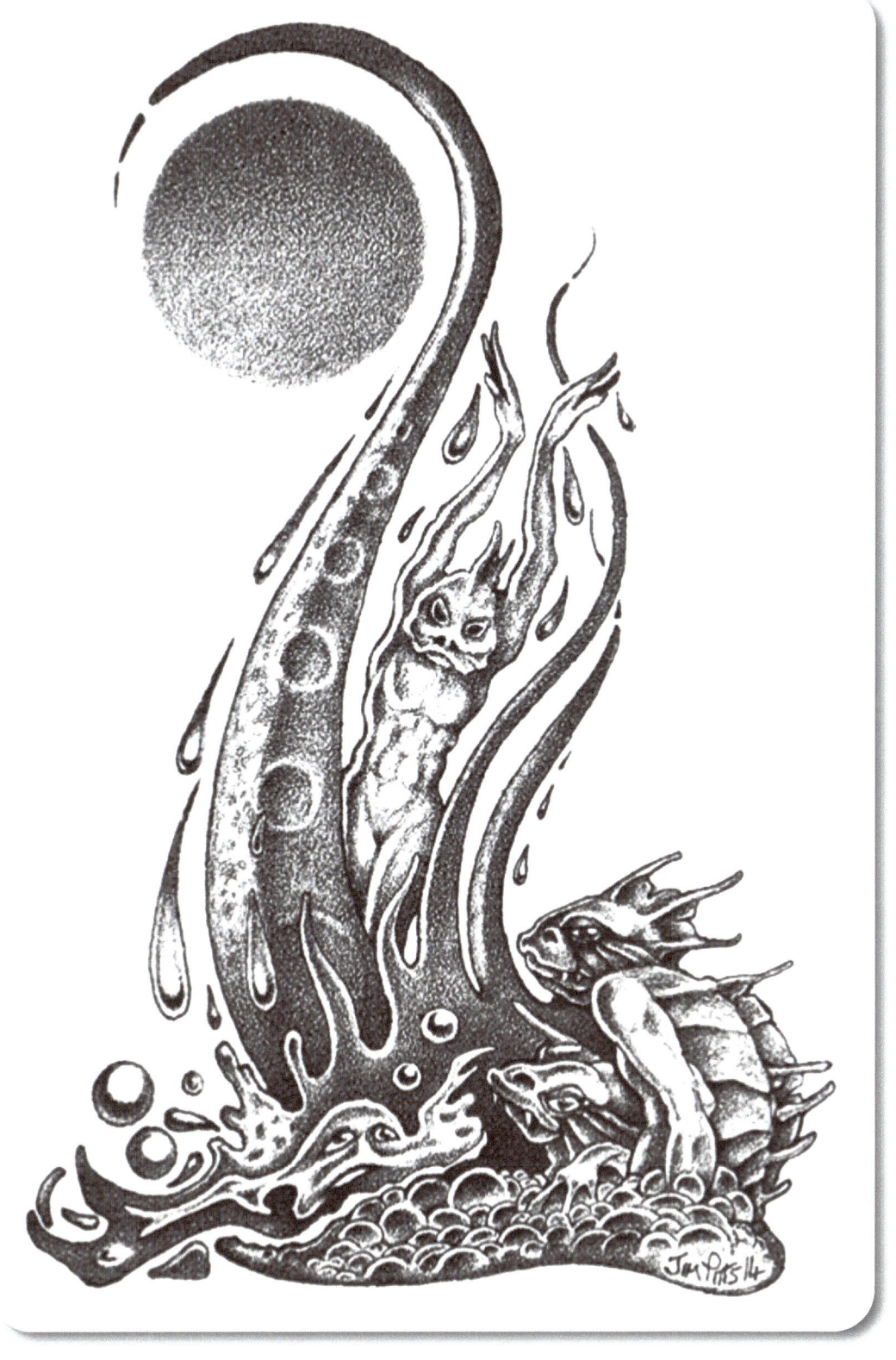

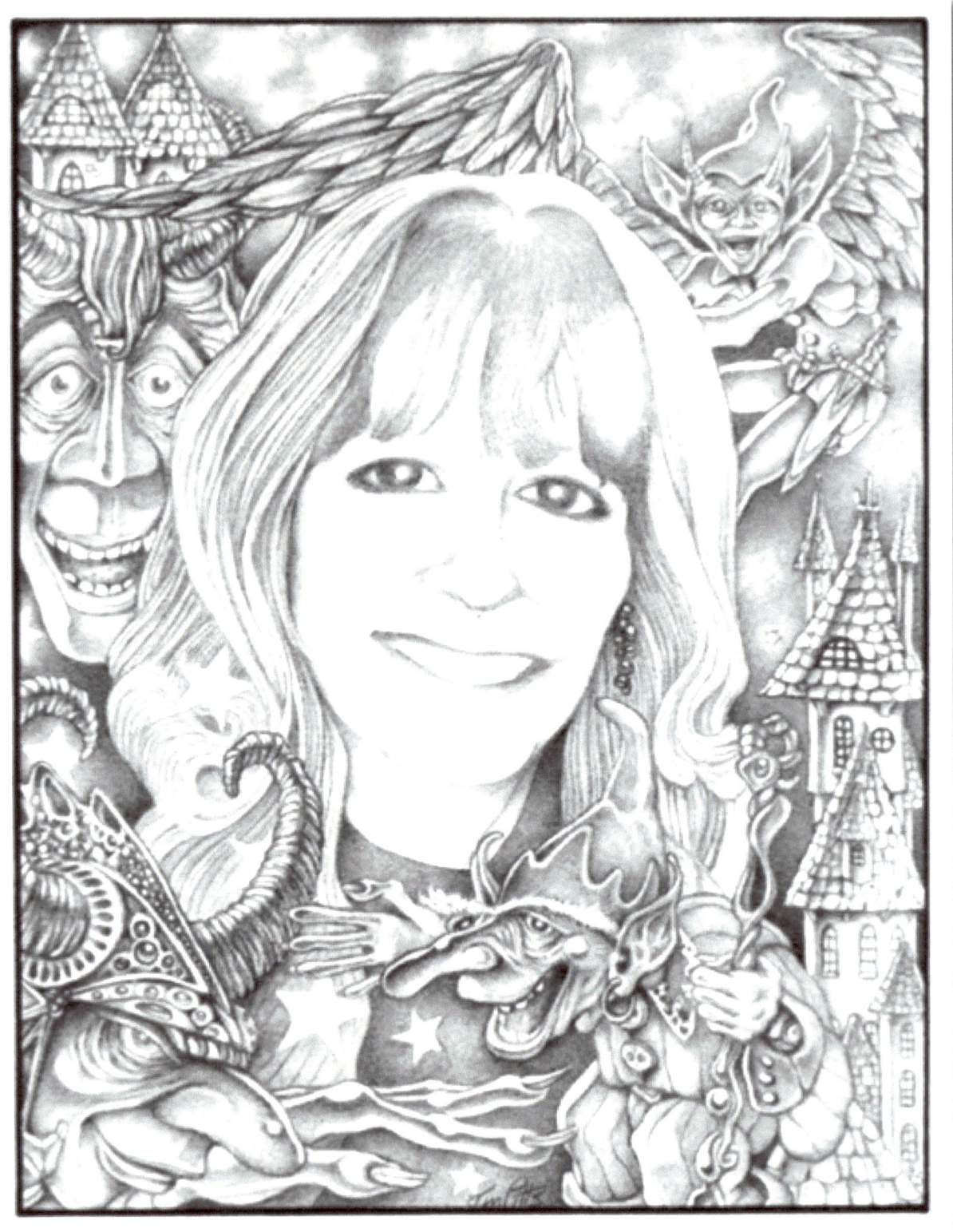

A Portrait of Rachel Caffrey (approx 1995)
From the collection of John Caffrey

Interior artwork for *Cthulhu 6 - Fall Out* by D-J Tyrer

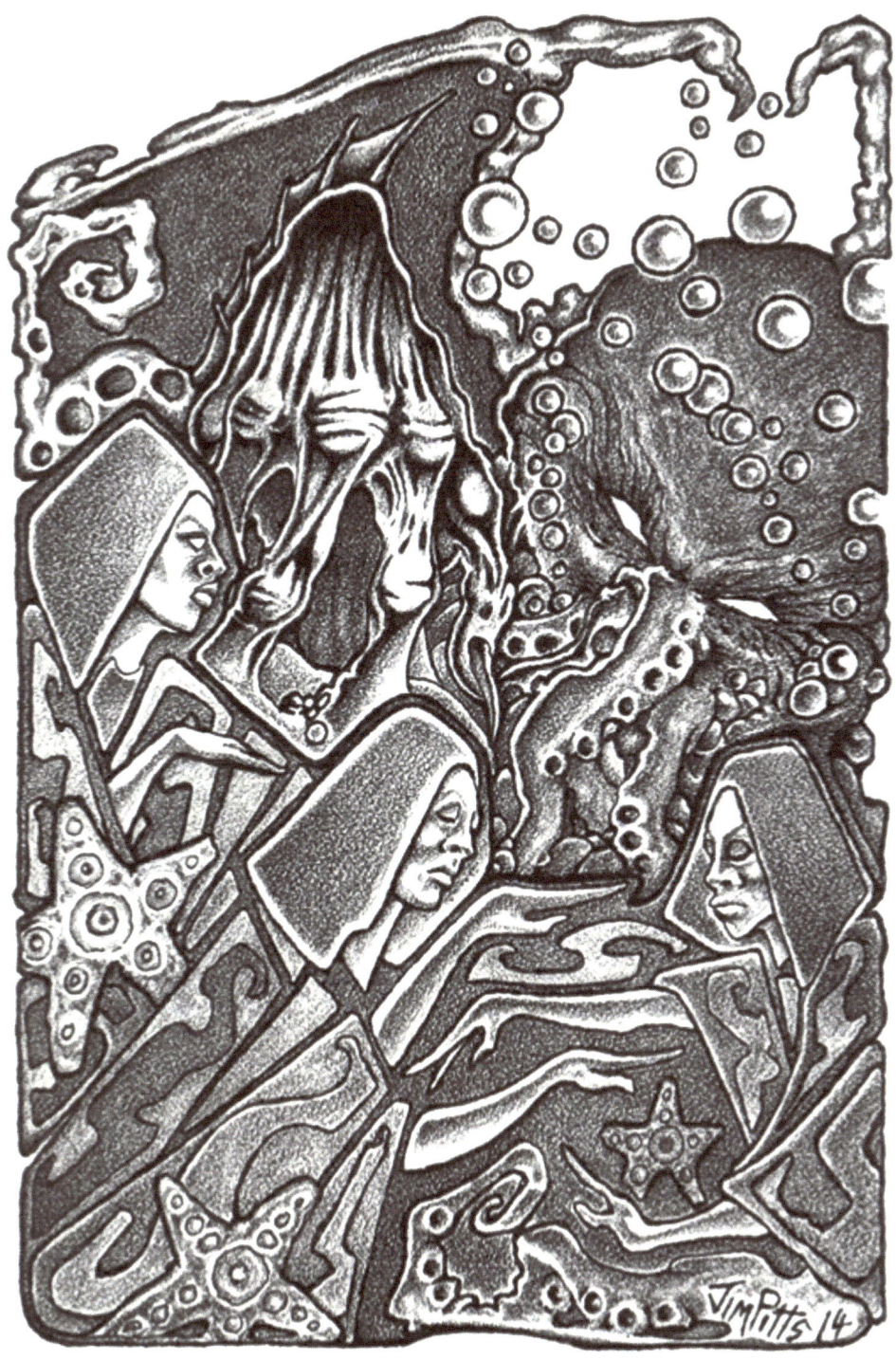

Cover artwork for *The Compleat Khash volume two: Sorcery in Shad* by Brian Lumley - Published by W. Paul Gamley 1994
Cover for *Cthulhu 6*

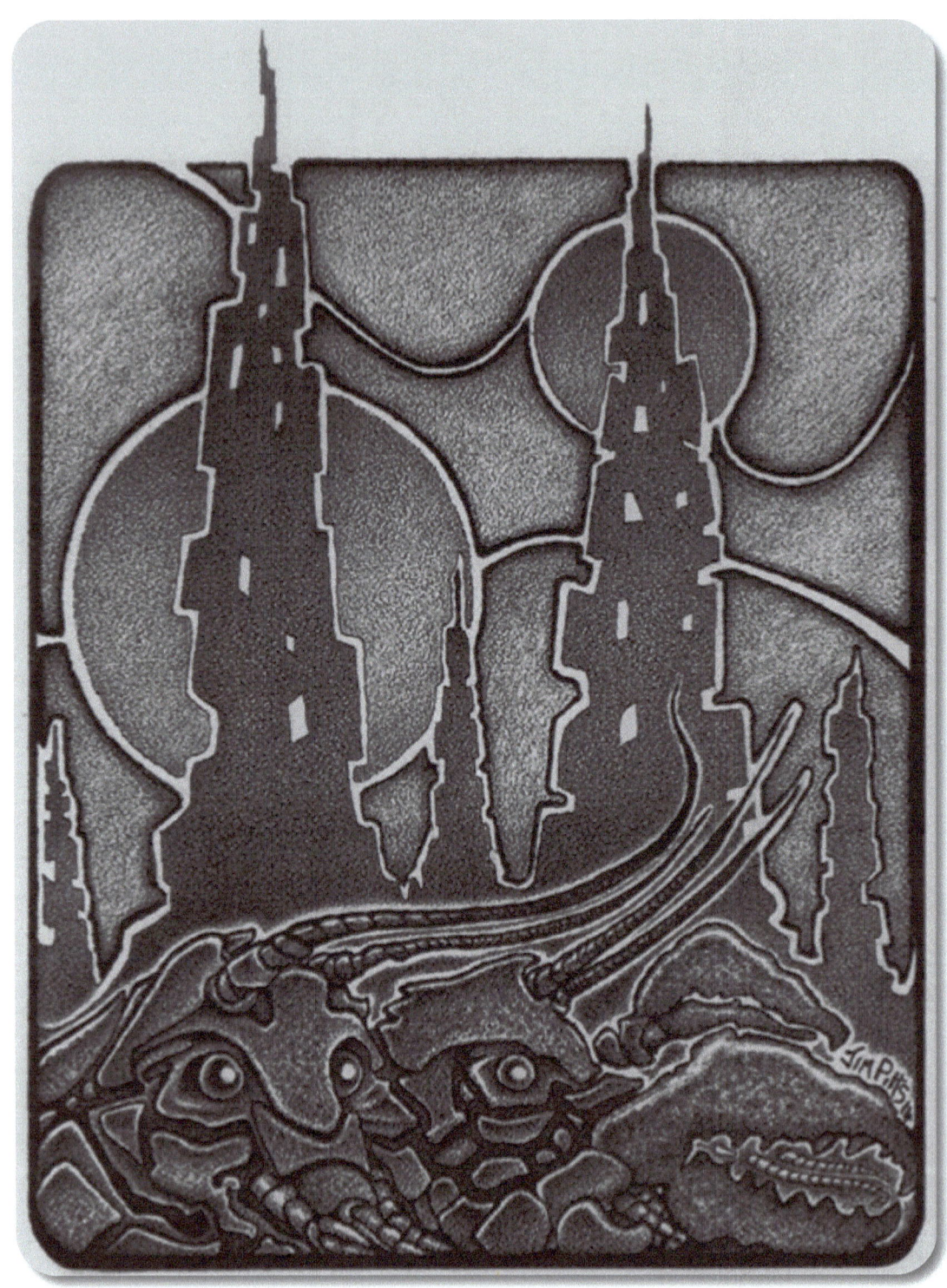

FISHHEAD
The Darker Tales of Irvin S. Cobb

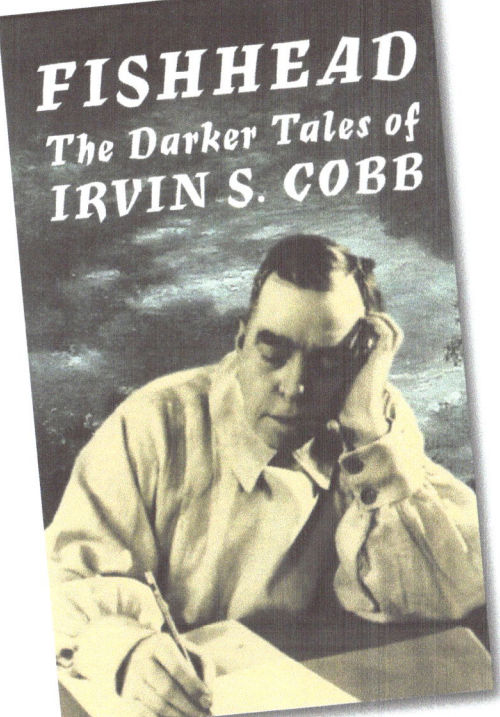

Fishhead: The Darker Tales of Irvin S. Cobb was published by Parallel Universe Publications in 2016. It was the first book published by PUP to have a frontispiece. The illustration below, by Jim Pitts, is for the title story.

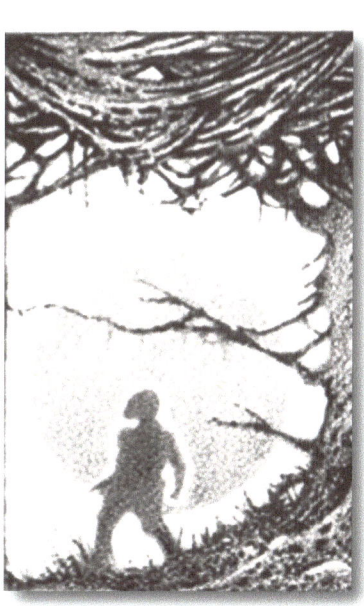

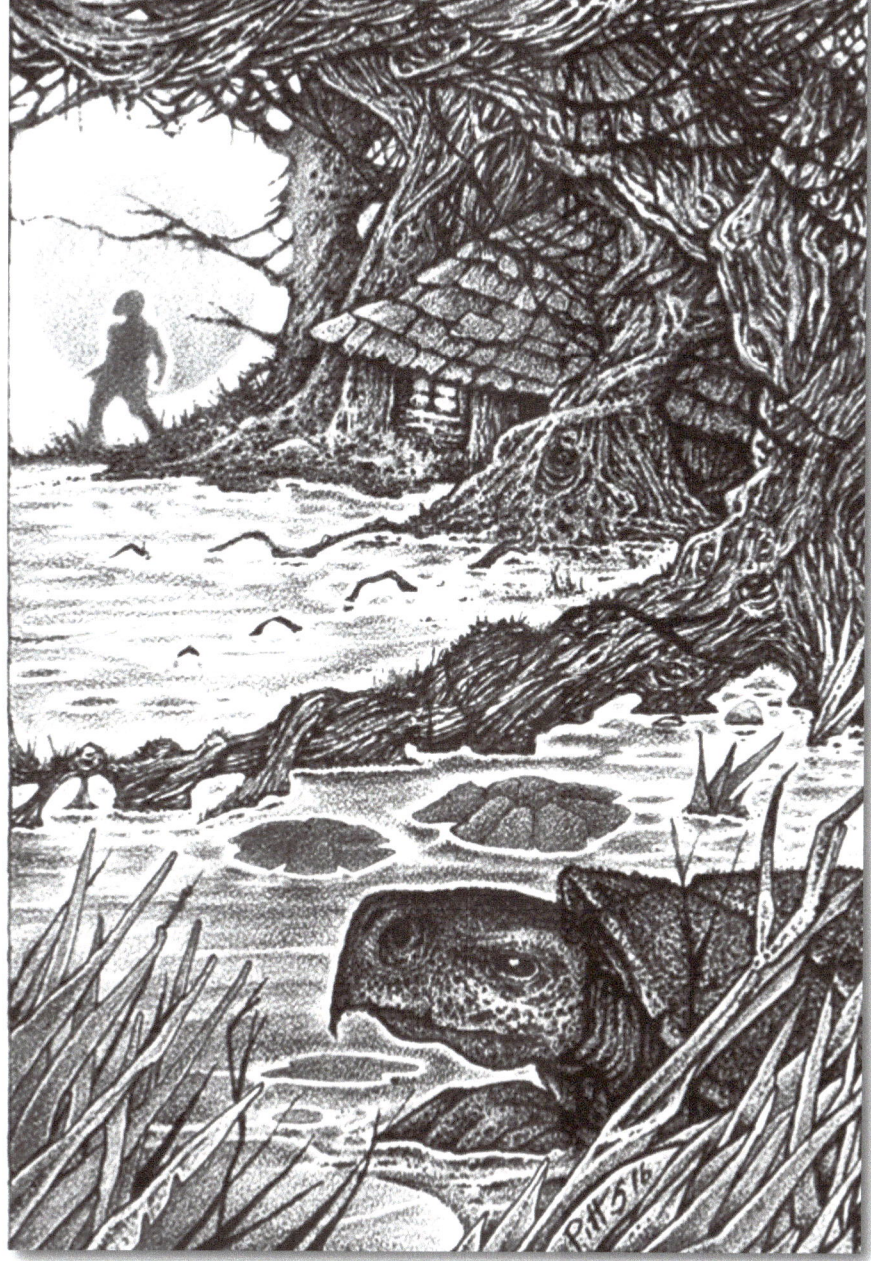

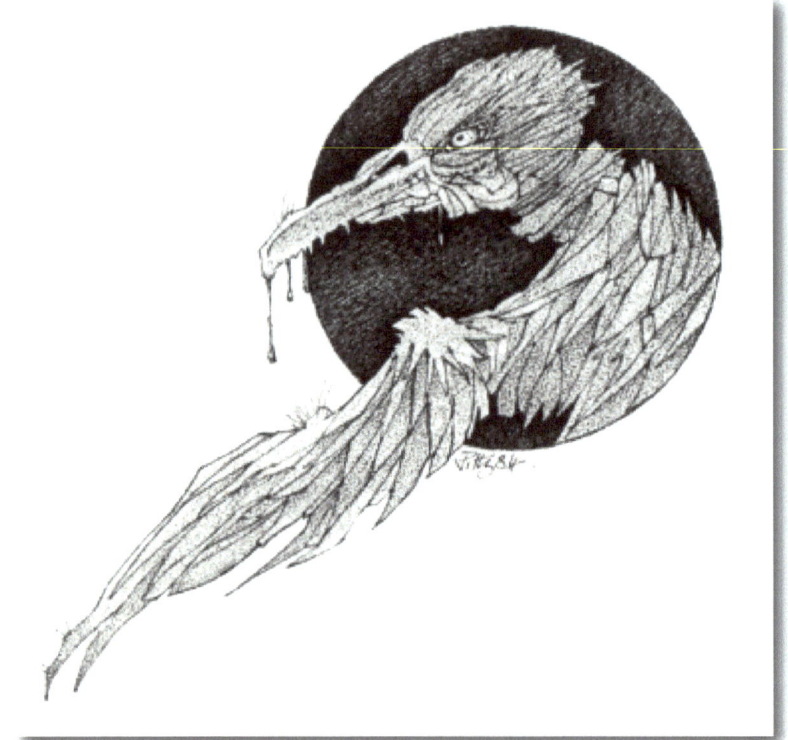

"Birdwing" - from the collection of Mandy Slater

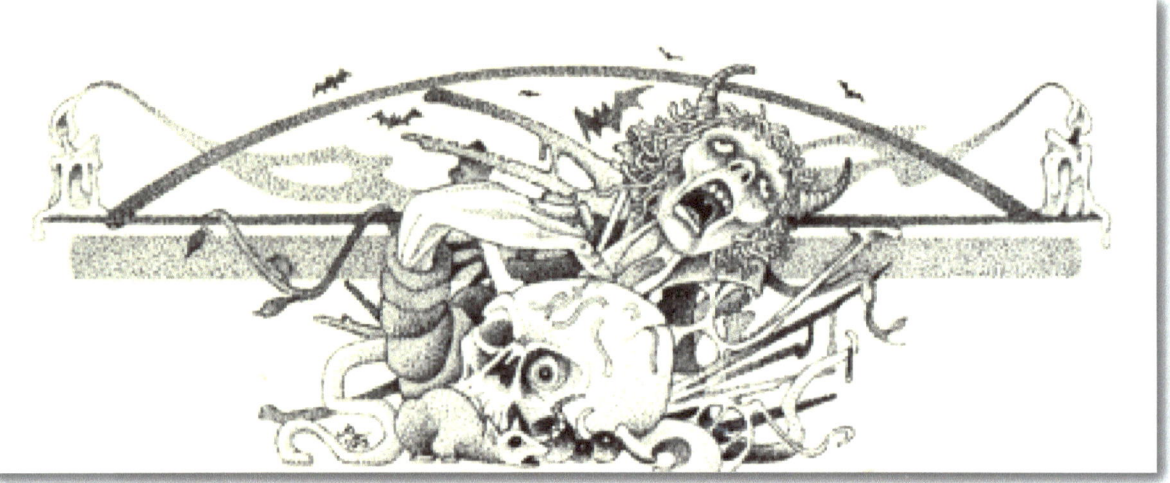

Letter-heading designed for Stephen Jones by Jim Pitts

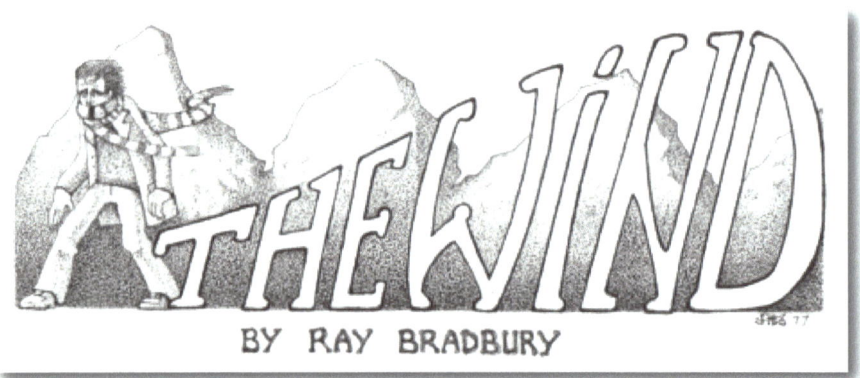

FEAR

"Artist in Residence: JIM PITTS"

August 2016

The first issue of the newly revived horror/fantasy/Science Fiction magazine, *Fear*, edited by John Gilbert, saw an extensive interview with Jim Pitts, along with some of his recent illustrations. This issue also included a tribute to the film director Robin Hardy (*The Wicker Man*), who had recently died, and interviews with horror writers Ramsey Campbell, Gary McMahon, and Jonathan Mayberry.

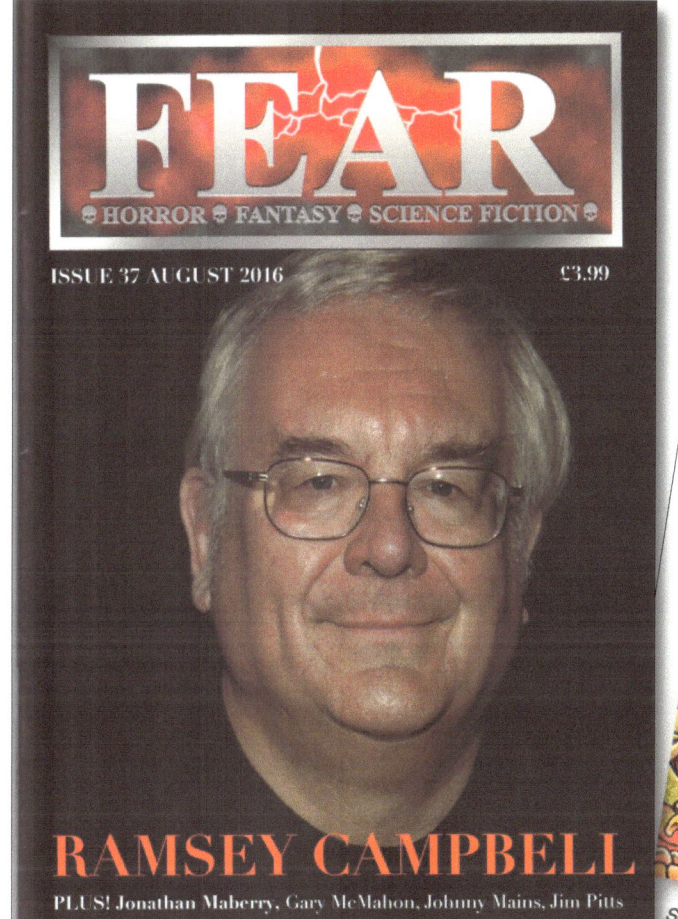

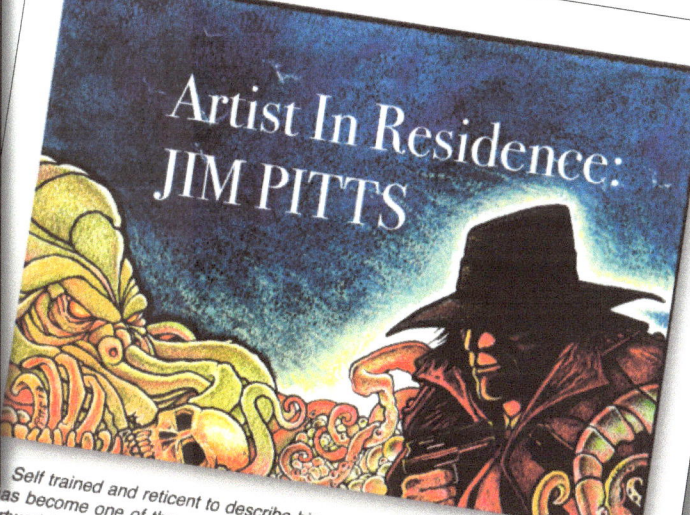

MARIANNE DREAMS
by Catherine Storr
Puffin Books

Marianne Dreams was first published by Puffin Books in 1964. The edition with Jim's cover was in 198,1 with interior illustrations by Marjorie-Ann Watts.

"I sent some photographs of some colour work to Penguin Books and I received a phone call from the Art Editor of Puffin asking me to go straight ahead with a commission for *Marianne Dreams*. There was talk of some more commissions but a change of Art Editor put paid to that. At the same time I sent pictures to Penguin, I also sent some copies to *Radio Times* who asked me to call in the next time I was in London, which I did.

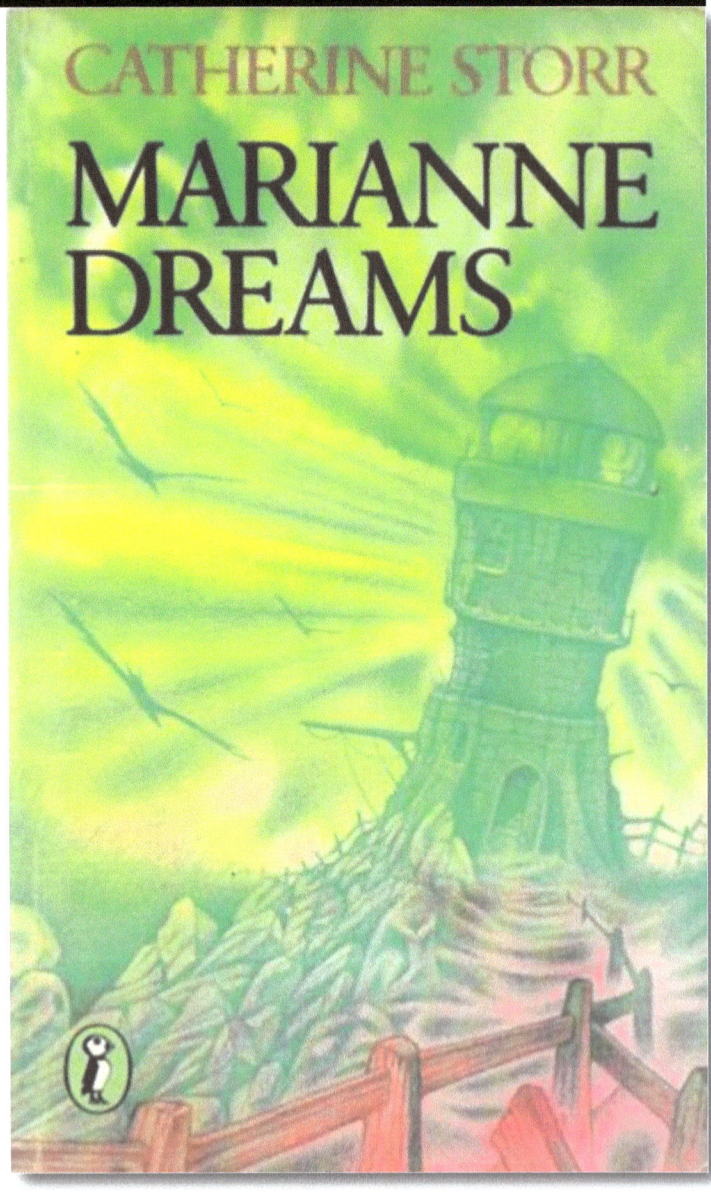

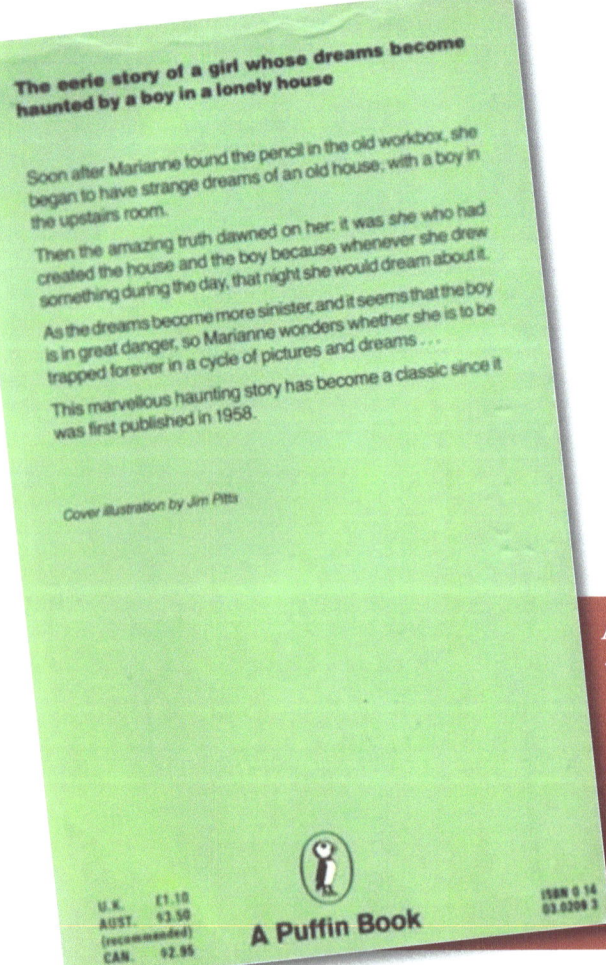

A very positive meeting followed. The only problem was that I lived in Lancashire and they worked on the basis they commissioned you and you went away, roughed it out and showed them your idea. They gave the nod and would want the finished item, all over a couple of days. Impossible for me before computer days... Of course, now I can work anywhere in the world..."

Illustration for *Climbing Those Stairs* by David Ieuan in *Worlds of the Unknown* Vol 1 (Spectre Press)

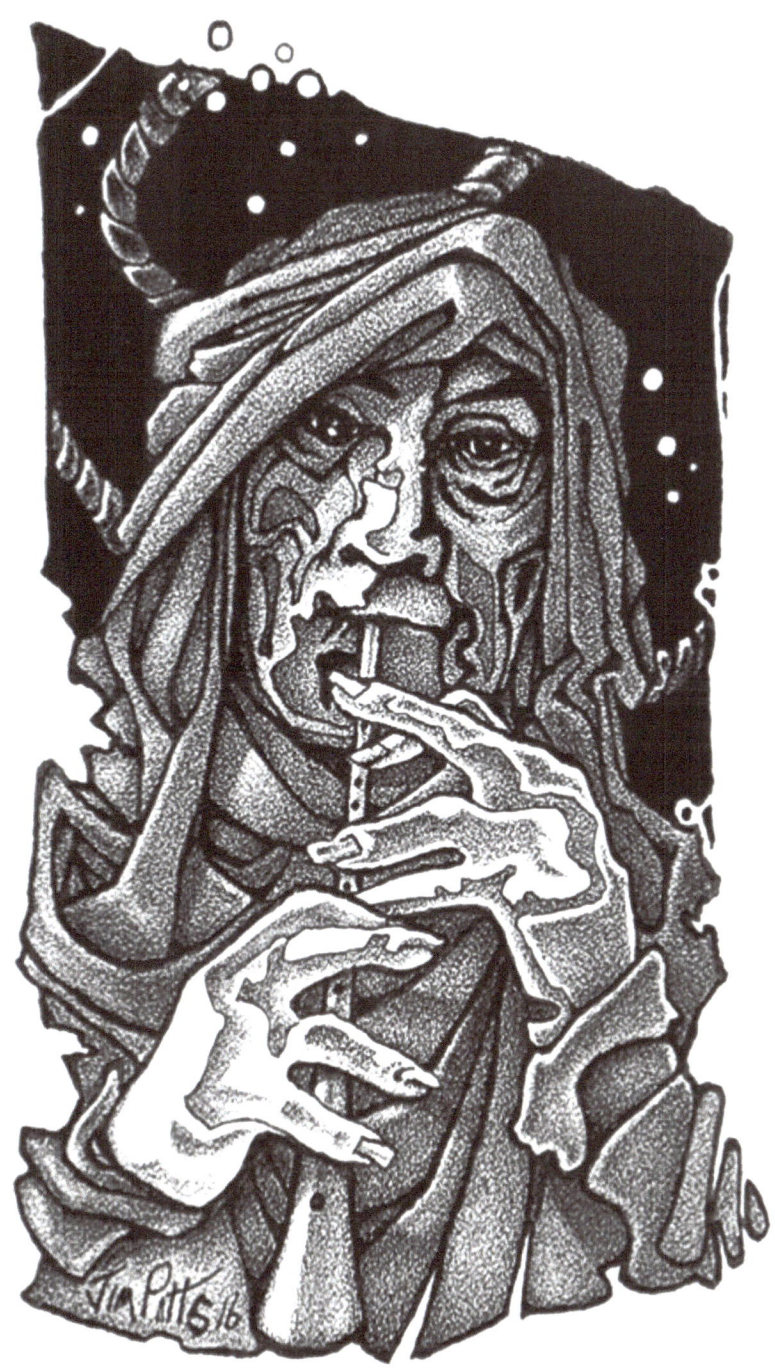

Cthulhu illustration appeared in, *The Hyborian Gazette No 2*

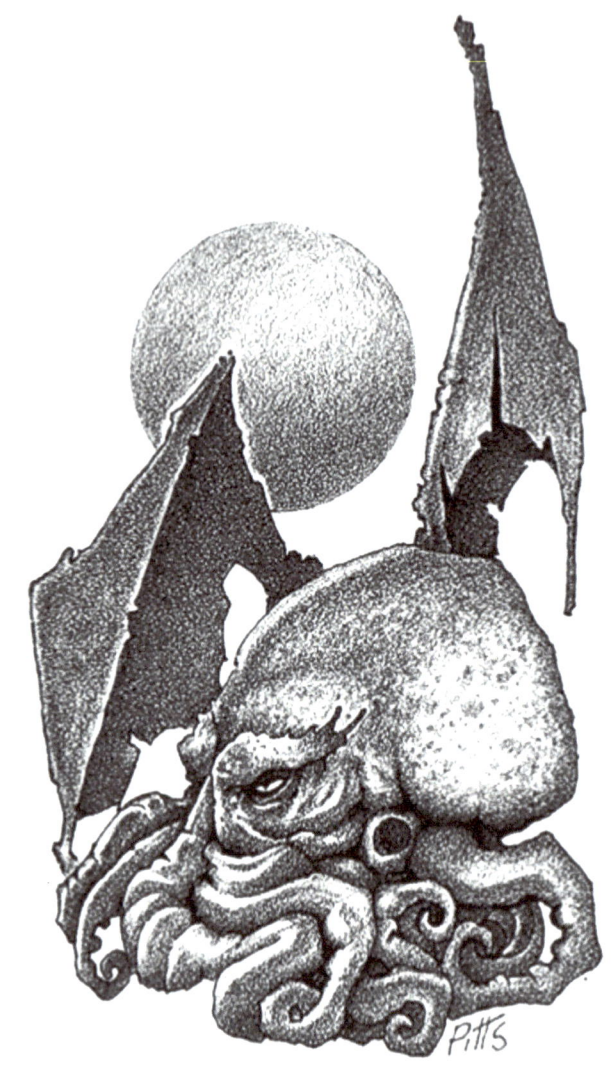

The Writer's Chair by Anthonie Holslag appeared in *Worlds of the Unknown* Vol 2, Spectre Press

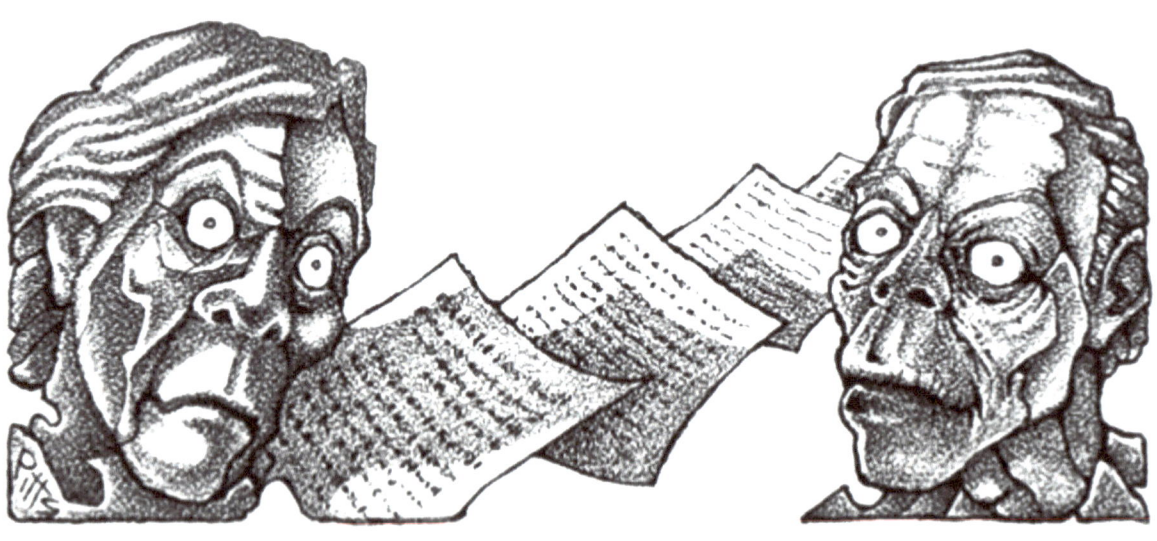

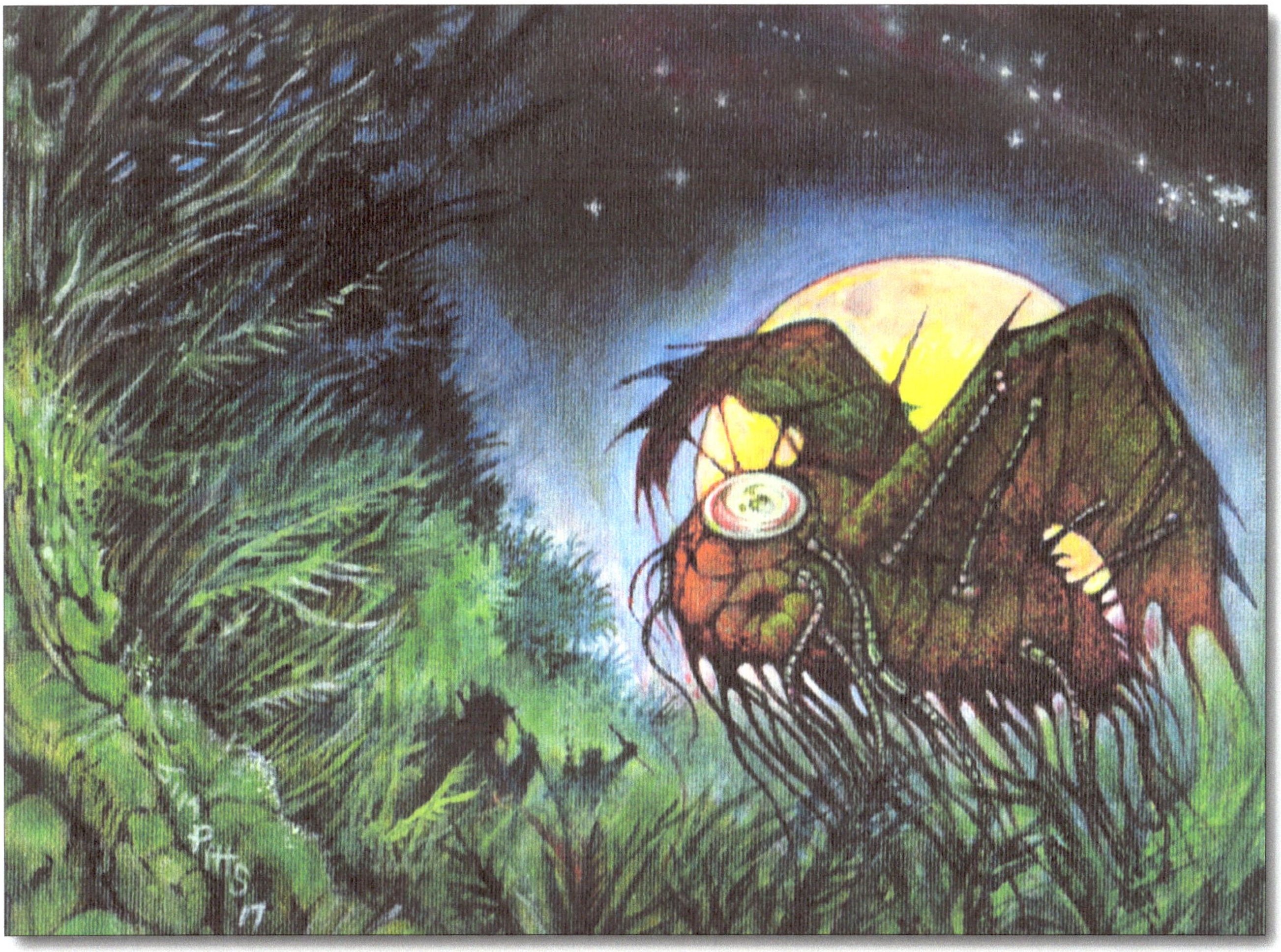

A wraparound cover illustrating Adrian Cole's Pulpworld yarn, *Steaming into Wonderland*, published by Spectre Press, *Worlds of the Unknown 5*, edited by Jon M. Harvey.

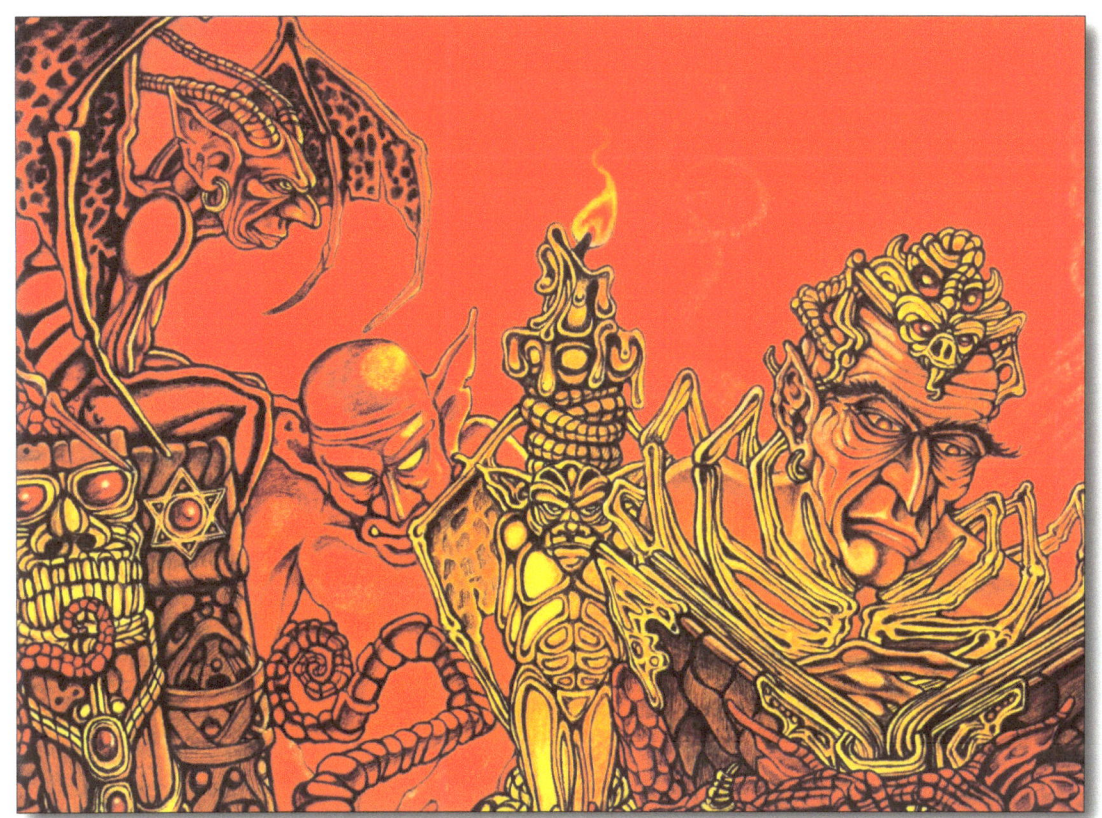

Inspired by Clark Ashton Smith's Zothique stories

SHADOWS OVER INNSMOUTH
edited by Stephen Jones

The Great Collaboration
(Jim Pitts, Dave Carson and Martin McKenna)

Shadows Over Innsmouth, edited by Stephen Jones and published in 1994 by Fedogan and Bremer, had a unique wraparound cover, a great collaboration between artists Jim Pitts, Dave Carson, and Martin McKenna. It also boasted interior black and white illustrations by all three artists, plus stories by Basil Copper, Jack Yeovil, Guy N. Smith, Adrian Cole, Ramsey Campbell, David Sutton, Peter Tremayne, Brian Mooney, Brian Stableford, Nicholas Royle, David Langford, Michael Marshall Smith, Brian Lumley, Neil Gaiman, and, of course, H. P. Lovecraft.

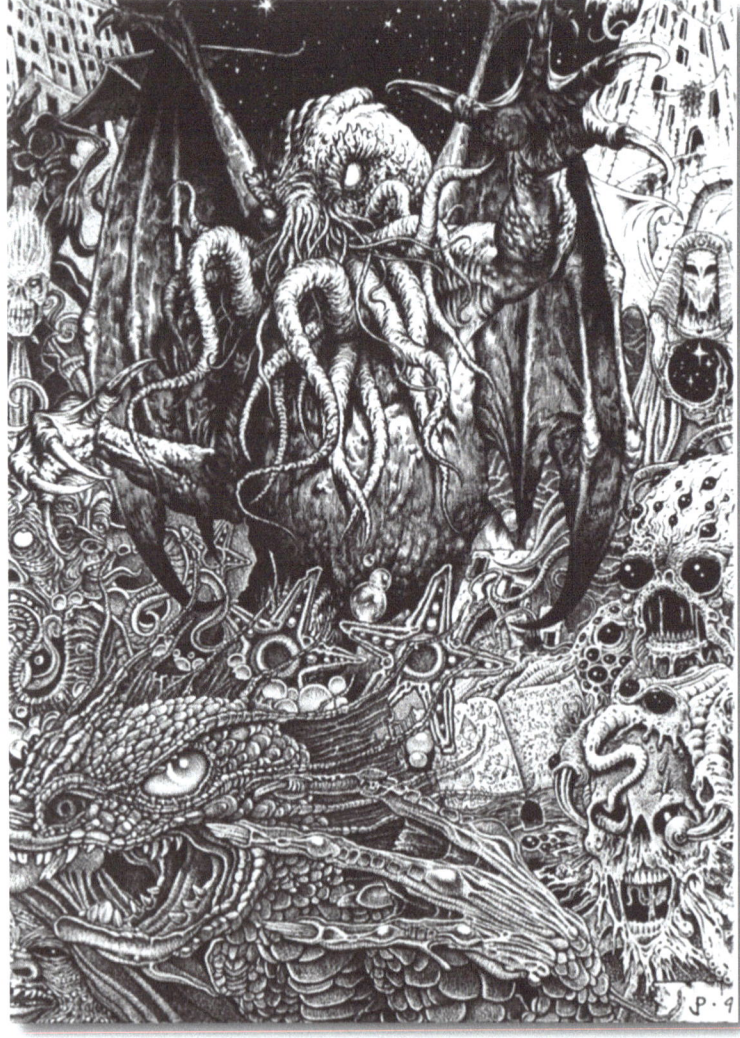

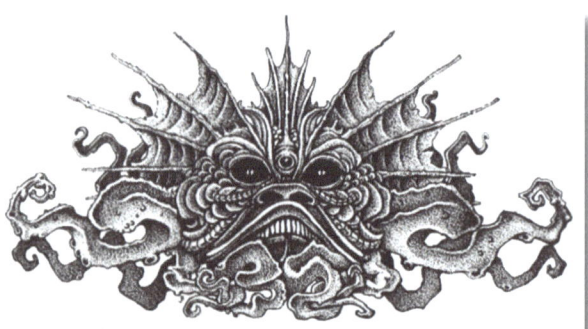

This drawing of Cthulhu started with the central figure by Martin McKenna, who passed it on to Jim and Dave Carson, who finished it. This picture led to the commission from Stephen Jones for *Shadows Over Innsmouth*.

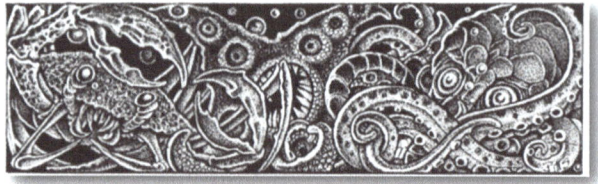

Two of three headings in the book created by Jim Pitts

The wraparound cover of *Shadows Over Innsmouth* was a collaboratiuon between Jim, Martin McKenna, and Dave Carson. The monster on the back cover is the work of Dave Carson. The Innsmouth figure on the front is by Martin McKenna. The houses and wharf in the background are by Jim, plus the figure on the spine. Martin McKenna was responsible for all the colouring of the wraparound cover.

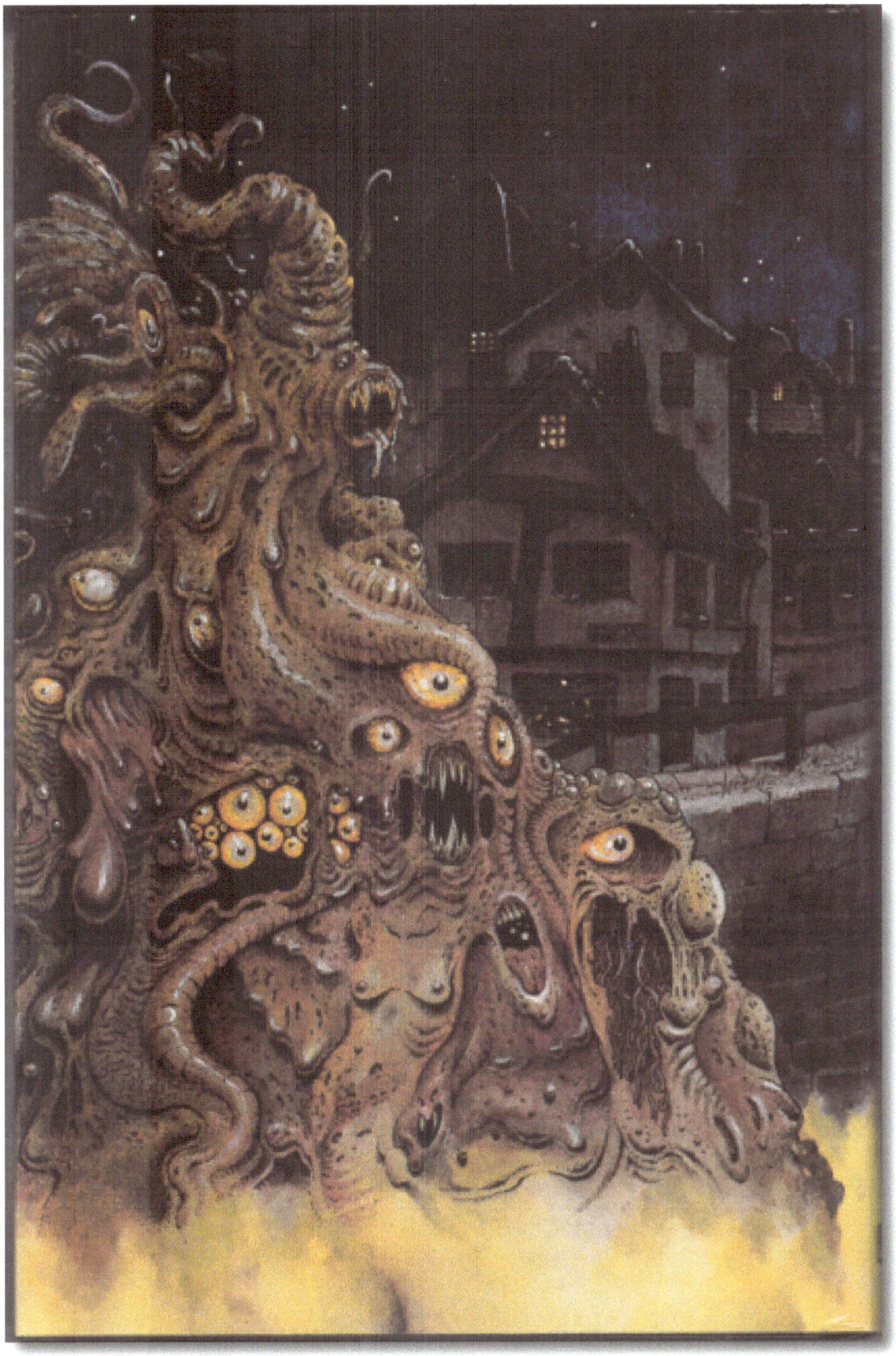

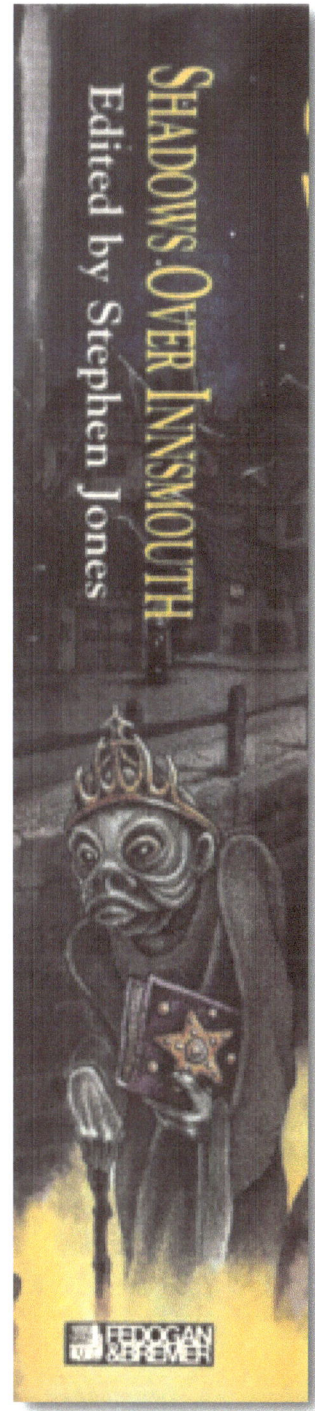

Many thanks to both Dave Carson and Martin McKenna for having readily given their permission to reproduce their artwork here.

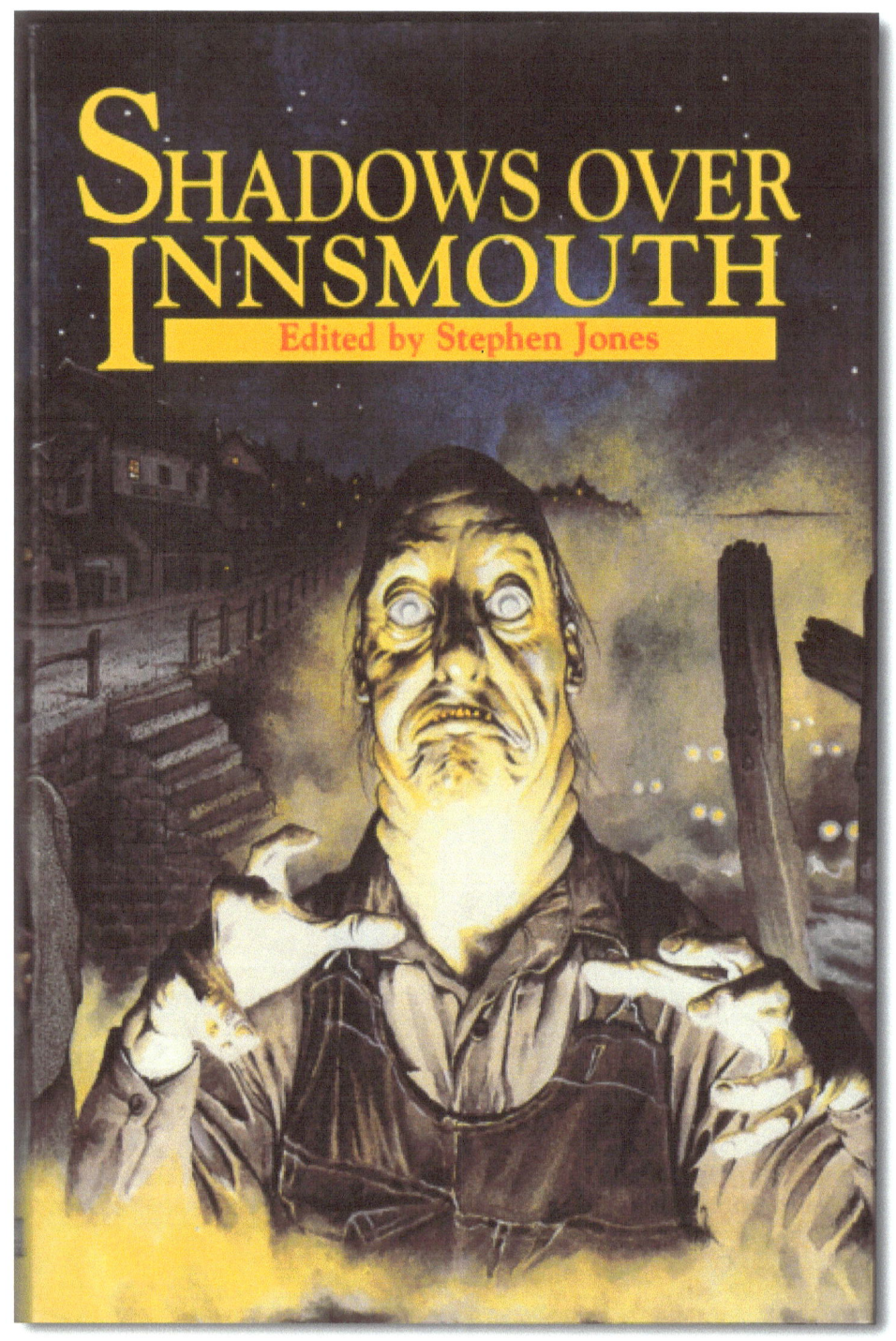

Jim's share of the picture below - *Old Man Marsh* (the main figure), the buildings and the background. The rest was the work of Martin McKenna and Dave Carson.

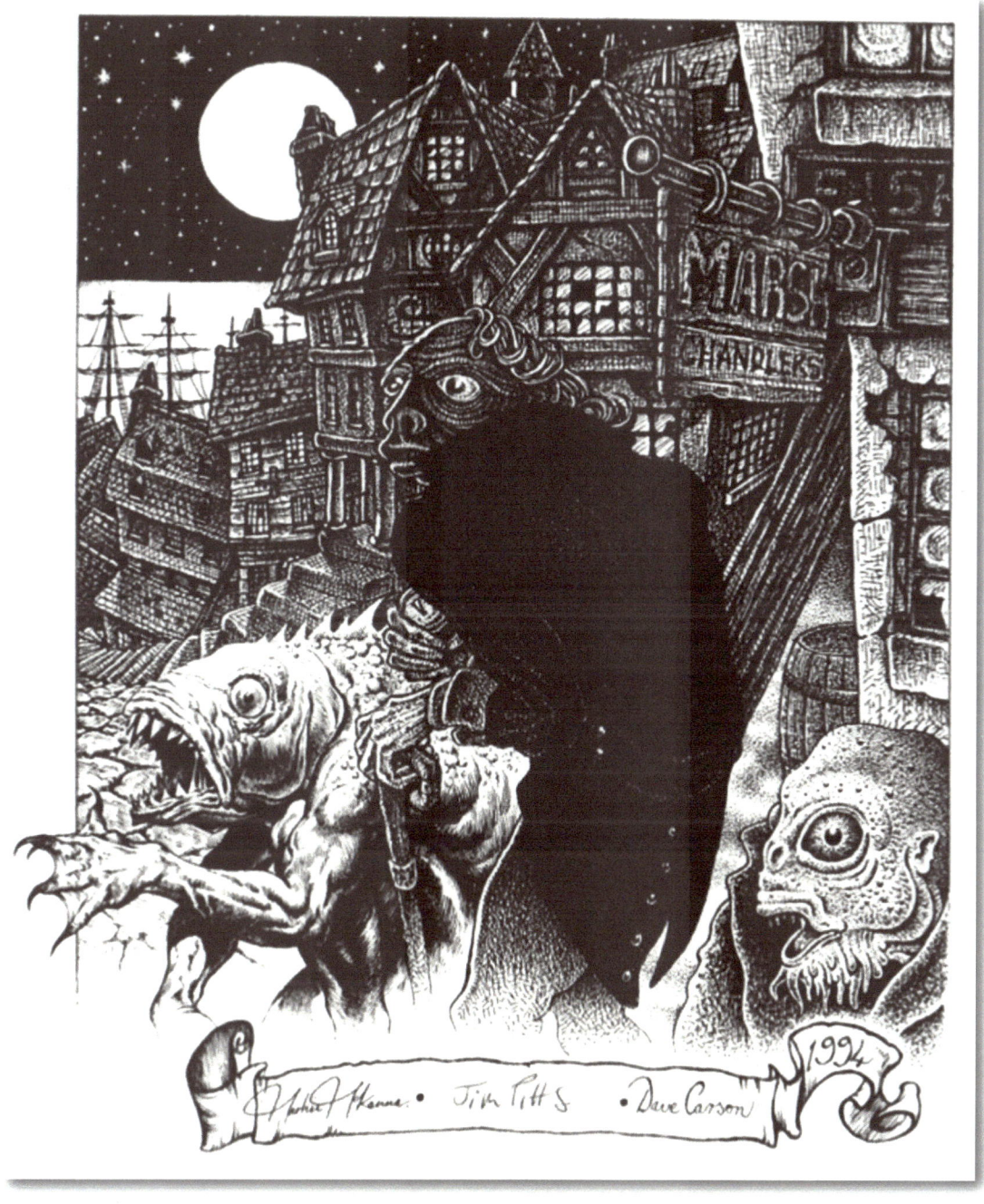

The figure below is Father Dagon. This is Jim's share of the picture.

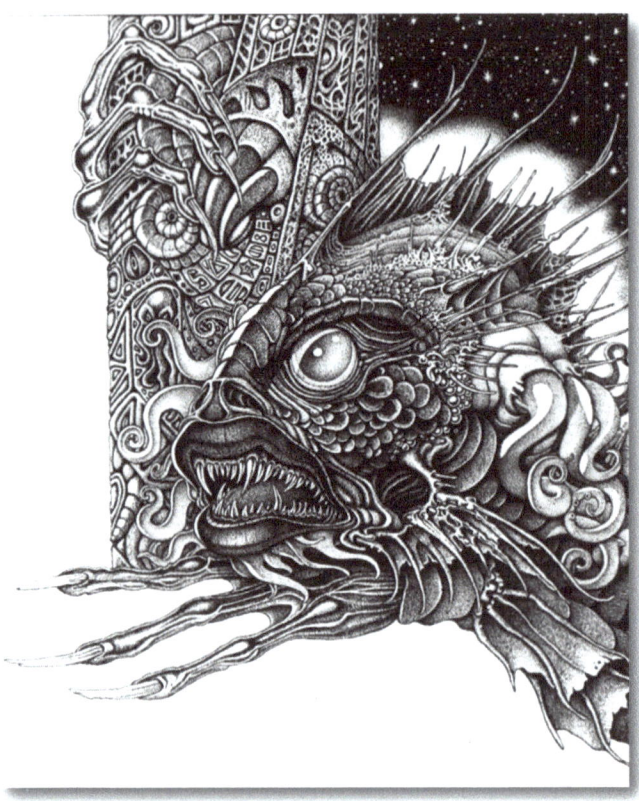

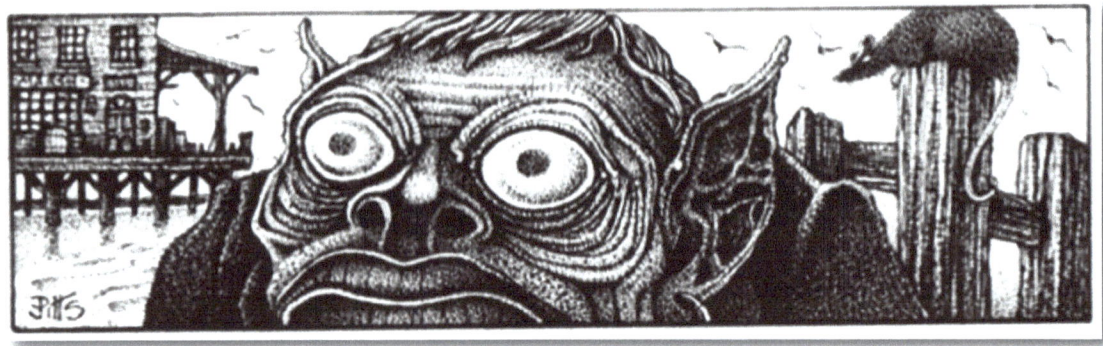

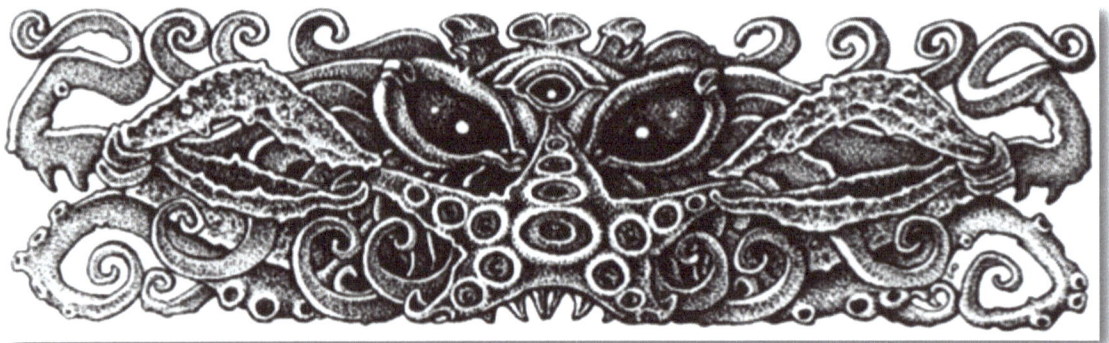

The top heading (Innsmouth resident) was an extra that was not used. Jim later coloured this and sold it privately. The bottom header was used in the book.

M. R. James "Oh Whistle and I'll Come to You, My Lad"

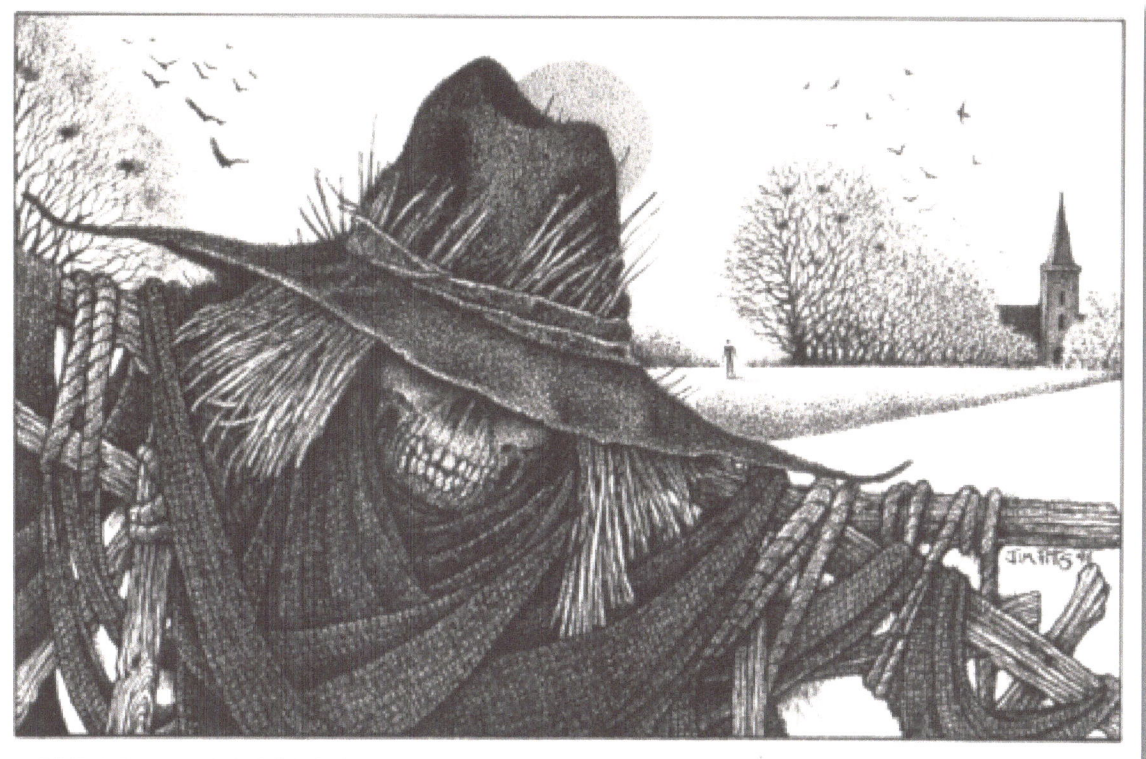

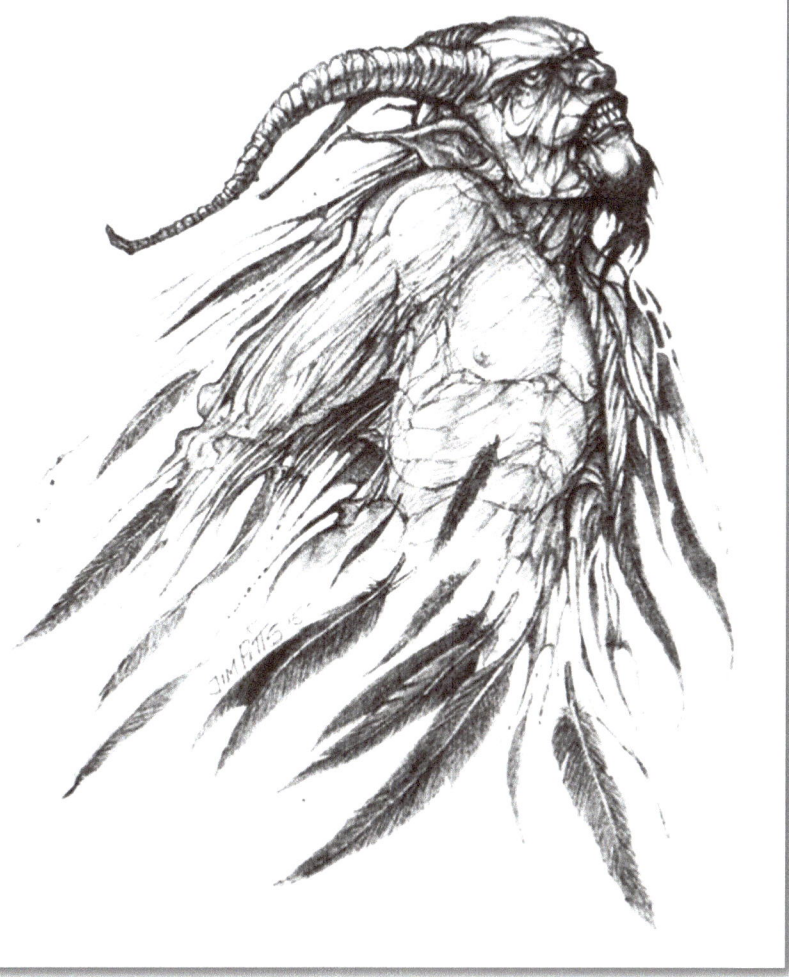

Inspired by the "Charlie Parker" novels of John Connolly

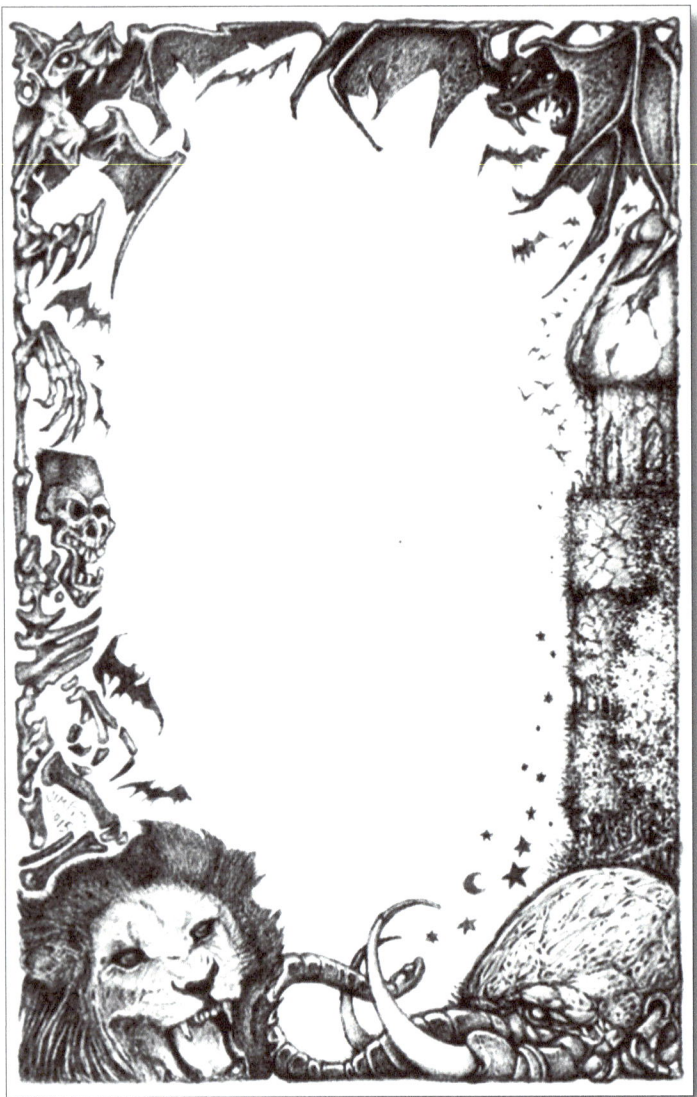

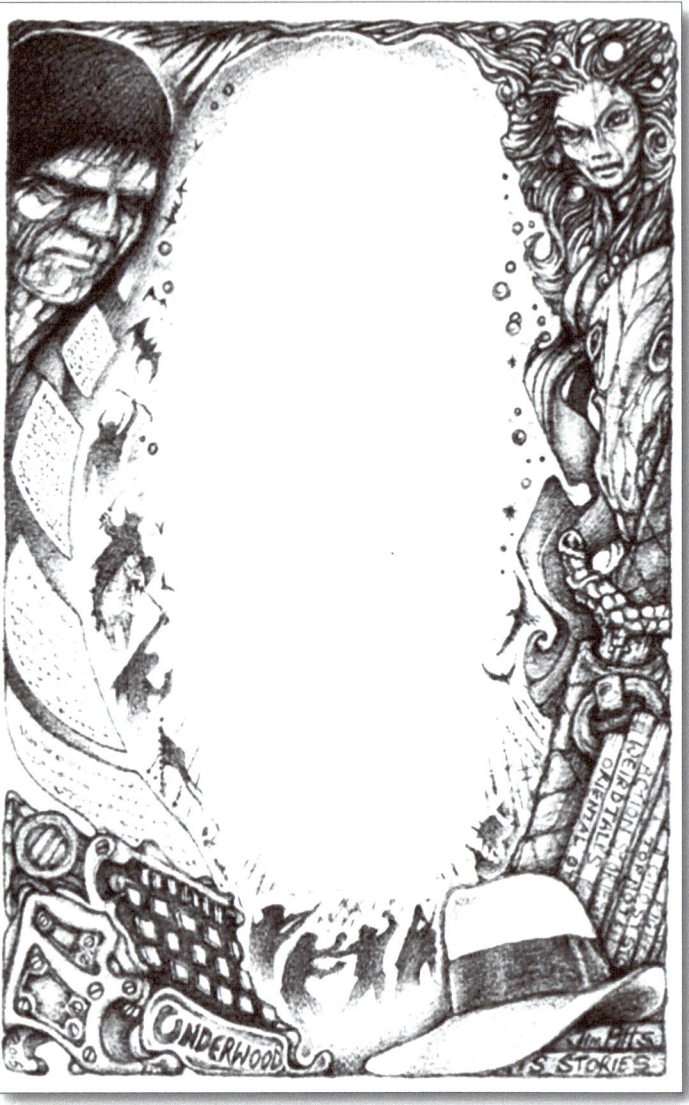

The top framework was used for "A Rogue Rhyme" - *Yara's Pride* by Jason Hardy. The lower framework was used for *Perception*, again by Jason Hardy.

Both appeared in *The Hyborian Gazette*, No 1.

Heading for *The Oath and the Unicorn* by Marion Pitman, *Worlds of the Unknown* Vol 3, Spectre Press

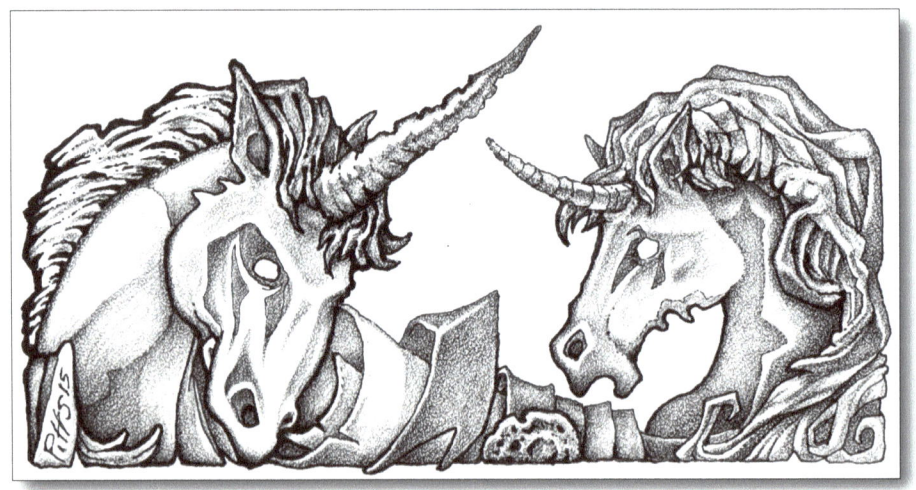

Contents page design for *Earth, Air, Fire & Water* by Brian Lumley. Fedogan & Bremer, 2017

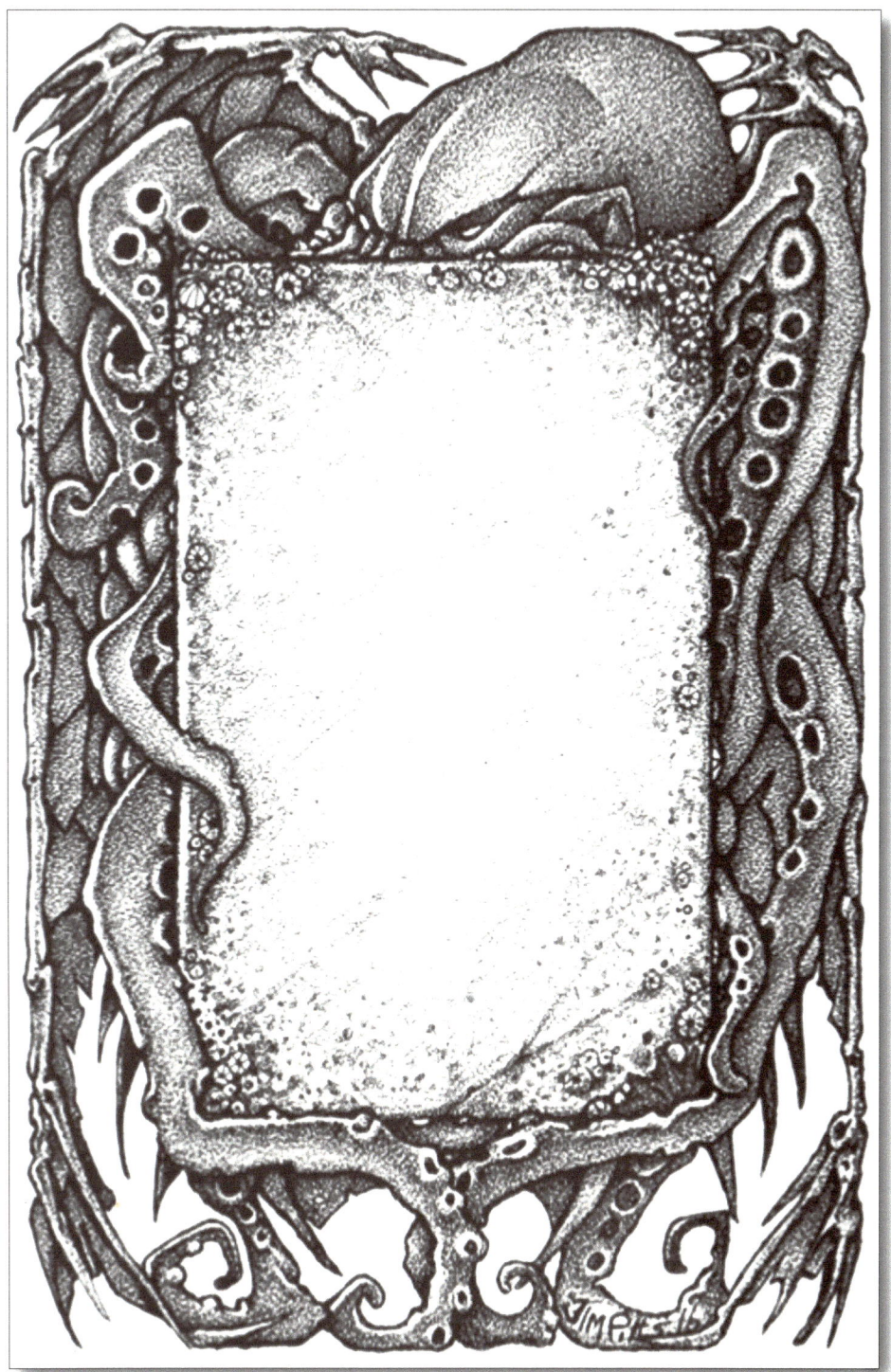

SOME SKETCHES

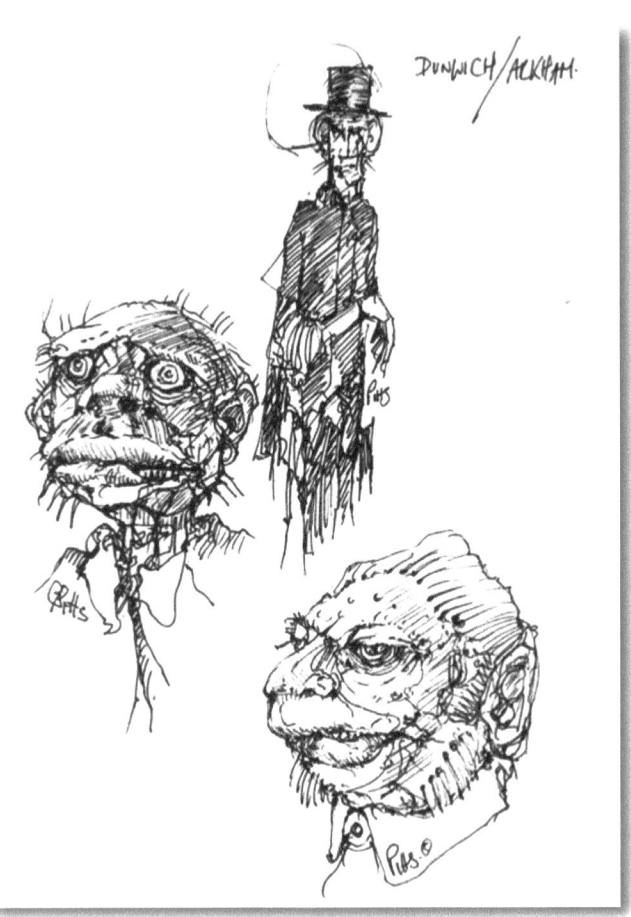
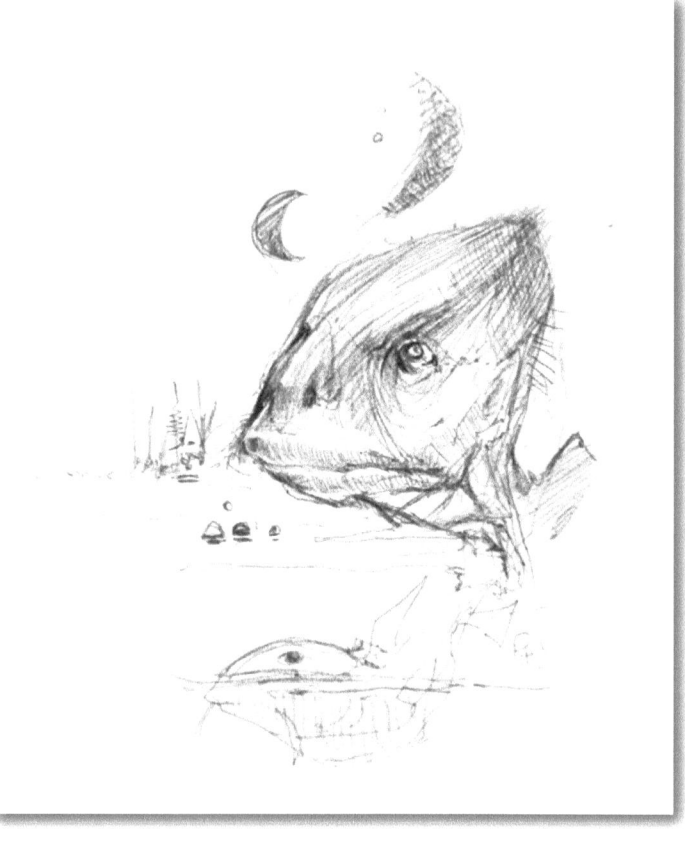
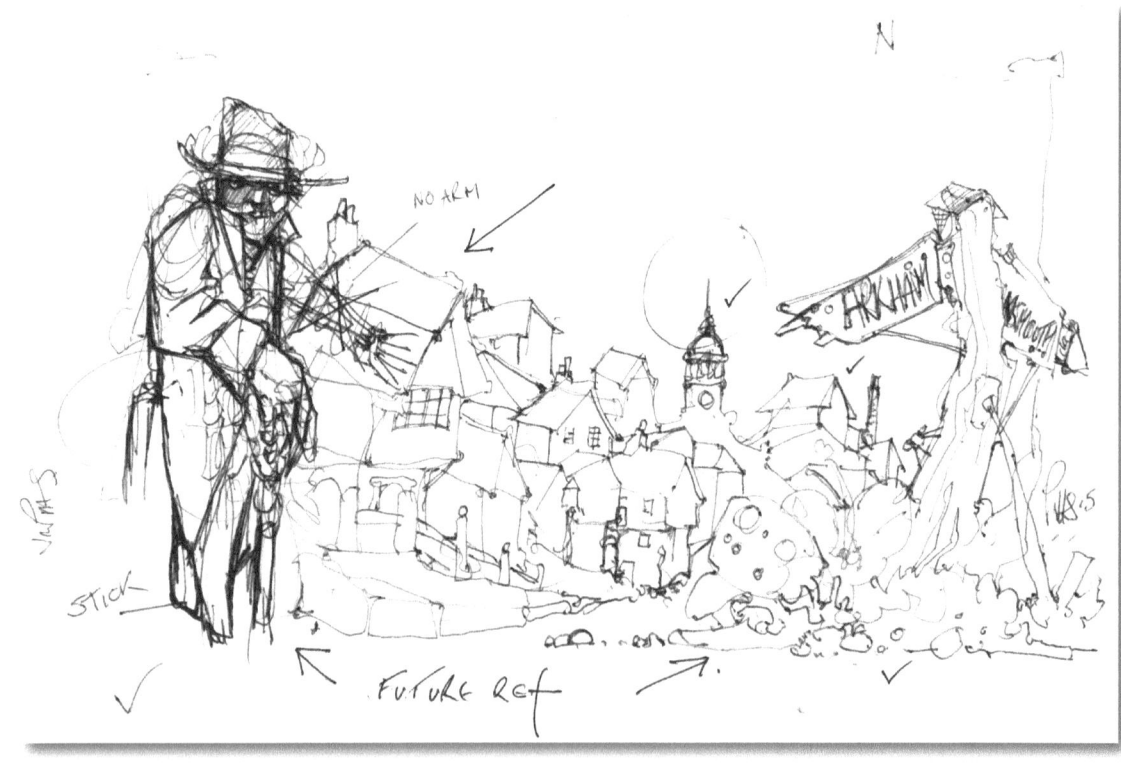

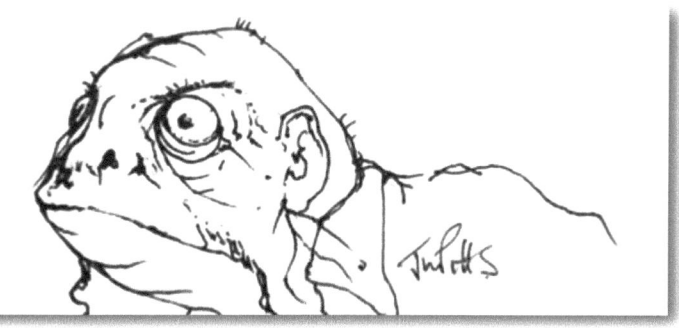
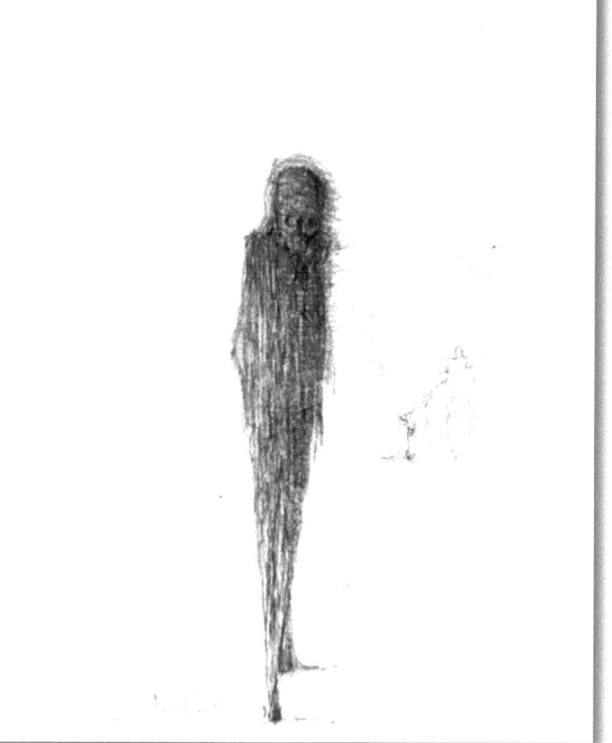
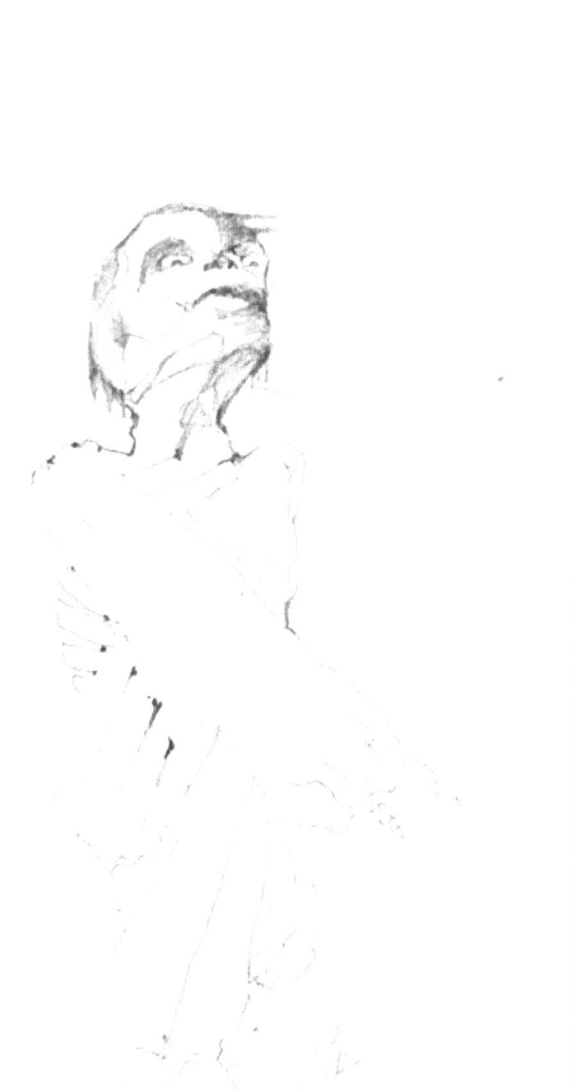
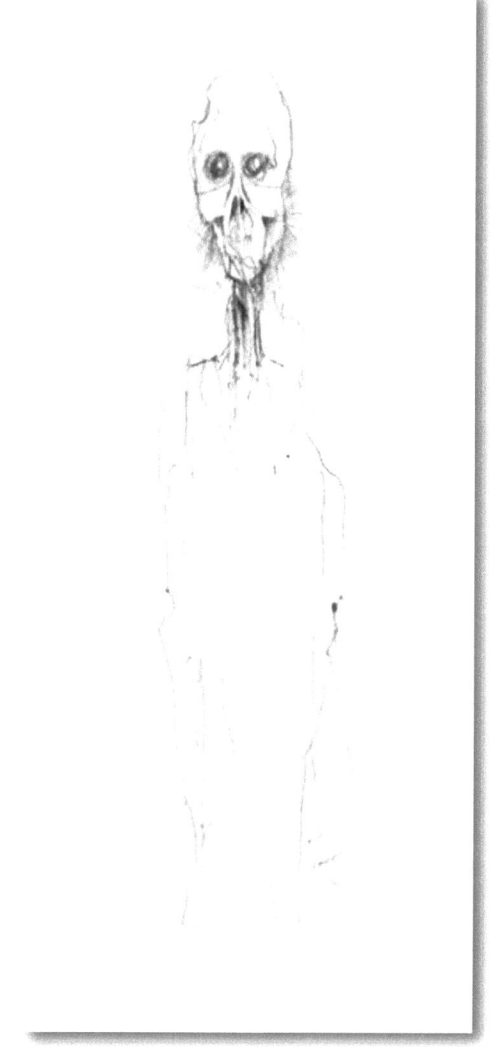

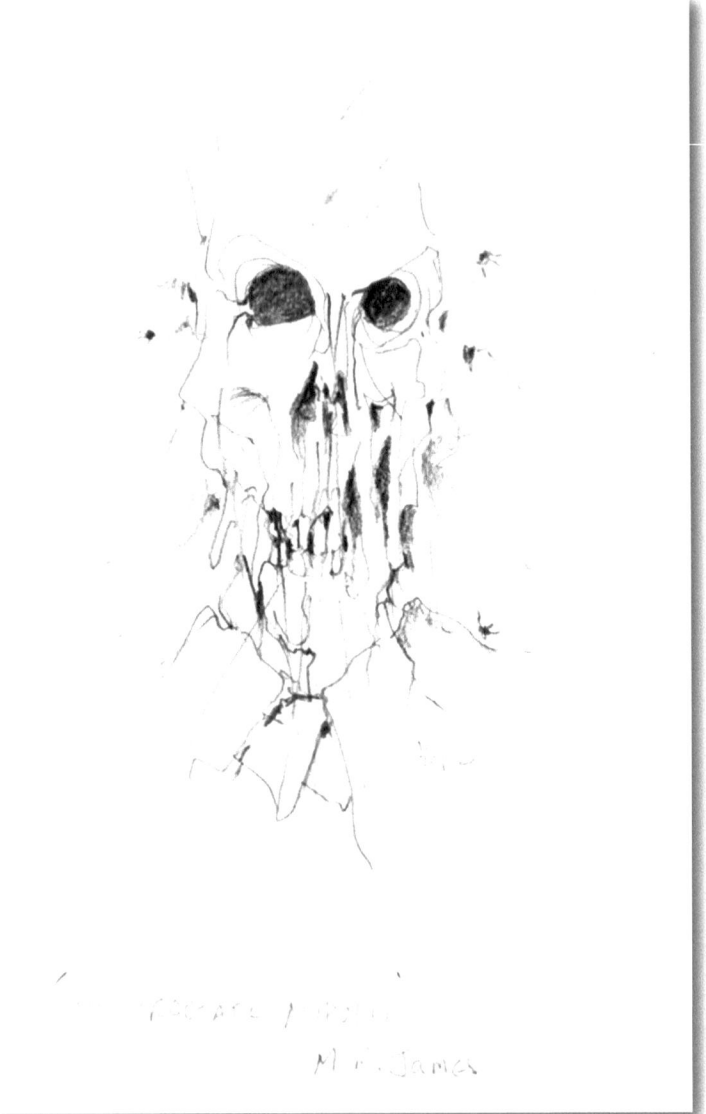
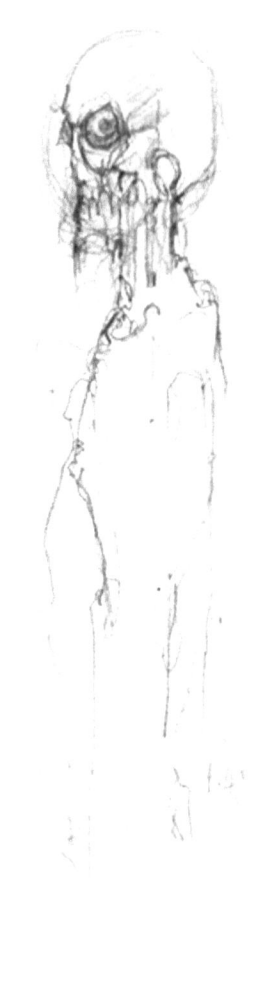
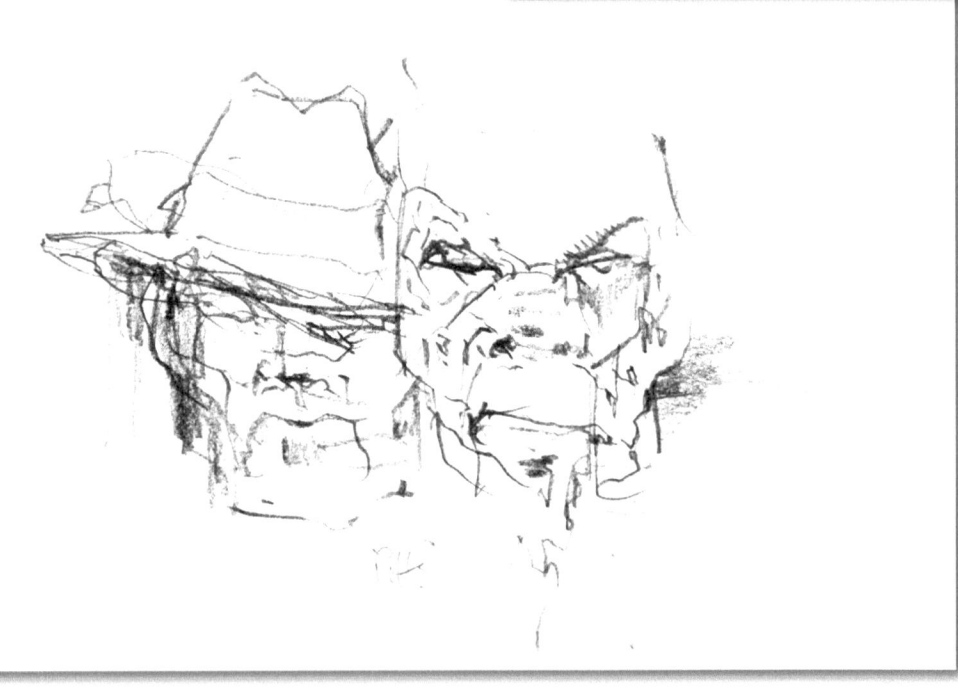

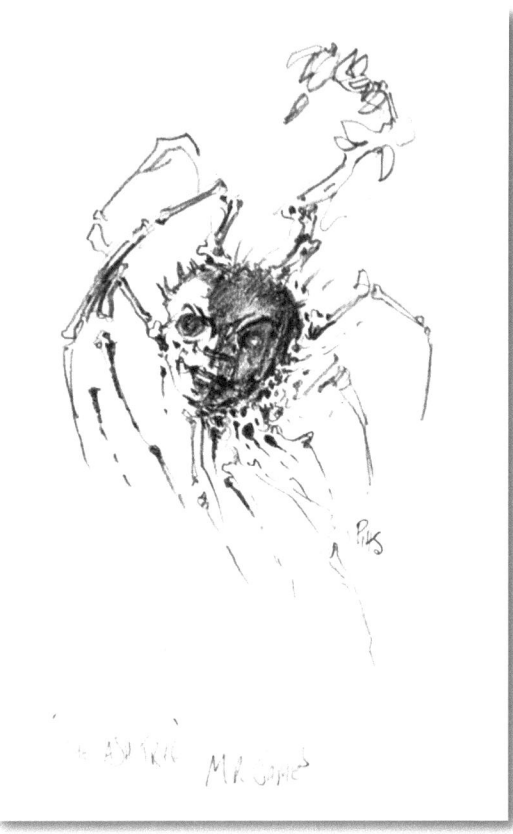
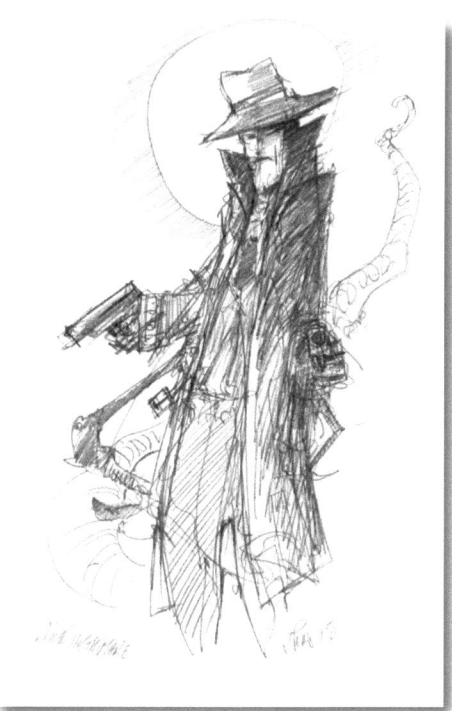
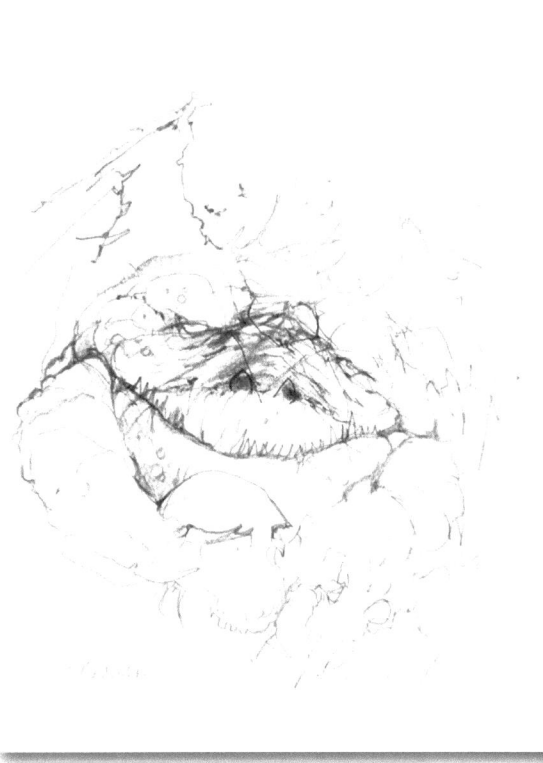
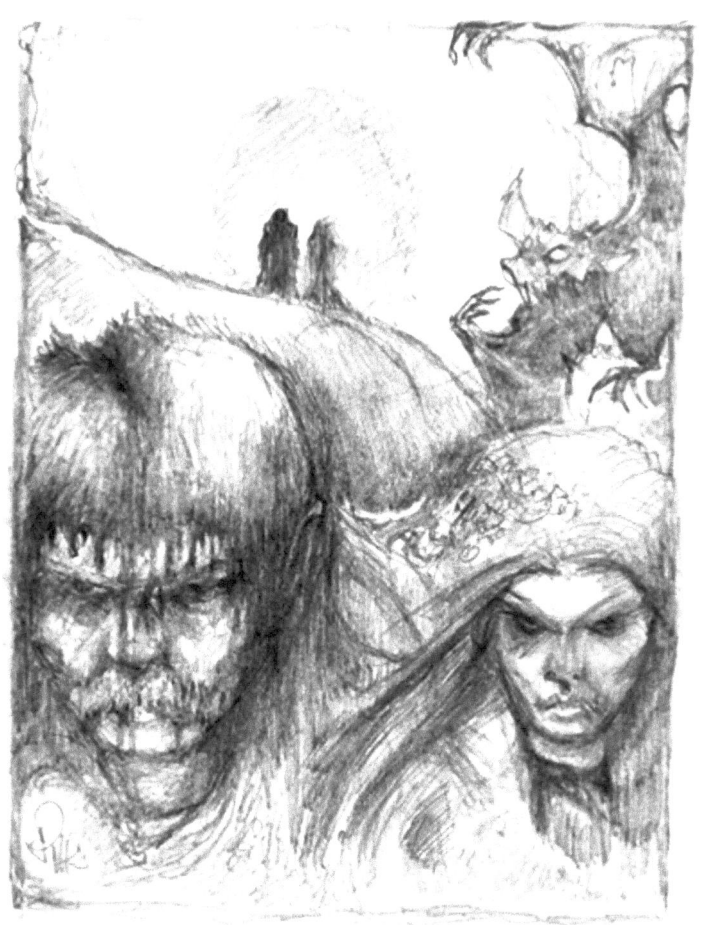

Whimsical piece inspired by H. P. Lovecraft's *Strange High House in the Mist* - watecolour and coloured pencil

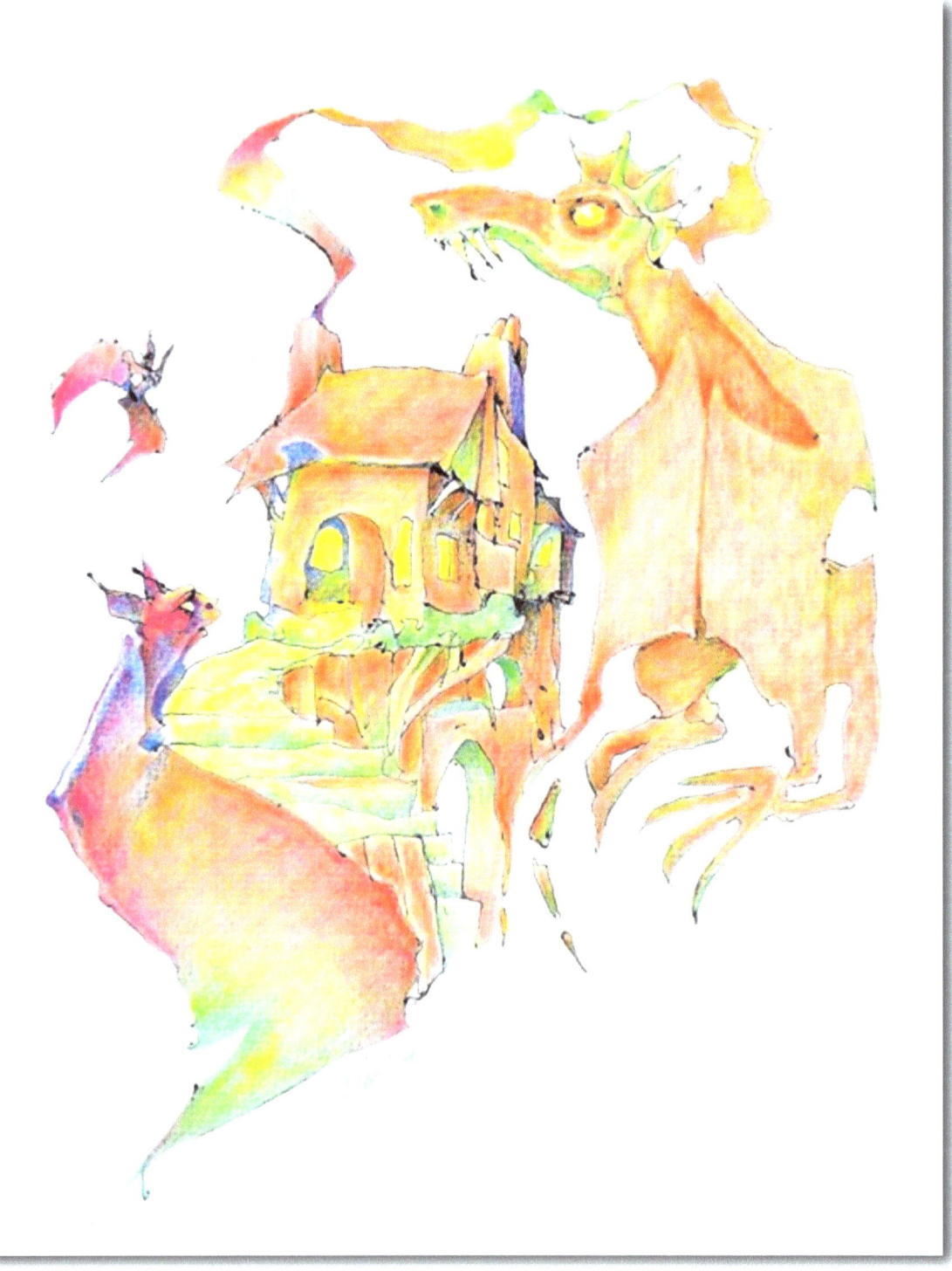

Front cover of *Horror on the High Seas* edited by David A. Sutton and published by Shadow Publishing in 2014

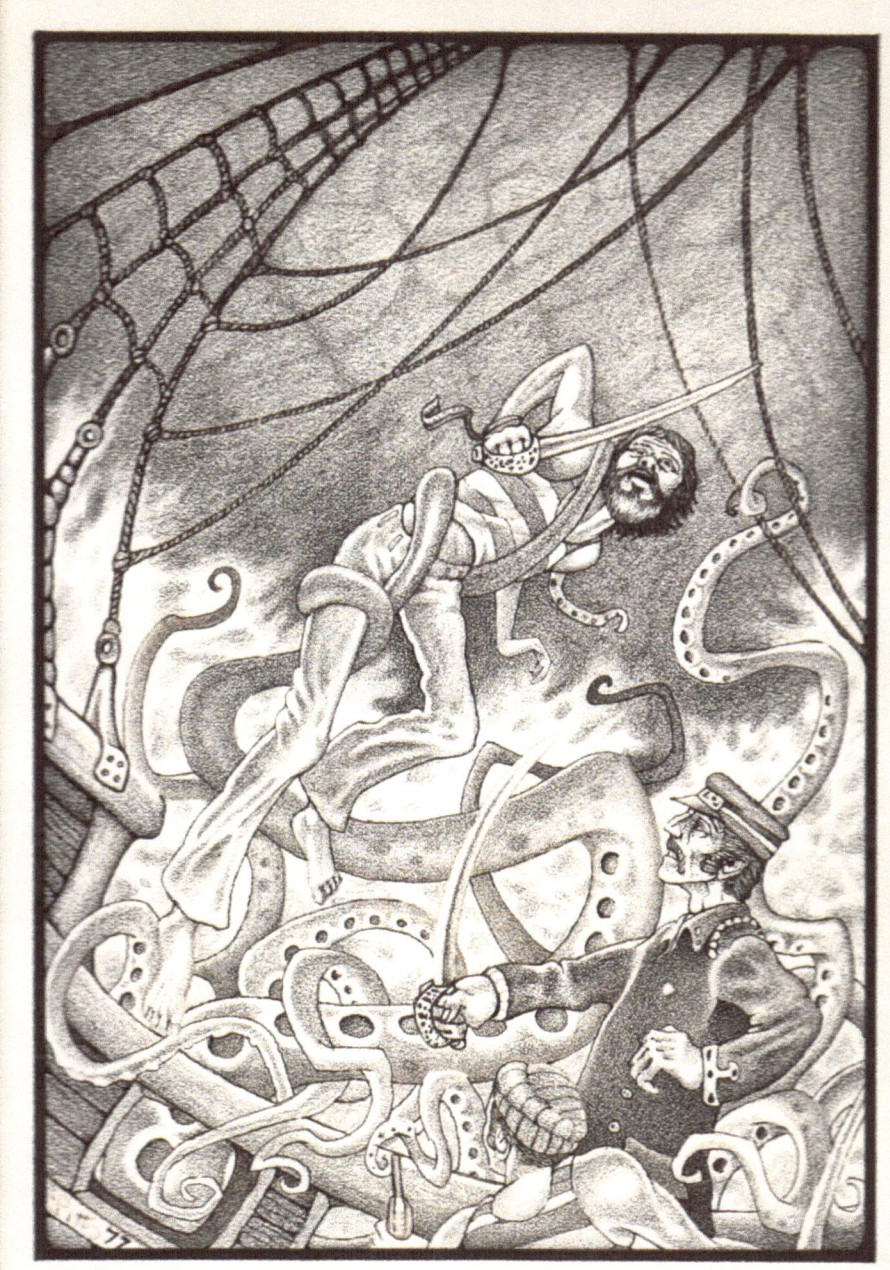

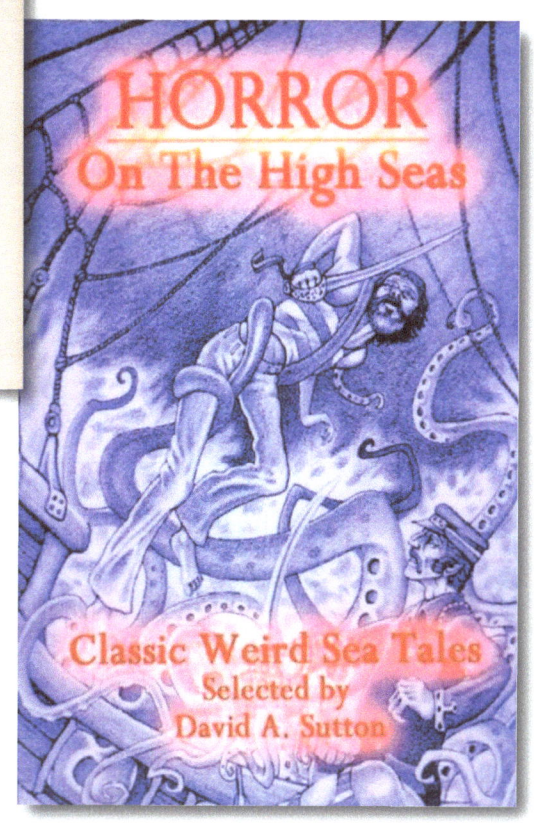

Illustration of William Hope Hodgson's story
The Riven Night

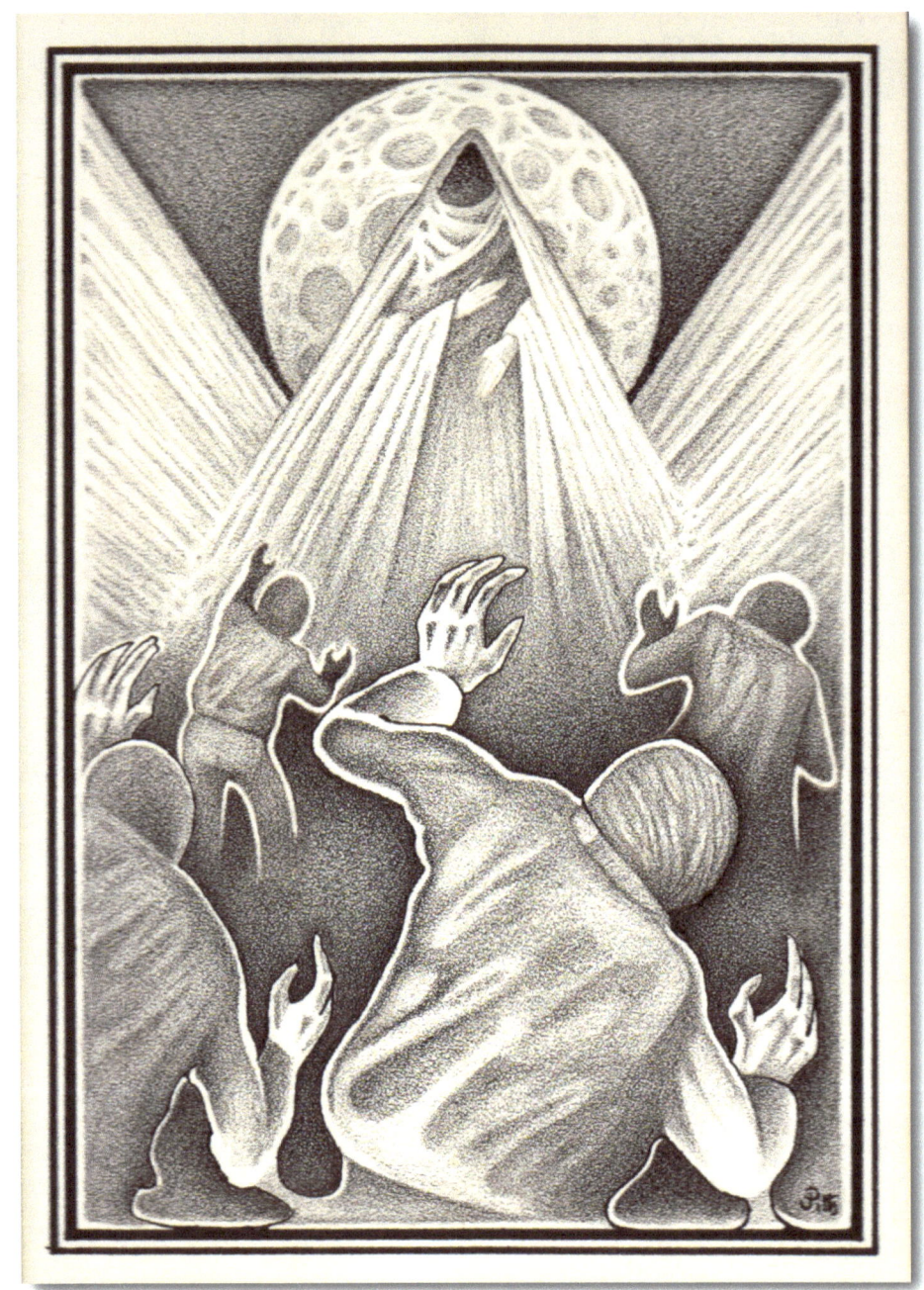

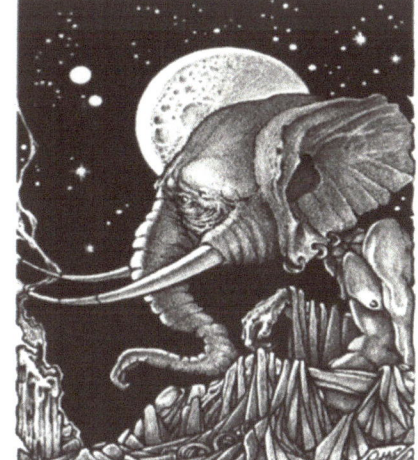

Issue 1 of *The Hyborian Gazette*, published by Carnelian Press, Summer 2015.

An illustration of Robert E. Howard's classic Conan story *The Tower of the Elephant*
The Hyborian Gazette No 1

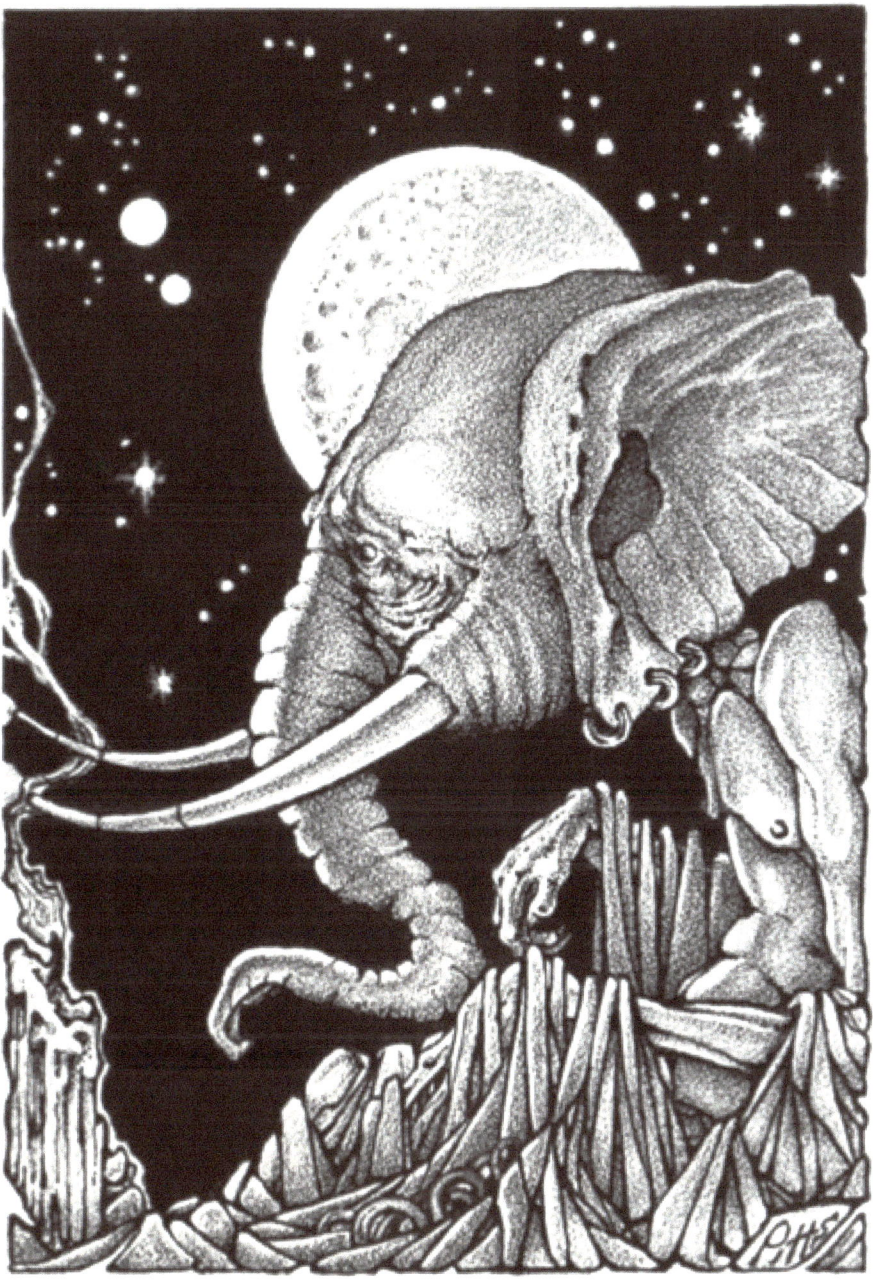

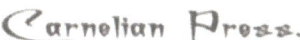

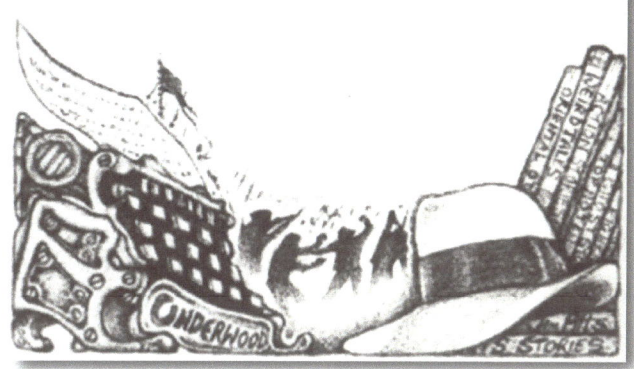

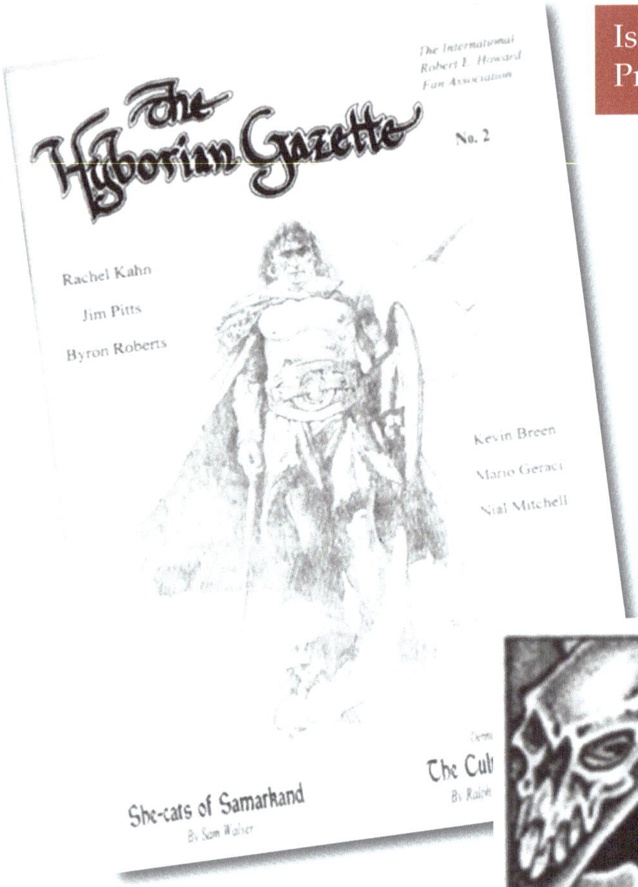

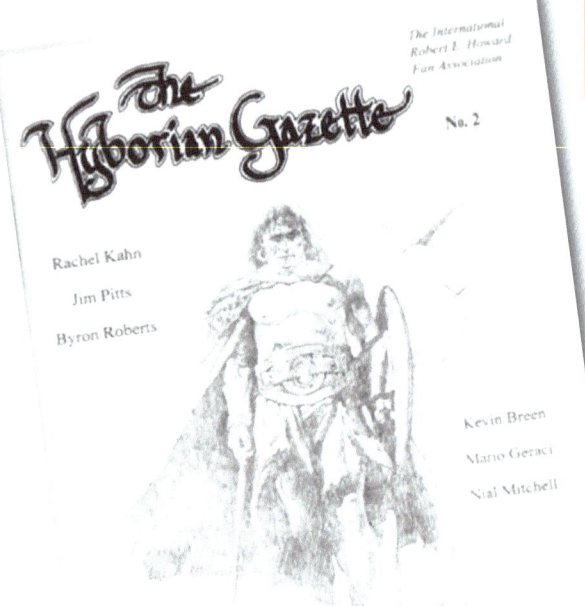

Issue 2 of *The Hyborian Gazette*, published by Carnelian Press, Summer 2016. Cover art by Sanjulian

The illustration below is for *The Cult of the Kraken* by Ralph Grasso and Steve Dilks

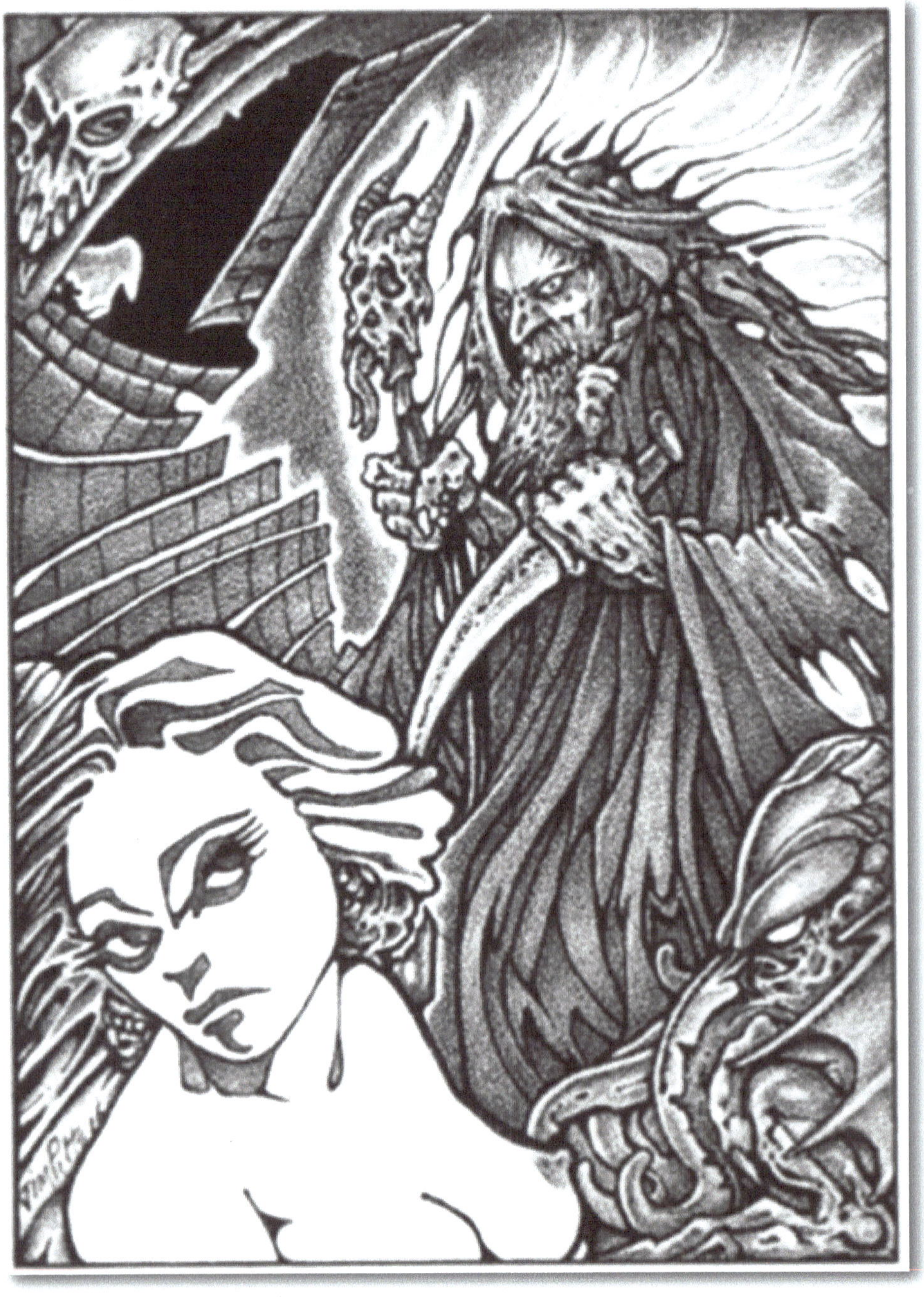

LOOKING FOR SOMETHING TO SUCK
by R. Chetwynd-Hayes

Looking for Something to Suck: The Vampire Stories of R. Chetwynd-Hayes, published by Valancourt Books in 2014, collected together sixteen tales by the author known as 'Britain's Prince of Chill', including such classics as 'My Mother Married a Vampire', 'The Labyrinth', 'Birth', 'Looking for Something to Suck', and 'The Werewolf and the Vampire'.
This first-ever paperback edition featured an additional story not contained in the original limited hardcover edition and also included a foreword by award-winning editor Stephen Jones, new illustrations by Jim Pitts, and an original cover painting by Les Edwards.

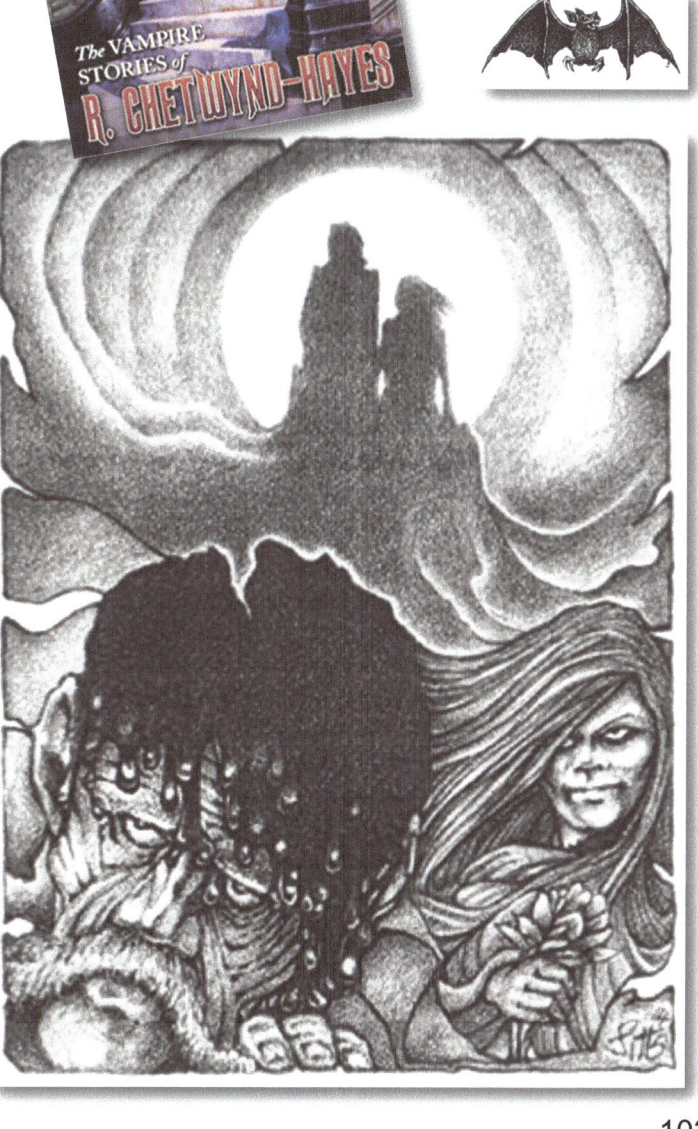
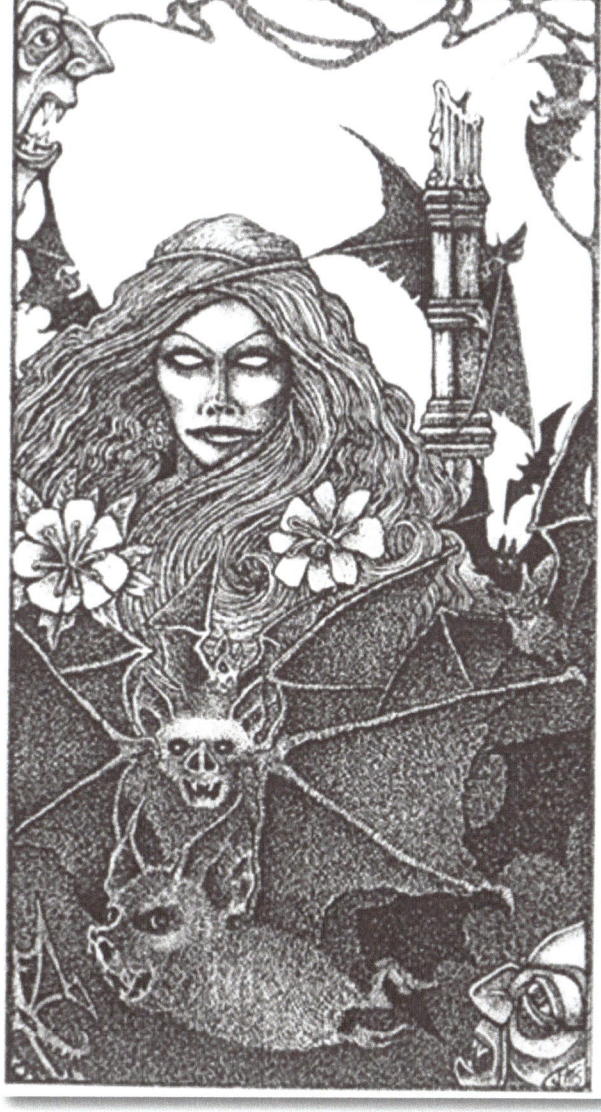

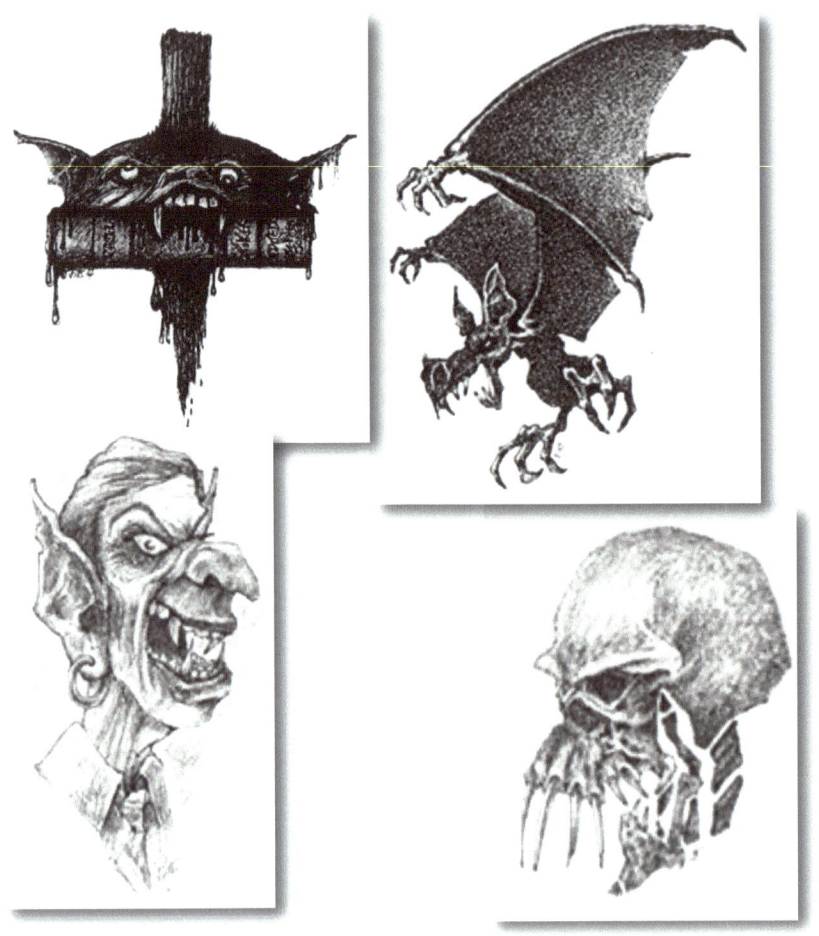
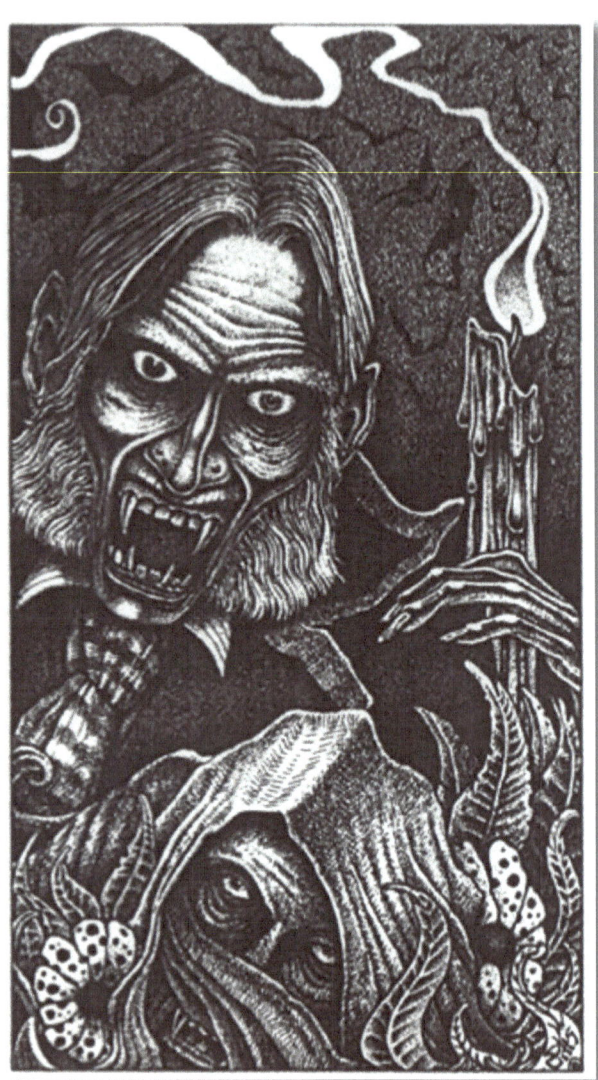
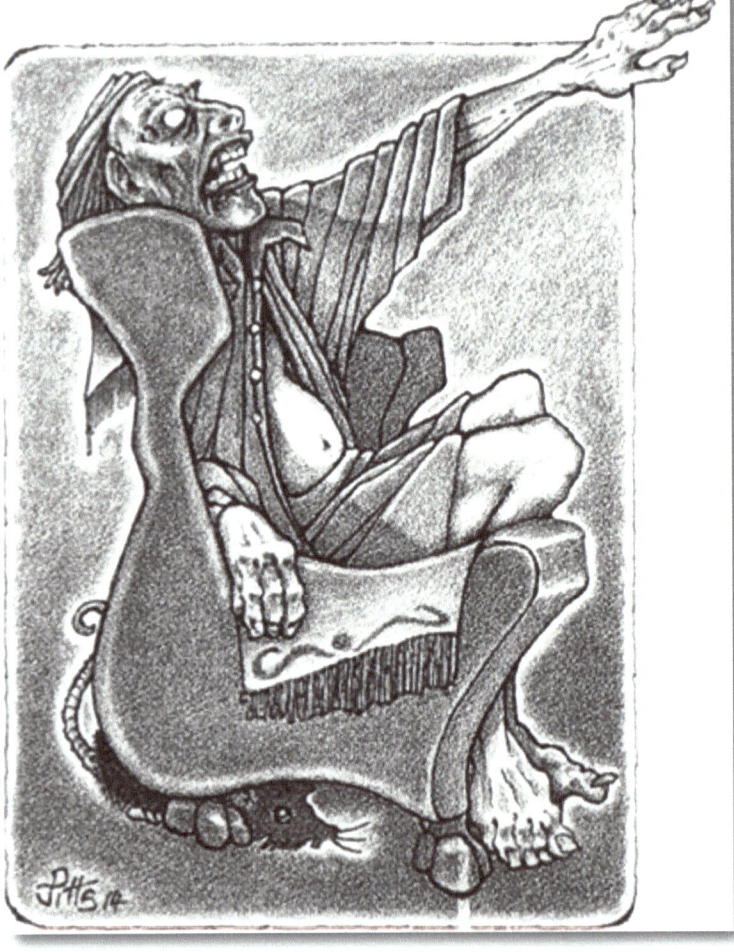
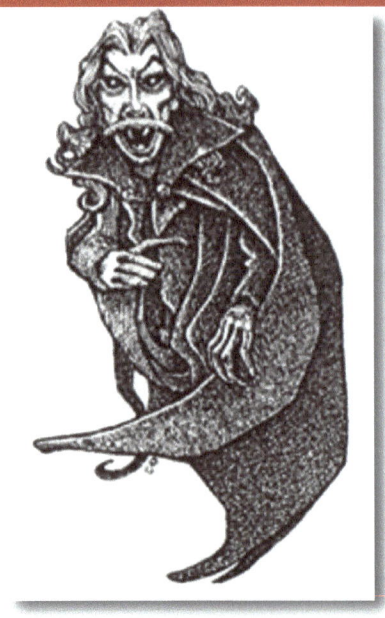

Above: *Family Welcome*.
Far left: *Keep the Gaslight Burning*
Facing page, right: *Amelia*
Immediate left: *Great-Grandad Walks Again*

Cthulhu - watercolour and coloured pencil

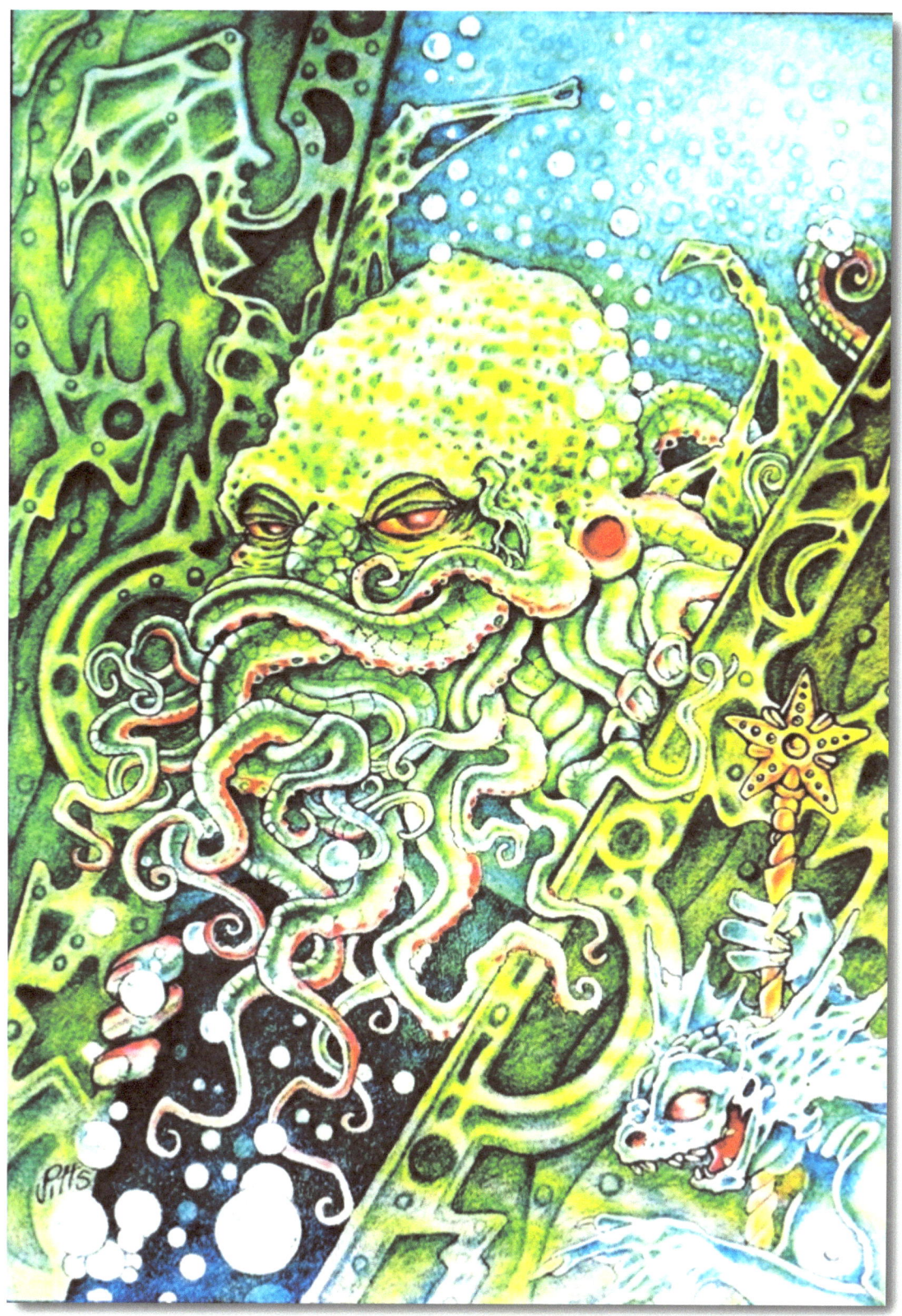

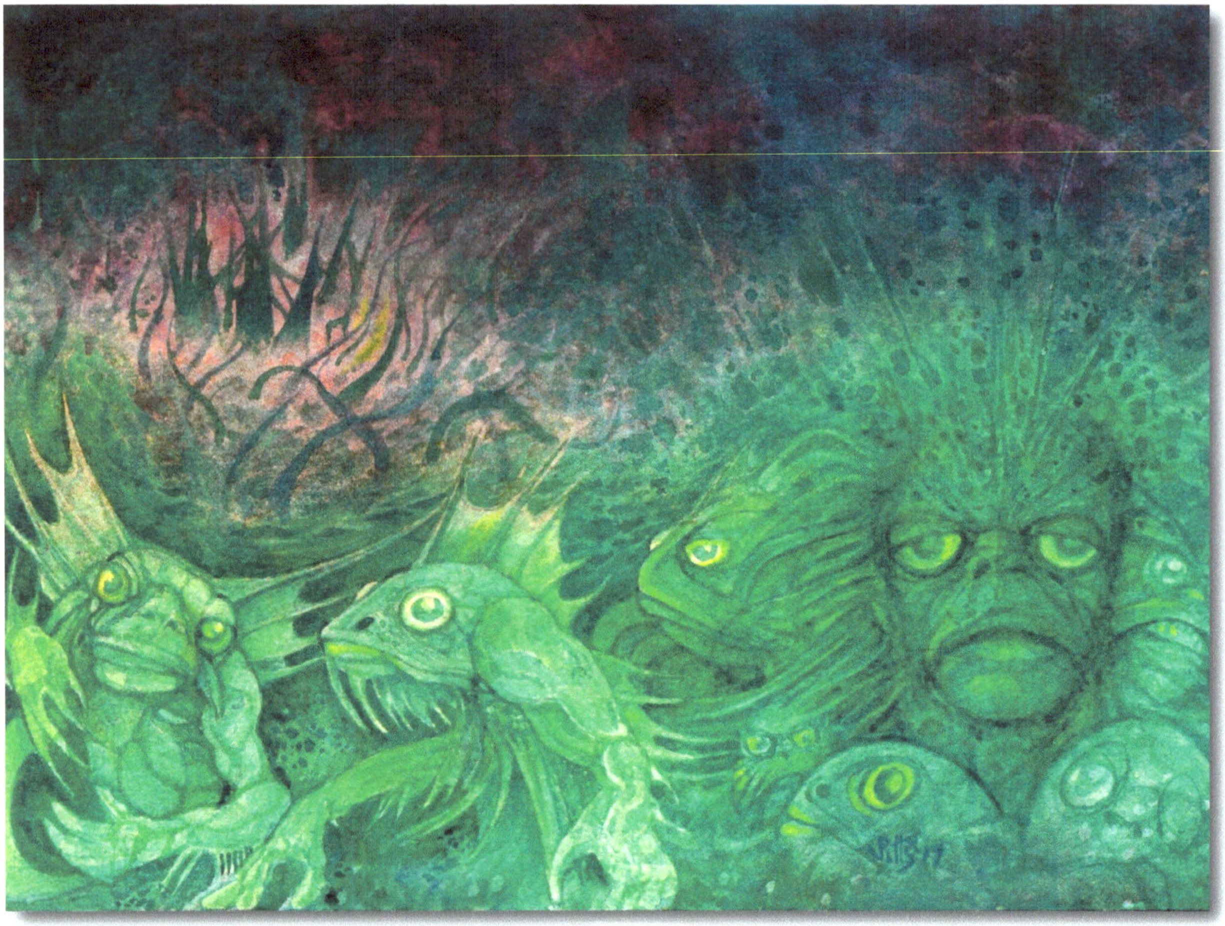

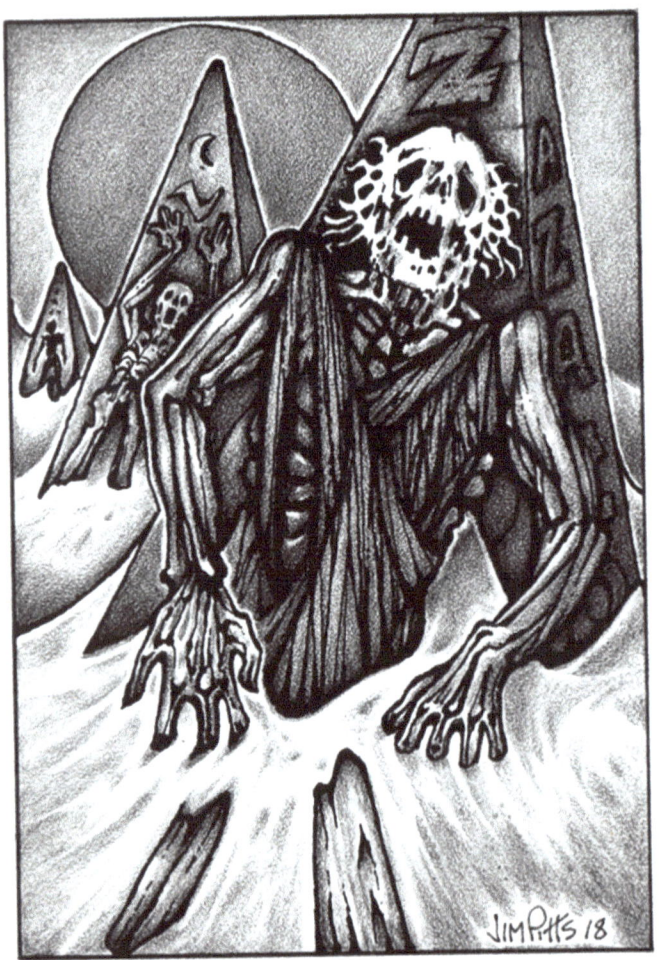
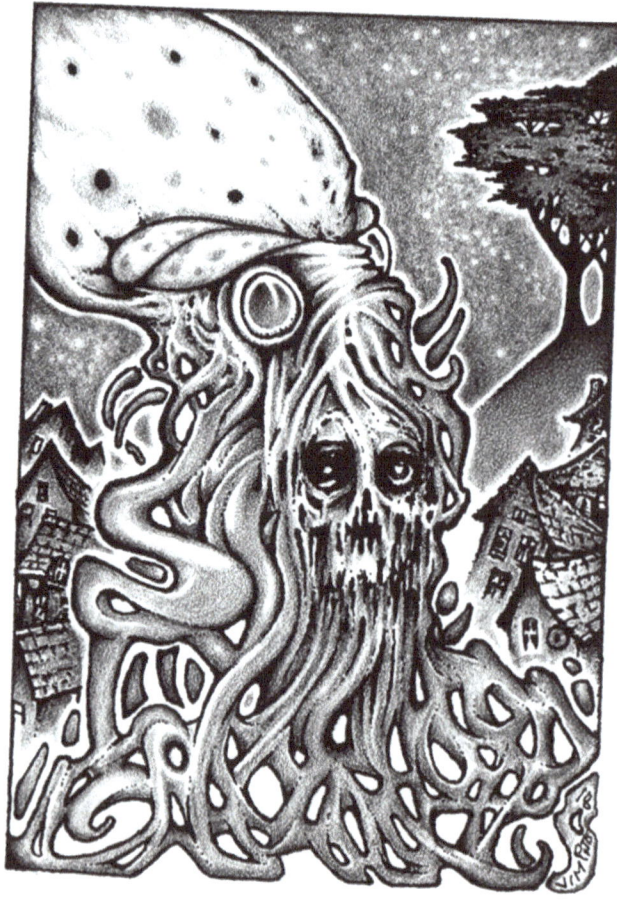

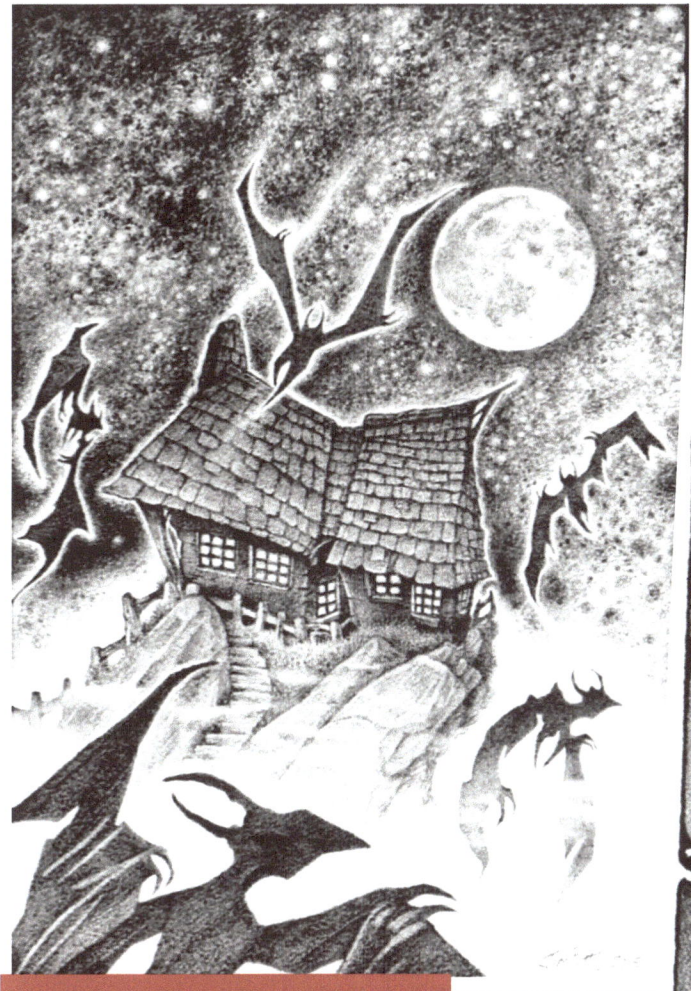
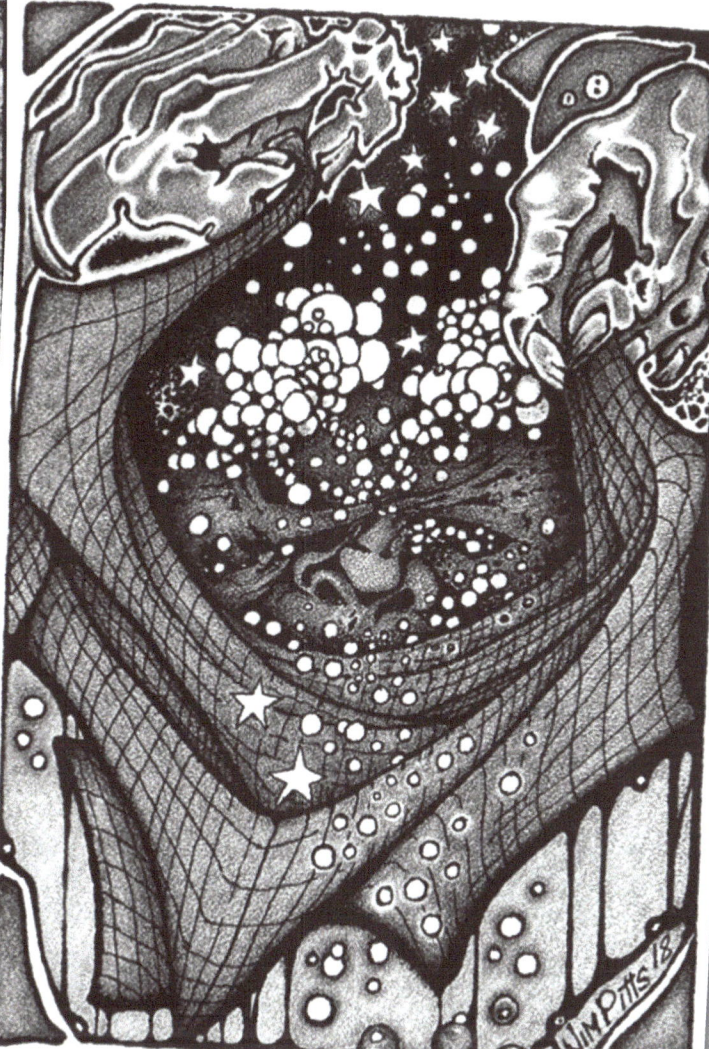
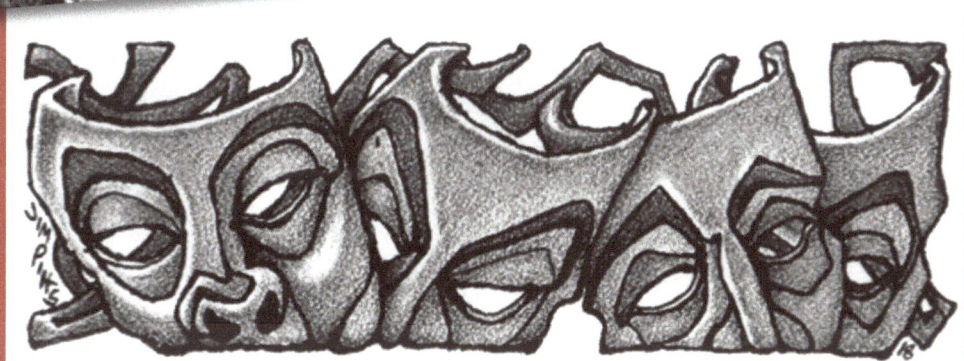

Facing page, top: Cover art for James Wade's *Such Things May Be*, Shadow Publishing, 2018
Facing page, bottom left: *Garden of Ashes* by Mark Howard Jones, Spectre Press, *Tales of the Cthulhu Mythos*
Facing page, bottom right: *Beneath the Pimple* by Bryn Fortey, Spectre Press, *Tales of the Cthulhu Mythos*
Top left: *Strange High House in the Mist* by H. P. Lovecraft
Top right: *The Mask of Nithon* by Martin Gately, Spectre Press, *Tales of the Cthulhu Mythos*
Right: Some headings for Alchemy Press collection.

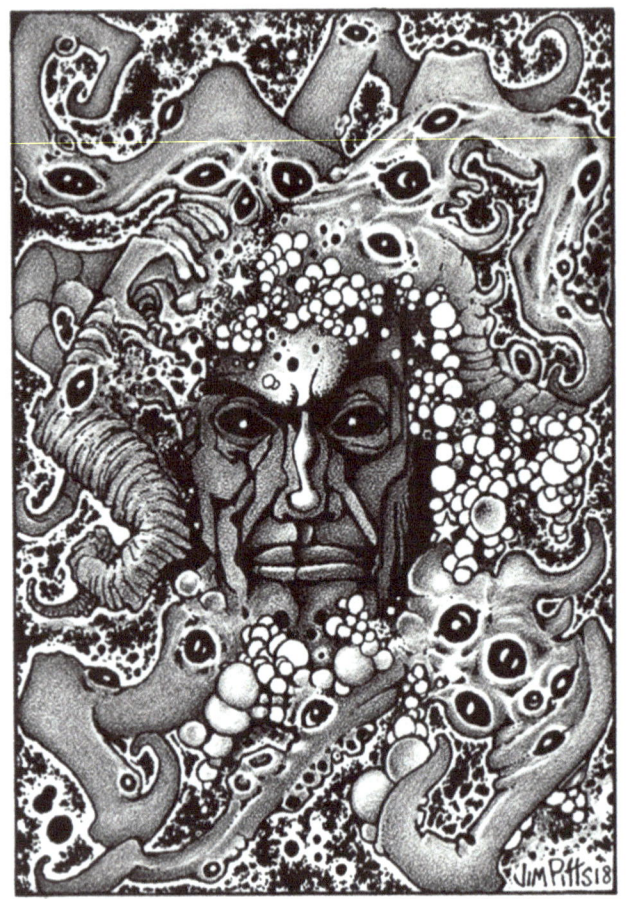
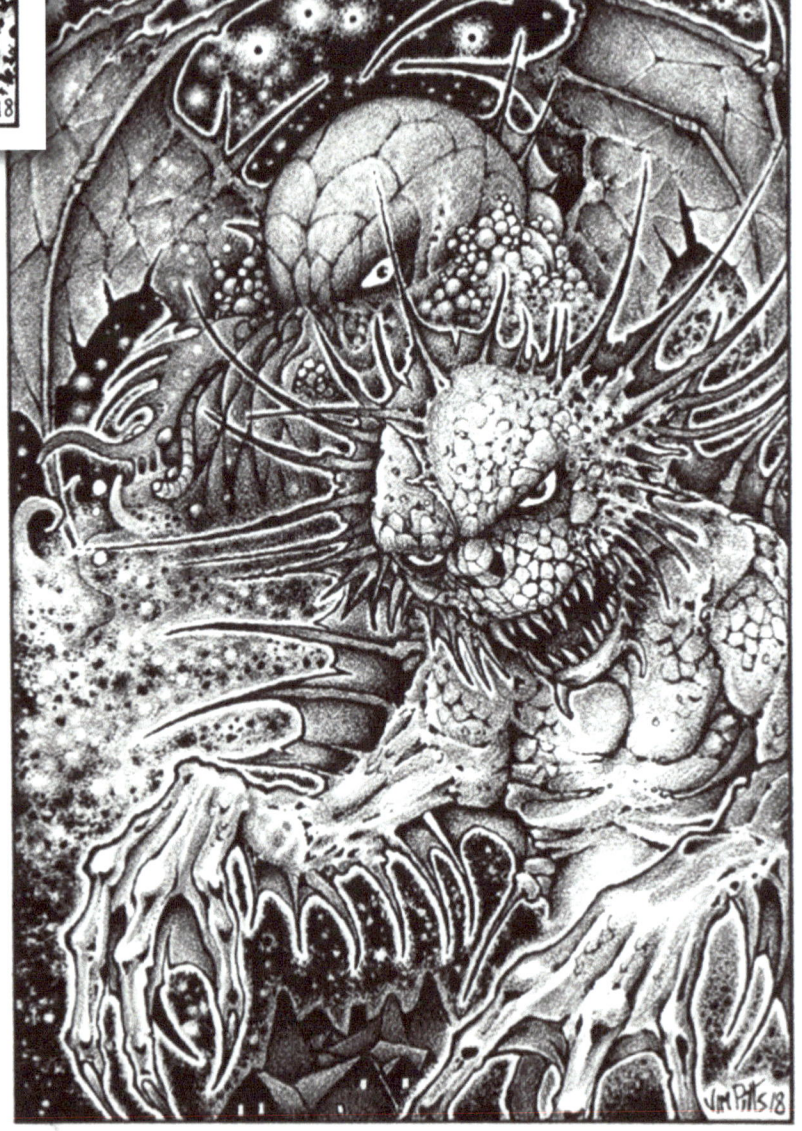

Above: *The Downfall of Bubastis* by Mark J. Ruyffelaert, Spectre Press, *Tales of the Cthulhu Mythos*
Right: *Sentinels* by Brian Mooney, Spectre Press, *Tales of the Cthulhu Mythos*

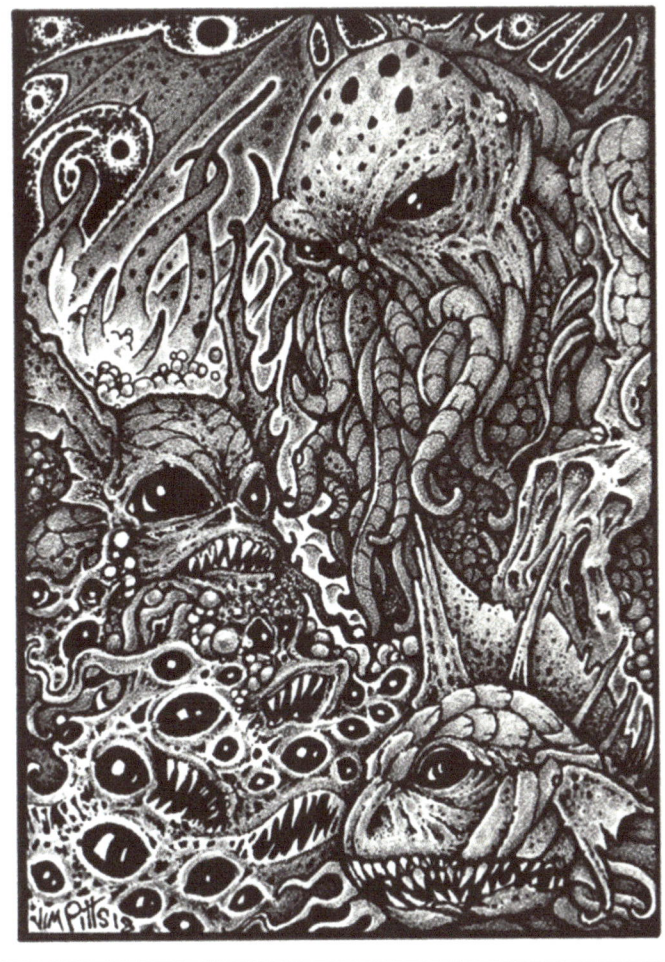

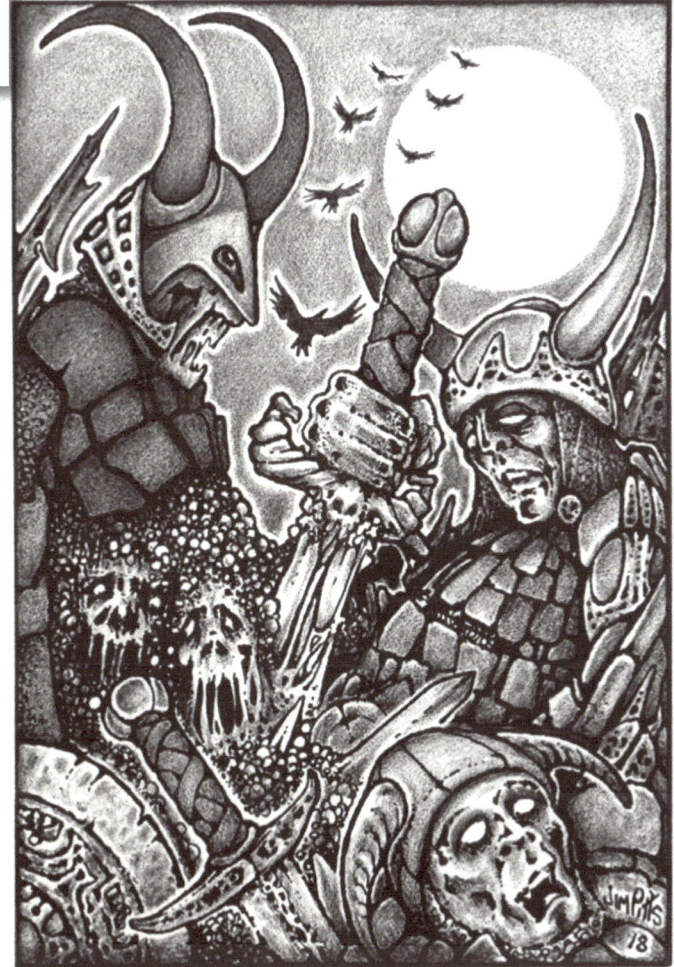

Above: *The Cthulhu Candidate.* by S. L. Edwards, Spectre Press, *Tales of the Cthulhu Mythos*
Right: *The Serpents of Albion* by Adrian Chamberlain, Spectre Press, *Tales of the Cthulhu Mythos*

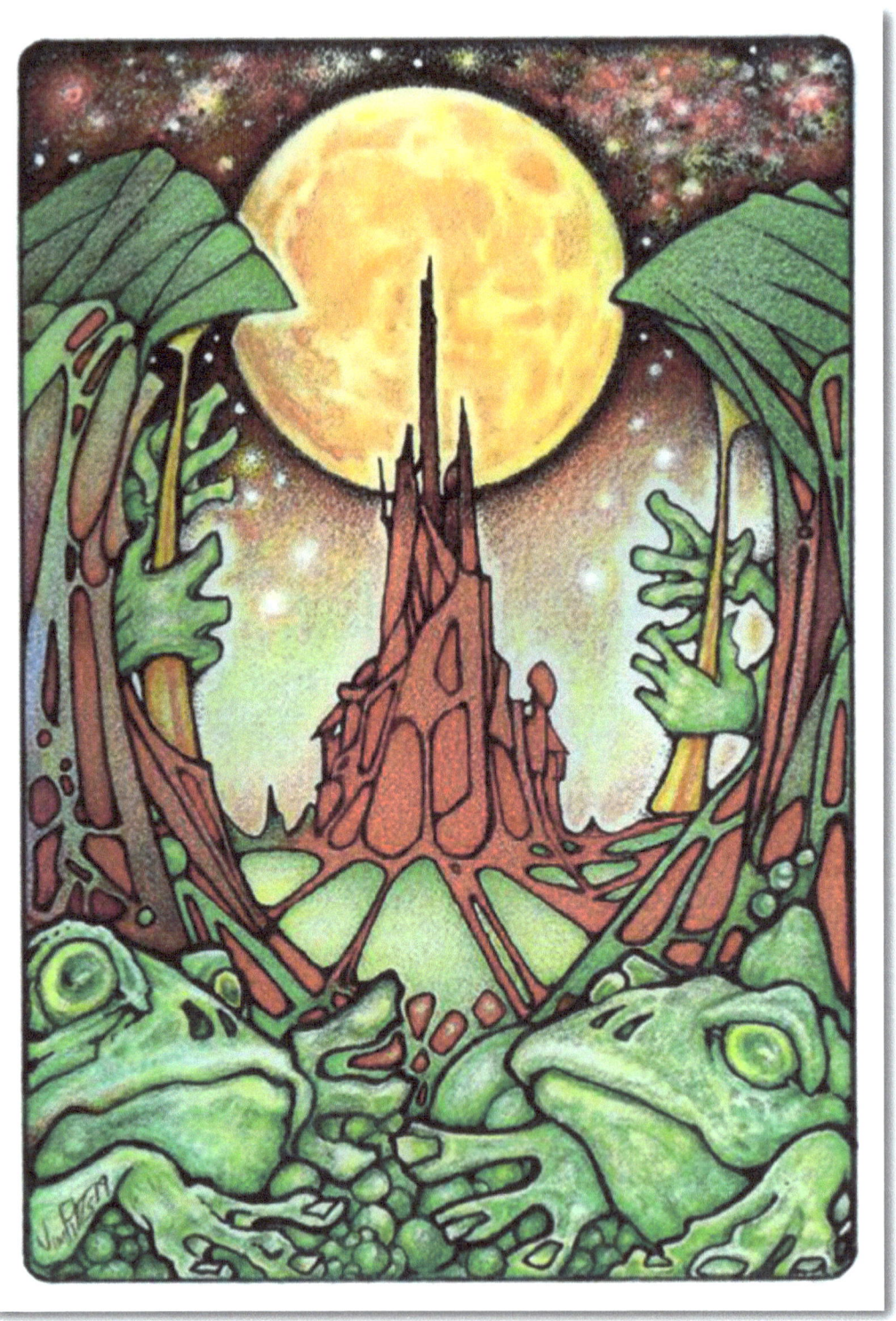

Above: *The Moon Bog* by H. P. Lovecraft, frontispiece illustration in chapbook published by Pegana Press, 2019

ACKNOWLEDGEMENTS & THANKS

Back in 1970-71 I submitted artwork to David Sutton and Jon Harvey. By 1972 I had gained my first accolade, the Ken McIntyre Award for Best Artist at Eastercon that year. Twenty years later and after the publication of numerous b&w and colour illustrations - in both professional, semi-professional and fan markets - I was awarded the British Fantasy Society Best Artist Award for the consecutive years of 1992 and 1993. Almost fifty years later - after retiring from industry - I am still illustrating magazines and books for various publishers and friends, both here in the UK and America. Without the following people none of this would have been possible. The first four guys are the real reason I was ever published in the first place:

David Riley, David Sutton, Jon Harvey, & Steve Jones

The rest of these ladies and gentlemen also deserve mentioning
for their friendship and help over the years...

Nick Caffrey, Peter Coleborn, Adrian Cole, Stuart Schiff, Brian Lumley, Jo Fletcher, Ramsey Campbell, Dave Carson, John Caffrey, Sylvia Starshine, Les & Val Edwards, Andrew Smith, "Whisperin'" John Carter, Mike Chinn, Rosemary Pardoe, Sandra Sutton,

and finally my thanks and love to **Joyce Tierney**, my partner for the last twenty years!

There are many more. I'm sure they know who they they are! It's been a great ride,
and the years are still rolling on!

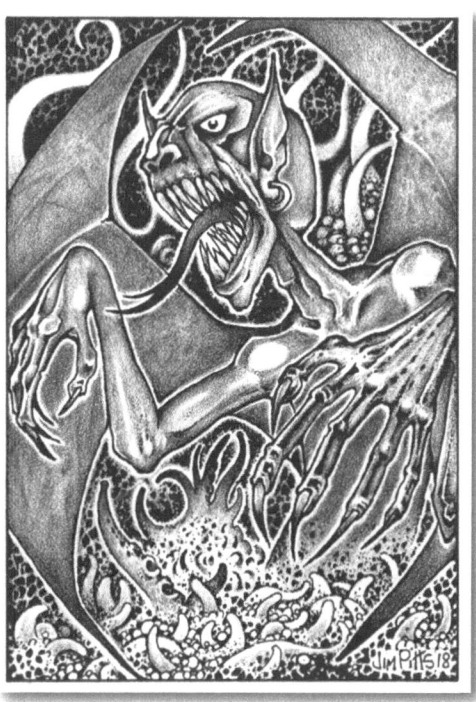

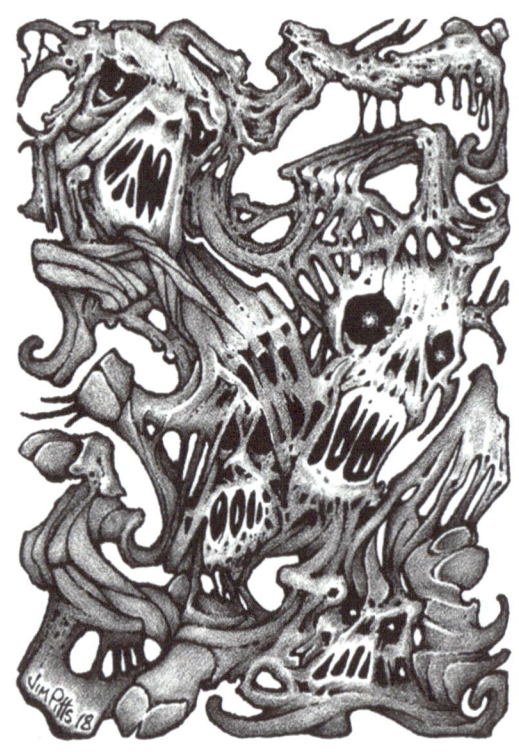

Bottom of page 111: *Biological* by Gail Barden, Spectre Press, *Tales of the Cthulhu Mythos*
Above: *The Devil's Stump*, Spectre Press, *Tales of the Cthulhu Mythos*

For details of all the books published by Parallel Universe Publications check our website:
paralleluniversepublications.blogspot.co.uk/

www.ingramcontent.com/pod-product-compliance
Lightning Source LLC
Chambersburg PA
CBHW051152220526
45473CB00003B/747